S0-DFT-579

HANDBOOK
FOR
PUBLIC
OFFICIALS

All rights reserved. No part of this publication may be reproduced or transmitted in any form or by any means, electronic or mechanical, including photocopy, recording, or any information retrieval system, without permission in writing from the author: Wayne K. Lemieux, Westlake Village, California.

Printed in the United States of America.

Copyright © 2008 Wayne K. Lemieux
All rights reserved.

ISBN: 1-4392-0544-2
ISBN-13: 9781439205440

To obtain additional copies, please contact us:
BookSurge, Publishing
www.booksurge.com
1-866-308-6235
orders@booksurge.com

HANDBOOK
FOR
PUBLIC OFFICIALS

Fifth Edition

Wayne K. Lemieux

Dedicated to my mother, Audrey Lemieux

TABLE OF CONTENTS

WARNING

ABOUT THE ONLY thing my high school, college and law school teachers agreed on was: don't apologize for what you say, people won't take you seriously. I want to be taken seriously but I must start with an apology.

Lawyers shouldn't write books about how to manage public agencies. Lawyers, particularly public agency lawyers, should speak when spoken to and the rest of the time get out of the way. But alas, 21st century California will not allow local public agencies to operate without more or less constant legal advice and it is getting worse. This book had to be written because public administrators, who should be writing this book, can't, without a long session with a lawyer.

State law should not confine local agencies. State legislators do not have the answers and local officials are not ignorant bumpkins. But this is not the heart of the problem. State legislators should not assume only they can overcome local parochial interests in the search for the public greater good. But this, too, is not the problem. State legislators should not believe local officials are corrupt (or at least more corrupt than state officials). Not the problem. The problem with the statutory straightjacket is much more fundamental. It is not democratic. The people imposing laws on local government should know it is not democratic but they are happy with the situation.

This is not an argument the state legislature is an undemocratic body. But think about it. What happens when the state adopts a law telling a local agency how to act? The statute is a hunting license for the state bureaucracy and court system to second-guess local decisions. Remember, in the United States (despite appearances, California is still part of the United States), government is supposed to be representative and the power of government is supposed to be separated among three branches: executive, legislative and judicial. Legislature can adopt any law it wishes as long as the courts say the law does not violate the Constitution. The State Legislature has adopted so many laws affecting local government that the state bureaucracy, not the legislative body of local agencies, will determine what is legal, what can occur, and what must not occur. When the state bureaucracy stands aside, courts become the *de facto* governing body for local government. Agencies must hire the best lawyer money can buy and let the lawyer make decisions. This is a sad state of affairs for which I apologize.

This book is a modest attempt to free the public administrator from the tyranny of the mandarin lawyer. Mr. or Mrs. Public Official: you still need your lawyer. You need to be a more informed consumer of legal advice. This book should help you identify the questions to ask. For my colleagues who share disgust with the degradation of local agencies, this book should allow your clients to be less dependent and allow you to allow your clients more freedom of action.

The structure of local government is not complicated. An elected governing body establishes policies and hires officers to carry out the policy. The officers hire employees to translate management directives into programs. A good structure goes a long way to ensure a well functioning agency. This structure is described in the first part of this book.

Structure isn't everything. The agency must adopt internal regulations describing how its particular system of government is to work. The second part of this book deals with how an agency governs itself.

For many in local government, it would be a perfect world if they only had to deal with fellow employees or other governments. But the agency must deal with "customers." It is a sign of well-being if this occurs sooner and more often than not. The third part of this work deals with how a local agency deals with taxpayers, customers and total strangers.

PART 1

STRUCTURE OF LOCAL GOVERNMENT

Agencies do not magically function without the hard work of a team of dedicated officers and employees. Like the New England Patriots, the team need not be stars to be champions. Teams succeed when each team member knows and fulfills a role. This part explains the roles of the team so an award-winning agency can emerge.

CHAPTER 1

THE GOVERNING BODY

The governing body of a local agency is usually elected by the residents of the agency. State law compels the body to meet in a certain way, decide things in a specified manner, be paid not more than a certain amount, and act ethically. State law says nothing about what is important: the role of the governing body (city council, board of supervisors, board of directors or board of trustees). It is time to address what is compelled and describe what is really necessary.

Role of the Board

The role of the governing body of a local agency is to establish the agency's policies within the context of the Act establishing the local agency ("principal act") and representations made to the electorate.

Determining policy is a full-time job. Even when everyone has a clear view of their role, it can be difficult. Fortunately, there is a method to avoid madness. The governing body should first create a clear *mission statement* containing broad principles such as, "this water district will serve water at a fair price." The mission statement should <u>not</u> contain detailed directives such as, "this water district shall buy staples from a specific vendor at a low price." The mission statement will not be at once apparent but with minimal effort, there should be unanimous agreement by the board on the statement. To avoid having the statement become window dressing, the board should refer to the statement for context when making other policy decisions.

When the mission statement is approved, the governing body should adopt programs to implement the statement. The programs can consist of services such as the delivery of sanitation service or projects such as the construction of treatment plants. Management can help by suggesting services and projects necessary to fulfill the statement. Of course, no program can be approved without examining the fiscal impact. Management must also explain whether the agency can afford proposed programs. This usually happens incrementally during annual budget deliberations. A wise manager will budget for new services and projects which may arise during the year and which cannot be delayed until the commencement of the next fiscal year. The budget process should be repeated during the year when unexpected programs arise.

The third role of the governing board, after the adoption of a mission statement and the approval of programs, is to oversee management's efforts to carry out the programs. The efficient operations of a local agency are jeopardized if the board does not supervise management. Supervision does not mean detailed instruction on how to carry out board directives. Elected officials should not criticize specific steps taken by management. This discipline is the most difficult skill for directors to acquire. The board must be result oriented. Have management explain whether specified programs are being carried out on time and within budget. Do not expect management to explain precisely how this is accomplished. The board's remedy if programs are not properly implemented is to confront and possibly replace management.

A shareholder would be horrified if the board of directors of General Motors tried to tell an assembly line worker how to do her job. Shareholders expect the directors to hire competent management, oversee management, and fire the managers when they don't do their job. For some unexplained reason, many elected officials seem to believe the voters (their shareholders) expect them to tell the assembly-line workers how to operate. In this case, what is not good for General Motors is not good for local agencies. The board has enough to do without meddling in day-to-day operations. If the board thinks there is something wrong with operations, the board must interrogate the manager. If satisfactory answers are not given, the manager must be fired.

One way to ensure the board maintains the proper prospective on the role of the board is to adopt a written policy. A formal written policy on board and on staff relations can prevent embarrassing confrontations. Such a policy might state:

- A majority of the board shall establish district policies, i.e., mission and programs, at public meetings.

- The general manager shall recommend programs to implement policies to the board.

- The manager shall carry out the programs approved by the board.

- The board will not instruct management how to implement the district's programs. But management is responsible if the policies are not implemented.

- Directors will ask the general manager about the status of projects. The general manager shall promptly provide requested information.

- Directors can call on management for a reasonable amount of attention and assistance. However, a director should not expect management to devote significant time to individual questions without concurrence of the board.

- Individual directors will not instruct management how to perform.

Compensation and Benefits

Principal acts provide two basic compensation plans for a governing board: monthly salary or per diem. Cities and counties pay monthly salaries based on the population of the entity. This is simple, compared to per diem compensation where directors are paid for each day devoted to the business of the district.[1]

District boards must determine what constitutes the business of the agency. Meetings of the board are covered. Attendance at industry conferences can be covered. Other activities can be the subject of a per diem if reasonable and necessary to accomplish the purposes of the agency and attendance is approved by the board. The number of per diems a director can earn and the amount of each per diem is specified in the principal act. For example, airport district directors can earn up to six per diems a month at a rate of not more than $100 per meeting.[2] Water agencies can substitute a uniform act for the principal act by adopting an ordinance following a public hearing.[3] Under the uniform act, the directors can be paid for up to ten meetings per month. The per diem rate under the uniform act starts at $100/day but annual cost of living increases are possible.[4] (The IRS has ruled directors of a government agency are "employees" and are therefore subject to Medicare and income tax withholding even though directors of a private corporation are not considered "employees" and are therefore not subject to income tax withholding.[5])

Directors can be reimbursed for usual and necessary expenses if the board has an expense reimbursement policy. The board should actively oversee each director's expense reimbursement because the entire board will be embarrassed when a director abuses the privilege for frivolous expenses. The board should audit director expense reimbursement because persons appointed by the board cannot be expected to say no. Expense reimbursement is typically limited to travel, meals, lodging, and registration fees. If expense reimbursement is for an industry conference, the reimbursement amount for lodging cannot exceed the lodging rate provided by the conference.[6] (If the official is unable to secure rooms made available by the sponsor, the rate cannot exceed a reasonable amount.) In the case of travel, the board can specify a reasonable rate and if it doesn't, the reimbursement rate permitted by the Internal Revenue Service will apply.[7]

There is no prohibition for reimbursing directors for alcoholic beverages, however, most agencies refuse to reimburse for alcoholic beverages. Similarly, there is no *per se* prohibition against reimbursing for expenses incurred for a spouse of a director who attends a conference. However, spousal expense cannot be paid unless the spouse's presence was "necessary" for the director.[8] In most cases, spouses are not "necessary" for the director to perform the work of the conference. Agencies are well advised to preclude reimbursement of spousal expense.

Directors can obtain many of the benefits provided to employees. Many employee benefits have no application to part-time personnel such as directors. A director could accrue a vacation from the agency but a director could not take a vacation from a board meeting and still earn a per diem. Directors can be covered by travel insurance, can be enrolled in the agency's group medical health plan, and can be covered by worker's compensation insurance.[9] Participation in the agency's group health plan is an exception to the maximum amount of "compensation" a director would otherwise be entitled to receive. (An agency cannot provide the director with a cash payment amounting to the difference between the agency's group plan and the directors' personal insurance plan.[10]) Worker's compensation is a mixed blessing. Directors can be enrolled based on per diem. A director injured while performing agency business will be entitled to care under the worker's compensation plan but will be precluded from an action against the agency for personal injury.

A director can appear before the agency the director serves as an advocate for a person or cause. A director who does so may be disqualified from acting on the request of the person or cause due to conflict of interest (if the director received income) or based on due process.[11] Ironically, a director cannot act as an advocate for a person or cause <u>after</u> leaving office for a period of one year.[12]

Directors do not make agency decisions; boards make agency decisions. The decision of a board must be made by a majority of the board. Even the presiding officer cannot speak with authority unless a majority of the board has acted. Usually, the Principal Act states the board acts only by "motion, resolution or ordinance."

A motion (or minute order) is adopted when a motion is made, seconded and carried by a majority. The minutes are the only permanent record of motions. Determining a majority is not always as easy as counting one, two, three (for a five-member board). For some agencies, "majority" means the affirmative vote of a majority of the quorum.[13] A five-member board would require three affirmative votes; two affirmative votes, and one abstention will not carry a motion. For some agencies, a majority of those voting is sufficient.[14] A five-member board would pass a motion with two affirmative votes and one abstention. Some types of motions require more than a majority vote. For example, a motion to add a subject to the agenda after the Brown Act deadline needs a four-fifths vote to find the need to take action has arisen subsequently to the posting of the agenda.

Sometimes action must be taken by resolution or ordinance. Usually, this occurs for more important matters. Director's compensation must be established by resolution or ordinance. An agency can act by resolution to create a clear record of action even when not mandated by law. Typically, resolutions require the same number of votes as a motion but some resolutions may require more than majority vote. The vote on resolutions is recorded in the minutes of the board meetings and a separate resolution is prepared for the resolution book.

The most important decisions of the board are contained in ordinances. Some ordinances can be enforced as a misdemeanor.[15] Not all agencies can adopt ordinances.[16] When an agency acts by ordinance, the process can be stated in the Principal Act. When the Principal Act is silent, the process required for cities can be safely employed.[17] This requires two "readings" (or votes) at least 5 days apart and a waiting period of 30 days after second reading before the ordinance is effective.[18] The ordinance must be published within 15 days of second reading. The delay between introduction and effectiveness is to allow the electorate the opportunity to present a referendum on the ordinance. In fact, one reason the law requires certain decisions be made by ordinance is to expose the decision to a referendum.

Voters can repeal an ordinance by a referendum.[19] A referendum petition must be signed by more than 10% of registered voters in districts in which the total number of voters is less than 500,000, and by more than 5% of registered voters in districts that contain 500,000 or more registered voters.[20] The petitions must be filed by a deadline after circulation commences.[21] If the requisite number signs the petition, the board must rescind the ordinance or call an election.[22] If the majority of the voters approve the referendum, the ordinance is repealed.

An agency or its voters can also enact an ordinance by a direct vote – initiative.[23] An initiative is legislation approved directly by the electorate.[24] Because the initiative is "legislation," the scope of the initiative power is the same as the scope of the agency's power to legislate. For example, an initiative cannot eliminate an agency's power to act.[25] The initiative cannot be used to "impair essential functions of government."[26] The agency may be forced to place an initiative on the ballot because voter approval is necessary, e.g., to levy a special tax.[27]

Citizens may also propose measures an agency refuses to enact. The initiative process is similar to the referendum process. Before circulating a petition, the proponents of the initiative must publish a notice of intention in a newspaper of general circulation (if available) or in a newspaper within the county (when there is no newspaper of general circulation) and post in at least three locations.[28] Within 10 days of the publication, the proponents must file the notice of intention with the county clerk.[29] The agency attorney gives the initiative a title. An initiative petition must be circulated within 180 days after the receipt of the title from the attorney.[30] The petition must be signed by 5% of the voting public.[31] (But, if the agency has a registration of 1,000 or less, 25% of the voters must sign the petition.[32]) If the petition does not have the required number of signatures, no further action is taken.[33] If the petition has the required signatures, the clerk submits the petition to the governing board.[34] The board must pass the ordinance or submit the initiative to the voters at the next general or special election within 88 to 103 days of the presentation of the proposed ordinance.[35] If the majority of voters favor the initiative, it become a valid enactment.[36]

From the perspective of the public, the most important law affecting public agencies mandates public meetings. Even accidental violations cause acute embarrassment because the local press is particularly vigilant in guarding the public's access to the decision-making process. The Brown Act is important. It deserves and will get its own chapter.

Meeting Decorum

The Brown Act does not specify the rules for meeting procedures. The most commonly used formal rules of procedure are Robert's Rules of Order. The basic purpose of Robert's Rules should be understood:

> ...(T)hese rules are based on a regard for the rights
> - Of the majority,
> - Of the minority, especially a strong minority—greater than one-third,
> - Of individual members,
> - Of absentees, and
> - Of all these together.
>
> Fundamentally, under the rules of parliamentary law, a deliberate body is a free agent – free to do what it wants to do with the greatest measure of protection to itself and of consideration for the rights of its members.[37]

With few exceptions, the agency's meetings are meetings of the governing board. "Members" who enjoy rights under Robert's Rules are the members of the governing board.

A majority of the members of the council, governing body or commission constitutes a quorum. Additionally, certain officers are necessary to convene the meeting: (1) the presiding officer, i.e., mayor, vice mayor, president, vice president, commission chair or vice chair; and (2) the secretary or clerk who records the minutes.

The presiding officer must call the meeting to order when a quorum is present and the time for the meeting has arrived. The chair announces: "The meeting will come to order."

During the meeting, the presiding officer should be called "Mr. Chair," "Mr. President" or "Madam Chair," or simply "The Chair." The presiding officer also should refer to herself by such a title, e.g., "The chair rules..."

The following order is often used for the meeting:

(1)   Pledge of allegiance,

(2)   Reading and approval of minutes,

(3)   Reports of officers and standing (permanent) committees (or commissions),

(4)   Reports of special or *ad hoc* committees,

(5)   Special priority matters,

(6)   Unfinished business from preceding meetings,

(7)   New business (matters initiated at the current meeting),

(8)   Audience comments,

(9)   Adjournment.

Business is brought before the assembly by motion of a member. The motion may be made before or after the presentation of a report on the matter. A motion bringing a matter up for decision on a topic is entitled a *main motion*. Other motions that propose some other action, e.g., to call the question, are subject to rules of priority.

Before a member can make a motion or participate in a discussion, the member must *obtain the floor*, i.e., the chair must recognize the member as having the exclusive right to be heard then. The chair must recognize any member who seeks the floor while entitled to it. The proper way to obtain the floor is to state: "Madam Chair." The chair gives the member the floor by stating: "The chair recognizes Ms. Jones." The first recognized member to ask for the floor has the first right to it.

The three steps for bringing a motion before the assembly are:

(1)   A member makes a motion such as, "Madam Chair, I move that…"

(2)   Another member seconds the motion. (Recognition of the member by the chair is not necessary in the case of a second.)

(3) The chair states the question (motion), e.g., "A motion has been made by Ms. Jones and seconded by Mr. Smith to approve the budget."

Then the chair states the motion is pending and open to debate, although the chair may allow brief informal discussion even before the motion is made. Until the chair states the question, the maker may withdraw or amend it and the second may withdraw in such a case.

The second merely implies the motion should come before the meeting and not necessarily that the second favors the motion. The second may offer modification of the motion to the moving party who may approve or reject the proposal. The purpose of a second is to avoid unnecessary discussion on motions that have no chance of passage.

If the motion is unclear or out of order, the chair, instead of stating the question, may request the maker to clarify it or rule the motion out of order, whichever is appropriate. Once the motion is made, seconded and stated, only a second motion may amend it.

After the motion is stated, the members debate the motion. Debate must be confined to the pending motion or else it is out of order. The presiding officer should not participate in the debate at least until all other members have finished their discussion. The chair, recognizing the maker of the motion, begins debate. A contrary member is then recognized and so forth until all members are heard. A member can speak a second time after every member has been offered a turn to comment. The chair may limit further discussion.

Following debate, the chair "puts the question" to vote by saying, "Are you ready for the question?" (Response) "The question is..." Then, the members vote. If the question calls for a roll call, the secretary or clerk calls the roll. If voice vote is permitted, the chair says, "All in favor signify by saying aye." (Response) "Those opposed, signify by saying nay." (Response) The chair announces the result of the vote, e.g., "The ayes (or nays) have it; the motion carries (or fails); (state the effect of the motion). The next item of business is ..."

A majority vote of those present will carry the motion (unless the law requires a specified number of votes). A member can change his vote until the chair announces the vote. The chair is entitled to vote on all matters.

Frequently, the rules of priority are adequate to deal with the problems under discussion. In a few cases, however, a "secondary motion," such as a "motion to table" will follow a main motion. Robert's Rules become complex in the area of secondary motions:[38]

(1) Main motions
(a) Original main motion
(b) Incidental main motion
(2) Secondary motions
(a) Privileged motion
(b) Subsidiary motion
(c) Incidental Motion
(d) Motion to bring the question before the assembly again

A basic principle of parliamentary law is that only one question (main motion) can be considered at a time. The question must be decided before other questions may be considered. A secondary motion covers issues that may be considered while the main motion is pending without violating this principle. Consequently, secondary motions take precedence over main motions. Further, certain types of secondary motions take precedence over other secondary motions. All privileged secondary motions take precedence over all subsidiary motions. The rank of an incidental secondary motion depends upon the character of the main motion.

Rules have also been developed that rank the various types of privileged motions between themselves and subsidiary motions among themselves. The ranking rules may be summarized, in order of preference, as follows:

(1) Privileged
(a) Fix the time to adjourn

(b) Adjourn

(c) Recess (when a question is pending)

(d) Raise a question of privilege (not debatable)

(e) Call for the Orders of the Day

(2) Subsidiary

(a) Lay on the table

(b) Previous question (to close debate)

(c) Limit or extend debate

(d) Postpone to a certain time

(e) Refer

(f) Amend

(g) Postpone indefinitely

The Legislature mandates open meetings to compel communication between the electorate and the elected. The agency can adopt rules of order to force orderly proceedings. But no law or rule ensures an effective meeting. Good meetings are the products of hard work by the governing board, particularly the chair.

Ethics

The State Legislature has mandated local elected officials to have a least two hours of "ethics" training every two years. This statute specifies topics to be considered, most have little to do with ethics. The "required subjects" will be discussed below in a separate chapter. Real ethics will be discussed now.

Ethics can be defined in many ways, but, in the end, ethics has one meaning: you must act with propriety. To satisfy public expectations, government officials must be honest, respectful, compassionate, fair, responsible, and courageous. These characteristics are not mandated by statutes, rules and regulations. Legal standards provide the minimum. Government officials will be punished if they do not satisfy the minimum but they are also expected to do better. Ethics have developed for reasons from the profane to the profound. Theologians urge ethical behavior to promote conduct compatible with religious beliefs. For Christians, this usually means the Golden Rule: "Do unto others as you would do unto yourself." Secular philosophers promote philosophical values. For Aristotle, "goodness is happiness" of an orderly and peaceful society. For government, ethics means: "Obey the law and everything will be all right." Ethics is important for these reasons and more.

The Institute for Global Ethics concludes there are five core values shared across the globe: "compassion, fairness, responsibility, honesty and respect." The Josephson Institute lists six pillars of character for Americans: "caring, fairness, responsibility, trustworthy, respect and citizenship." The Boy Scouts among us will recognize these lists are remarkably similar to the twelve characteristics of a good scout: "trustworthy, loyal, helpful, friendly, courteous, kind, obedient, cheerful, thrifty, brave, clean and reverent."

Ethical conduct is important to politicians for very pragmatic reasons. Being perceived as ethical can result in election victory. Everyone – particularly voters – would choose the high-road-official if they know how. The electorate may have difficulty finding the ethical official, but an official doesn't have a problem being ethical.

Ethics is important everywhere. Good ethics will be on display at public meetings. Elected officials lose the respect (and support) of the electorate by rudeness at public meetings. The public does not appreciate brilliant riposte. The public sees nastiness where officials see cleverness. The public believes acrimonious debate is a sign of failure. In short, the public expects more of their leaders than of themselves. (A vocal few constituents will encourage rude behavior by directors. The "give 'em hell, Harry" syndrome wears thin.) Rude behavior leads to gridlock and gridlock to more rude behavior. The business of the agency is not accomplished. Eventually, the thoughtful majority will throw contentious bums out.

Rules of decorum are like table manners. Every adult is expected to know them and no one appreciates being told what they are. The lack of decorum becomes a difficult cycle. No one has a vested interest in calling a halt to rudeness. No one except the elected official who realizes boorish behavior is demeaning.

The program for restoring (or preserving) decorum has several phases. Be patient:

- *First, debates and decisions must be public.* Even the most hardcore orator will tone it down when the public is watching. Take advantage of public access channels offered by the local cable operator. They need the business. The board is more likely to behave. They can never be sure who is watching.

- *Attempt to reach a consensus*: At least initially, avoid secondary issues threatening a consensus. Build up to the potentially divisive issues by agreeing on basics. When the divisive issues must be confronted, everyone will have a stake in preserving the earlier consensus.

- *Be respectful*: Even the most obnoxious, deceitful and lazy director enjoys the support of a few honest and energetic voters. Treat the director as if you are dealing with these voters. Come to the aid of other directors if your supporters are disrespectful of another director or else you will be perceived as adopting (or promoting) your disrespectful supporter's view.

- *Make a decision*: Make a decision even if a consensus is not possible after appropriate time for reflection, otherwise you reward and encourage obstreperous behavior. Citizens rightly criticize government for inaction when hard decisions are continually avoided. An expeditious, honest decision will satisfy an honest citizen even if the citizen disagrees with the outcome. On the other hand, not-so-honest citizens will do everything to delay an adverse decision, including demanding a consensus.

Courteous behavior is more than moral behavior. Courteous behavior honors the official and the agency.

Respect is also a key trait. Officials must respect the roles of others. Local agency officials are "legislators" when adopting laws or policies. The chief executive officer (often called the "general manager") is the executive branch when carrying out these laws. The judicial branch enforces these laws when necessary. Three branches of government must work together for the public good. Ethics requires officials in each branch to be respectful of the roles of other officials.

The roles of officials must be understood. Because the right to direct government is the heart of democracy, elected officials are the most important personnel of a local agency. Elected officials are most effective if they understand their role and the role of other public servants. Officials must represent the voters by determining what the electorate wishes. The ability to hear the electorate is no small feat. Officials who have this ability can be proud. The board must communicate the wishes of the electorate to the staff and communicate the recommendations of the staff to the electorate by adopting agency policy. When this discourse is effective, an agency should enjoy the support of the community necessary for successful operations. The electorate will withhold support and the agency will suffer when the elected officers fail to articulate agency policy.

Ethics are important when a law (policy, resolution or ordinance) is adopted. A moral process for adopting laws is described in the landmark work, The Morality of Law, which offered eight requirements for moral legislation. A moral "process" will tend to create moral "substance." The eight elements of Lon Fuller's thesis are:

1.	The rules must have general application. The ordinance cannot be written to favor or punish a particular person or group.

2. The public must have <u>notice</u> of the rules. Constituents must have the opportunity to conform behavior to the new law to reap benefits.

3. The laws cannot be <u>retroactive</u>. Constituents must have the opportunity to avoid penalties. For instance, the current rush to adopt safe water regulations is producing *de facto* retroactivity by encouraging litigants to sue agencies for serving water in compliance with past laws.

4. The laws must be <u>clear</u>. An unclear law is an open invitation for bureaucratic blackmail through interpretation.

5. The laws must <u>not be contradictory</u>. Another opportunity for bureaucratic abuse.

6. The laws must <u>not require the impossible</u>. Laws which ignore science can be impossible to follow.

7. The laws must <u>not be amended too often</u>. There must be constancy of the law through time. A constant turnover makes notice impossible. The rash of drinking water regulations violates this rule.

8. There must be <u>congruence between official action and the declared rule</u>. <u>The laws must be enforced as they are written</u>. <u>They must be clear and feasible without exceptions for opponents or supporters</u>.

"Ethics" can become a rationalization for misconduct. The Josephson Institute has identified several common rationalizations:

- If It's Necessary, It's Ethical
- The False Necessity Trap

- If It's Legal and Permissible, It's Proper
- I Was Doing It for You
- I'm Just Fighting Fire With Fire
- It Doesn't Hurt Anyone
- Everyone's Doing It
- It's OK as Long as I Don't Gain Personally
- I've Got It Coming
- I Can Still Be Objective

More specifically, as pertains to decisions by public officials, does anyone disagree the following standards are correct:

(1) Public office should not be used for personal financial gain even if such gain is not a violation of law.

(2) A person should be appointed to office solely on the basis of merit and without regard to: race, religion, national origin, gender, or medical condition.

(3) A person should not be appointed to office on the basis of family or personal relationship.

(4) Public officials should not threaten the use of the power of office for personal gain – financial or otherwise.

(5) Public officials should not disparage political opponents or fellow officials unless the comment is necessary to protect the agency and the official knows the statement to be true.[39]

When a law is violated, there are penalties. There is no legal sanction for unethical conduct unless a law is also violated. However, agencies can punish unethical behavior:

- Employees can be disciplined for violation of codes of conduct.[40]
- An elected official can be removed from committee members and barred from being the agency's spokesperson.

Vacancies

The public agency begins its corporate life with a vote. The governing body starts by having members elected or appointed. Some governing bodies are appointed. Some members are elected by landowners. Elections are governed by state election laws. There is little opportunity for the exercise of local initiative, but there is some. The agency can decide several things about the form of the election, such as whether the candidate statement shall be five hundred words or two hundred and fifty words in length and whether the cost of printing and distributing the statement shall be borne by the candidate or the agency.[41] Local agencies can impose campaign contribution limits more severe than is imposed by state law.[42]

A vacancy can occur on the governing board outside the regular election cycle by the death, disability, or removal of a member or by the member's abandonment of office. Vacancy occurs when an officeholder abandons the post. A statute describes events creating vacancy, including:

> ...absence from the state without the permission required by law beyond the period allowed by law...ceasing to discharge the duties of his or her office for three consecutive months, except when prevented by sickness or when absent from the state with the permission required by law... conviction of a felony or of any offense involving a violation of his or her official duties...commitment to a

> hospital or sanitarium by a court of competent jurisdiction as a drug addict, dipsomaniac, inebriate or stimulant addict, but in the event the office shall not be deemed vacant until the order of commitment has become final.[43]

Agencies have great discretion in deciding who to appoint to fill a vacancy. There is no prescribed way for a member to resign. Good practice dictates the creation of a good record. The agency should require members to resign in writing with a specified effective date.[44] The remaining members should "accept" the resignation on the record at a public meeting. However, a member cannot be forced to resign in writing and the resignation is effective even if it is not accepted. Any qualified "elector" may be appointed. Employees of an agency can serve on the governing board but once elected, the employee must resign as an employee.[45] An elector is someone eligible to vote. This usually means the person must live within the territory which elects the member and be at least eighteen years old. In some cases, the person to be appointed must actually be a registered voter but this is not a universal requirement. The office is assumed when the loyalty oath is taken.[46]

Within ten days of a vacancy, the agency must notify the county clerk of the vacancy.[47] The vacancy can be filled no sooner than fifteen days after a notice is posted that an appointment may be considered by the board of the agency.[48] Some agencies simply put a vacancy on the agenda and the board votes to fill it. Some agencies solicit written applications. Some agencies interview candidates. The selection process is not regulated, but it must be during a public meeting. A person who is appointed will hold office for the remainder of the term if less than half the term remains.[49] The appointed director will serve until the next election if more than half the term remains. An appointed director is not entitled to be designated as an incumbent until at least one election cycle.[50] The board of the agency may call an election to fill the vacancy.[51] The board of supervisors may appoint or call an election to fill the vacancy if the agency board fails to appoint or call an election to fill the vacancy within sixty days of the date of the vacancy.[52] If no one acts, the agency must call an election.[53]

Leaving Office

A person holding an elective office (whether elected or appointed to the office) can be removed from office in three ways: by the election of someone else, recall, or impeachment. The election of a successor is self-explanatory.

Recall is a "political" process. A recall election takes place when voters are dissatisfied with a director's performance.[54] Misconduct is not a prerequisite to recall.[55] The process is described in the Elections Code. It is lengthy and complicated. Any error will bring the process to the end. Opportunity for error is compounded because recall statutes are frequently changed.[56] Petitions containing a specified number of signatures must be filed with the agency secretary and then presented to the county election official who decides whether the requisite number of qualified signatures have been presented. If the petition contains enough signatures, the county election official schedules an election.[57] At the election, the official is recalled if a majority vote carries for the proposition. At the same election, the person receiving the most votes is elected to succeed the recalled director.

Impeachment is a judicial process. The impeachment statute was one of the first laws adopted when California became a state:

> An accusation in writing against any officer of a district, county, or city, including any member of the governing board or personnel commission of a school district, for willful or corrupt misconduct in office, may be presented by the grand jury of the county for or in which the officer accused is elected or appointed. An accusation may not be

> presented without the concurrence of at least 12 grand jurors.[58]

The District Attorney may attempt to remove an official if the grand jury decides the official is guilty of "willful misconduct." Willful misconduct is not defined. The first case interpreting this section was decided in 1890 when the California Supreme Court upheld the impeachment of a judge for imposing harsher, criminal penalties on "colored" people.[59] Most subsequent cases have held willful misconduct does not require criminal conduct; conduct shocking the conscience of the grand jury will sustain removal. However, a recent decision says the misconduct must be criminal.[60]

What right does a director have to call on staff for assistance? There is no statute on the subject. Several principles deal with different aspects of the question. First, a director can not obtain the assistance of the agency for personal matters such as business opportunities. For example, an agency can not provide direct or indirect campaign assistance. General information about elections can be provided to all candidates, including incumbents. Second, staff must secure approval for services requiring expenditures which would require board approval. Third, the staff must treat all directors the same or violate the electoral rights of the excluded director and the voters who elected the director. Fourth, some requests are covered by special rules. The custodian of records must provide *public* records to everyone, including directors under the Public Records Act. Agency counsel must provide *confidential* records in counsel's possession to the district under State Bar regulations. Fifth, the agency must provide directors with a place and opportunity to meet and establish the policies of the agency. Under the Brown Act, the board is entitled to obtain an agenda of every meeting in advance of the meeting. Special meetings cannot be called without actual notice to all board members.[61]

CHAPTER 2

MANAGEMENT

Since the board sets policy and management carries it out, the most important decision of the board is who will be the manager. Most principal acts call for the appointment of the Chief Executive Officer and other officers. The CEO will appoint department heads. Most principal acts require the board to appoint a counsel, treasurer, secretary, and auditor to ensure these officers will be more likely to offer independent advice to the board.

The chief administrative officer of a county, the city manager, city administrator, or the general manager of a special district performs the same function as the chief executive officer ("CEO") of a private corporation. As we have already learned, the CEO must recommend programs to the board and implement programs approved by the board. Except in small agencies, the CEO must hire employees and contractors to carry out the policies and programs. Often, the CEO is the spokesperson for the agency. In short, the CEO must have the skills to deal with elected officials, staff, and the public.

The typical selection process for a CEO goes through stages. Commonly, agencies advertise job openings in trade journals, such as Western Cities News or the Association of

California Water Agencies' newsletter. The candidates are often screened by a committee of the board. The governing body will interview finalists. Sometimes, CEOs respond to a written examination. Laws are fairly liberal when it comes to the process for selecting a CEO. Agencies cannot discriminate against "protected classes." The board can interview candidates in closed session, but the board cannot discuss salary in closed session. If this is a problem, the governing body may delegate responsibility for salary negotiation to an *ad hoc* committee but the entire governing body must make the decision on the salary in public session.

The executive officer must possess a range of skills. The selection process is an opportunity to determine if the applicants have the appropriate skill sets. The CEO should reflect the personality of the organization. This attribute is difficult to discover in the absence of an interview. The CEO has to understand technicalities of administration and the specialties of the organization.[62] Tests or interviews can discover these attributes. The more difficult quality to discover in a job applicant is the ability to communicate with the governing body and with the public. The CEO must explain sometimes complicated subjects in simple terms to the governing body that spends just a few hours a week on the job. The CEO has to explain the board's policies to the public. Testing job applicants for communication skills requires a face-to-face interview.

A written contract is not required, but written contracts are common for CEOs, if for no other reason than to deal with termination. Typically, CEOs serve "at pleasure" or "at-will." The CEO can be fired at any time without cause. The CEO deserves some protection from a whimsical termination. As a consequence, many CEO contracts include a severance clause which says if the CEO is fired without cause within six months after a new board is elected, a severance payment of several months of salary will be paid.[63] Typically, termination "for cause" will not trigger the severance package.[64] As with employees, the CEO must take a loyalty oath before assuming office.[65]

A CEO who can be fired for no reason cannot be fired for a bad reason. For example, an otherwise competent executive cannot be fired for political activities.[66] However, the First Amendment does not protect government employees from discipline for speech pursuant to the employee's official duties.[67] The executive must be given the opportunity for a "name clearing hearing" if the reason for termination is made public.[68] As a result, if they can, the board should resist the temptation to give reasons when terminating an at-will executive.

The governing body must hold the executive responsible for the affairs of the agency. The executive's contract should call for regular performance evaluations. The evaluations should take place no matter how inconvenient or apparently successful the executive's performance has been. Directors can discuss the executive's performance in general terms in closed session with or without the executive. However, if the board wishes to consider specific charges against the executive, the executive (like other employees) must be given notice of those charges and an opportunity to attend the closed session.

The executive can be paid any salary and benefits approved by the board. The executive can be provided benefits not provided other staff. (The most common would be a company vehicle.) The executive can be reimbursed for usual and necessary expenses incurred in the performance of duties. In each of these instances, executive compensation and benefits are not remarkably different than for other employees. (For this reason, discussion is deferred until compensation and benefits for employees in the next chapter.)

The governing body must also understand the roles of other officers so an intelligent choice can be made in selecting the right person for the job.

The role of the agency lawyer is often misunderstood and deserves comment, lest the district becomes the servant of a law office.[69] By now, you realize the job of the lawyer is not making policy. The lawyer advises the board when a proposed policy cannot be legally undertaken. The board should not expect the lawyer to conjure a rationale for every decision. Do that enough, the lawyer will join the board attending an involuntary school with bars on the windows in one of California's deserts. During the selection process, it is important to discover whether lawyer candidates think lawyers should be involved in policy making.

The lawyer represents the agency, not the CEO. The lawyer must ensure the CEO undertakes programs authorized by the board and follows the law in implementing those programs. The lawyer must inform the governing body when the CEO violates policies or the law. If the governing body refuses to discipline a CEO who violates the law, or the governing body itself violates the law, the attorney has a duty to the client, i.e., the agency, to do something. Most public lawyers and the State Bar believe public agency attorneys cannot report criminal violations to the District Attorney, except to prevent <u>future</u> violent crimes. Federal courts have taken a different view. In a famous case which arose during the Bill Clinton administration, the federal circuit court instructed house counsel to disclose documents developed for First Lady Hillary Clinton. The court's rationale is instructive:

> "We believe the strong public interest in honest government and in exposing wrongdoing by public officials would be ill-served by recognition of a governmental attorney-client privilege applicable in criminal proceedings inquiring into the actions of public officials. We also believe that to allow any part of the federal government to use its in-house attorneys as a shield against the production of information relevant to a federal criminal investigation would represent a gross misuse of public assets... <u>An official who fears he or</u>

<u>she may have violated the criminal law and wishes to speak with an attorney in confidence should speak with a private attorney, not a government attorney.</u>" (Emphasis added.)

The agency can resolve the question of the lawyer's duty by specifically authorizing counsel to disclose criminal violations. Surprisingly, lawyers are more reluctant than board members to take this step. Legal counsel, not the governing body, is usually responsible for the wall of silence because counsel does not wish to offend the directors by disclosing violations. Prospective lawyers should be quizzed on this subject before they are engaged. (Lawyer candidates can also learn much about their prospective client by asking whether the board would authorize the lawyer to contact the District Attorney.)

Business schools teach there are three ways to distinguish products: price, quality and service. Experts believe emphasizing one element sacrifices another, e.g., quality service costs more. Agencies seldom think of price, quality and service. Price usually plays a disproportionately large role in lawyer selection because the electorate will hector the board about high legal bills. Quality is often overlooked because non-lawyers feel they cannot really evaluate the quality of legal advice. Service is ignored altogether because lawyers usually blame bad service on complicated legal issues or the opposition.

Lawyers should not be hired solely on how much they charge. Hourly rates have little to do with cost. An inexperienced lawyer can charge $100 an hour but may need three hours to complete a task which an experienced lawyer can complete in a half an hour at $300 per hour. There's no way to evaluate lawyers on the basis of hourly rates. Cost comparisons are possible only if hourly rates are ignored. Lawyers usually know how much time is needed for transactional advice for the typical agency. The lawyer should be asked to provide a flat fee proposal for transactional advice.[70]

The governing body and the CEO are usually not very clear on what constitutes quality service. Because legal questions are complicated (why else would you ask a lawyer for help), clients often believe the answers must be complicated. Clients tolerate incomprehensible advice because they feel the matter is too complicated or because they are embarrassed to admit they don't understand what the lawyer is saying. Some clients even believe legal advice is not good unless it's incomprehensible! A lawyer's job is to explain complex legal concepts in simple terms. Abraham Lincoln had it right when he told the client: "Please excuse the length of this letter. I didn't have time to make it short." Unless you're Romanian, don't allow your lawyer to speak Latin. Quality service is provided when you understand what the lawyer is saying. The ability to communicate is easy to determine at the interview. Look the candidates in the eye and ask them a question. The best communicator will connect with a clear, concise answer.

Judging the quality of litigation service is also possible. A tally of wins and losses is <u>not</u> a good measure. A lawyer who wins every trial is probably settling cases which should be tried. This may be a sign the lawyer's advice is too conservative. Litigation-free clients and a successful litigation are only rough measures of quality. The typical legal problem can be solved in many ways. There is often no single right answer. That's why lawyers "practice" law. A lawyer who consistently offers complicated solutions even when the complicated solutions are clearly stated – is probably not offering quality service.

Lawyers must be scrupulously honest because sooner or later, the "other side" will attempt to obtain advantage in negotiation by accusing your lawyer of doing something wrong. When this occurs, you must have confidence in the integrity of your lawyer. Integrity is best judged by reputation. An agency's lawyer must protect the values of the agency. Sooner or later, the lawyer will stand alone among those dealing with the agency or the agency's constituents. The lawyer must accurately convey the *feel* of the agency to outsiders. Don't hire a "junkyard dog" unless you want to offend people. Don't hire a pacifist unless you want to surrender your rights. Ask the candidate how to approach a complicated problem.[71]

Public agencies are at the mercy of their lawyers once there is compliance with the Tort Claims Act and a lawsuit is filed. As with any combat, a moment will arise during every lawsuit when a client must rely on a lawyer's judgment in the assessment of the case. A client will have difficulty learning to trust a lawyer's judgment for the first time during litigation. Agencies must establish the long term relationship with their lawyers in anticipation of litigation because the opportunities for establishing trust during a lawsuit are few and far between. An agency must "test" its attorneys during the early stages of a lawsuit by meeting with their trial attorneys and questioning them closely about their methods and theories. A trial attorney who cannot explain the case to a sympathetic client will not be able to explain the case to a judge or jury. Do not be hesitant to replace the trial attorney who fails to develop confidence during the early stages of a lawsuit. Late in the case, the client will inevitably be asked to decide whether or not to accept a settlement offer. When this happens, the client must have confidence in the lawyer's recommendation.

Managing litigation is an art for the public administrator. Successful administrators seem to employ the same techniques. A few "rules" are helpful for lawyer management:

> Rule 1: Tell your attorney you are not anxious to spend money. (This is an easy rule but often overlooked.) Contrary to popular belief, most attorneys are not greedy. Attorneys are accused of being greedy when they are merely conscientious. This is especially true of younger attorneys. The key to a successful outcome in a lawsuit is preparation. When has the attorney devoted enough attention to the preparation of case? This depends on the

importance of the case and conscientiousness of the attorney. Lazy attorneys will not put in enough time, even on important cases. Attorneys who are too conscientious will put in too much time for cases which don't deserve it. The attorney and client must have the same understanding of the importance of the case and how much should be spent. The perfect case, a case which allows for an infinite preparation, does not exist. The client must recognize the attorney does not completely control the playing field. The opposition gets the vote. The other side can make a case more expensive by various tactics. The corollary to this rule is never let the other side know you are not anxious to spend money on the case. If the other side believes the agency is unwilling or reluctant to spend money on a lawsuit, the other side will announce its willingness to spend "whatever is necessary" in an effort to bully the agency into early submission.

Rule 2: Tell your attorney everything. Cases turn on facts and law. The lawyer must know the facts as soon as possible so you can be advised of the potential outcome. The corollary to Rule 2 is don't kill the messenger. Don't take it out on an attorney who advises you have a poor case. You need to know early so you can attempt to settle. If your attorney is a "yes" man, you will be happy up to the moment of verdict and then you will hear how the judge or the jury did something bad, crazy or stupid to produce the disappointing outcome. Mainly, judges and juries are not stupid, lazy or evil.

<u>Rule 3</u>: Litigation involves witnesses and this is where it gets expensive. Anyone who witnessed the events giving rise to the lawsuit will be asked to explain what was observed. This is done before trial with written interrogatories so the case can be evaluated. Usually, the most effective way to determine what a witness has to say is by deposition. The lawyer can appraise the witness's credibility. How will the witness appear to the judge or jury? Depositions cost at least $2,000 and a full-day deposition can easily cost $5,000. (Deposition expenses include your lawyer's time and the court reporter's time to transcribe, record, and transcribe the deposition. The losing side of a lawsuit can be assessed the costs of the other side's deposition.) If a lawsuit involves technical matters which cannot be easily explained by what an ordinary witness says, an expert witness must be called to testify. Expert depositions are particularly expensive. The deposition must be preceded by the production of the expert's documents. Experts often require the assistance of another expert. For example, in an eminent domain case, an appraisal expert will rely on planning experts to determine the future potential of the property. Furthermore, a separate expert is often hired to give confidential advice on how to examine the other side's expert and another to testify. Expert testimony is exponentially more expensive and complicated. A corollary to Rule 3 is the discovery process must occur before serious settlement discussions can take place.

<u>Rule 4</u>: Expend the appropriate effort for settlement. Once the facts are known and the law has been tested through pretrial motions, the parties can make a serious effort to settle a lawsuit. A mandatory settlement conference will be scheduled by the court before trial. A settlement judge – and not the trial judge who could be prejudiced by hearing settlement positions – will attempt to bring the parties together. Settlement judges have a full schedule and cannot devote much time to case. Usually, the mandatory settlement conference does not produce a settlement. However, in low value cases, this is the only practical path to settlement. In higher value cases, litigants often hire a professional mediator. Successful mediations do not just happen; mediation is expensive and requires preparation. A mediation brief emphasizing the merits of the case and the weaknesses of the other side is submitted to the mediator in advance of the mediation. Some mediators will bring both sides together in a large room to discuss the case in general terms before separating the parties. Some will separate the parties at the very beginning. The choice depends on how much animosity is in the room. Eventually, the mediator will have a heart to heart with each side explaining the weaknesses of that side's case while admitting the strengths. The mediation briefs may reveal an overlap between the positions of the parties so the mediator can quietly offer the shared position of each. (If the attorneys have been doing their job, they will have discussed settlement in general terms before the

mediation and discovered potential overlaps.) In the more typical case, the mediator must drag each side into the common ground. (A mediator can sometimes discover positions which even the parties did not know they held.) When the parties agree, the mediator will assist in drafting a settlement to be presented to the court.

Rule 5: Lawsuits take longer and cost more than expected. Sometimes the only way justice can be served is by presenting a case to a judge or a jury. Outsiders are often disappointed to find the public part of a trial usually doesn't start until 9:00 a.m. or 9:30 a.m. and usually ends at 4:00 p.m. or 4:30 p.m. with an ample lunch break. Actually, this is a very full day because between 8:00 and 9:00 in the morning, attorneys are conferring with the judge about the upcoming day by previewing difficult arguments and making the case for the exclusion of witnesses. During the lunch hour, attorneys are conferring with witnesses for the afternoon. During the evening, attorneys confer with the witnesses for the next day and prepare for the morning's trial. A serious case begins around 6:00 a.m. and ends around 10 p.m. Do that for six weeks and you will realize trial attorneys earn their keep.

Rule 6: Don't plan on appealing. After judgment is entered, the parties have sixty days to decide whether to appeal. The losing side is often too disappointed to make a rational decision for a couple weeks. Clients must be careful to not allow the aggressiveness of their attorney to pollute the decision on whether to appeal. This is not to say attorneys intentionally overstated the value of their case. Remember, for six weeks your attorney has been working hard to present only your side of the case. To show the right amount of enthusiasm, your attorney must believe in the righteousness of your position. It is not that easy to switch off the enthusiasm when an adverse judgment is given. (The English have a useful division of labor. Counselors do not appear in court and counselors advise clients and barristers outside the courtroom. Barristers appear in court and advise clients only in the courtroom. The counselor can evaluate the barrister's work dispassionately. California agencies usually cannot afford the luxury of a counselor and a barrister. However, agencies should make an effort to separate the two functions whenever possible. General counsel can act as "counselor" and the general counsel should assign someone else to act as "barrister.") The decision to appeal should not be taken lightly. Aside from time and expense, the appeal will continue to distract the agency from serving the public. Do not underestimate the distraction. Particularly at the appeal stage, staff will have a tendency to start rooting for the outcome. The corollary to Rule 6 is: begin settlement discussions when your attorney begins to say an appeal will be necessary to win the case. A successful appeal is more difficult than the trial.

Rule 7: The appellate court cannot cure every mistake. The Court of Appeals must defer to the trial court's findings of fact. If the trial court believed a witness who said the car swerved to the left, the appellate court will not grant your appeal based on another witness who said the car swerved to the right. Factual decisions by judge or jury will be assumed to be correct unless errors cannot be ignored. In the overwhelming number of cases, the only thing to appeal is incorrect legal decisions. Even here, it is necessary to be cautious: an incorrect legal decision can be based on an incorrect reading of the facts and not subject to being overturned on appeal. Of course, trial courts can make incorrect legal decisions. Laws are not always clear and sometimes the courts change the law with a dose of judicial legislation. Sometimes agencies will appeal an adverse judgment as a matter of principle or establish new law. But, realize "principle" is music to the ears of the lawyer. It means you are willing to spend more than the case is actually worth.

The office of treasurer has more variation in roles among agencies than any other office. The treasurer can be purely ceremonial. Directors can be appointed to serve as treasurer to receive the reports of a "deputy" treasurer who does the actual work of managing investments and accounting for money. In other places, the treasurer actively manages the books, oversees investments, and reports to the board.

By statute, the treasurer must recommend investment policy and certify investments have been made in accordance with the policy approved by the board. The treasurer must present the board with an accounting of money received, money spent, and cash on hand. In short, the treasurer is supposed to keep the governing board informed about the condition of the balance sheet and what is known in the private sector as the profit and loss statement. The treasurer should also make recommendations to the board on other financial matters, including accounting practices, selection of depositories, and financial consultants. The role of treasurer is best filled by a person with a financial or business background. Failure to appoint a qualified treasurer is a missed opportunity to obtain first-hand quality advice on financial matters.

The secretary is a ceremonial office with many small agencies. Directors are often appointed to serve as secretary; they immediately appoint a deputy secretary from the staff to perform the actual work.

The job of the secretary is time-consuming. The secretary keeps the minutes of the board meetings and manages the records of the agency. These jobs require a level of experience and education. The minutes need only recite: the time and place of meeting; the directors in attendance and votes of issues taken (roll vote when required by law). Typically the secretary will include statements made by the directors "for the record." The board, not the secretary, should decide how expansive to make the minutes. The secretary also is typically responsible for the preparation and posting of the agenda for every board meeting. This requires knowledge of the Brown Act (more about that below), and the cooperation of the CEO and presiding officer of the board.

One of the most difficult tasks of the secretary is to act as custodian of records. The Public Records Act requires most documents be made available to the public. Laws specify when records can be destroyed. These laws require an interpretation. A specific person, usually the secretary, must be designated the custodian of records so decisions on public records, inspection and destruction, can be consistent.

Some principal acts say the auditor is an officer of the agency. Other laws refer to an auditor as an outside, independent consultant. The two uses of the same term causes confusion. If the principal act says an agency shall have an auditor, the act is usually referring to a finance officer, not an independent, outside auditor. The finance officer may be responsible for maintaining the books in good order, but the finance officer type of auditor does not eliminate the need for an annual or biennial independent audit performed by an outside consultant.

The rules for public agency audits are different than the rules of private sector audits. An agency should select an independent auditor familiar with public agency auditing practices. In addition to what has been said earlier about price, service and quality, like the attorney, the auditor should exhibit independence. The auditor must be trusted to express an independent opinion, even if it is critical of the CEO, other members of the staff, or the governing body itself. A new auditor will need a certain amount of "get acquainted" time (mobilization, if you want to be technical). This suggests the same auditor should be used every year. However, at some point, the auditor becomes too familiar with the cast of characters and the auditor's independence may be compromised. This suggests auditors should be appointed for short durations. The governing body must decide how much independence is to be sacrificed to save money for other agency work.

Local government faces a multitude of rapidly emerging techniques, instruments, and complex policy issues in the area of capital financing. Recognizing this, local government has responded by seeking and retaining knowledgeable outsiders for financial advice. The financial advisors can address fiscal shortfalls facing government. Financial advisors can provide advice on how to structure borrowing. These consultants can also advise on how to invest monies.

Selecting a consulting engineer is one of the most important decisions a board can make. Engineers provide expertise and creativity which can save millions of dollars. They provide planning, design and administration services essential for the construction of a billion dollars of facilities in California every year. Selection requires a careful review of an engineering firm's experience, personnel, availability, reputation, and many other factors. The selection process must be fair and competitive.[72] When hiring a consulting engineer it is important to determine the role of the consulting engineer with the District staff. The consulting engineer should be viewed as "part-time" staff and part of the management team. District management should have a role in selecting the engineers (subject to approval by the Board) since the engineer will be working day-to-day with the District staff, not the Board.

The relationships between design engineers and the engineer who supervises construction should be understood. Every construction job will generate at least one dispute. Everyone on the site will try to avoid responsibility by blaming someone else. Sometimes this is appropriate. The construction manager must honestly evaluate the contractor's claims the work was not properly designed. To ensure independence, a construction manager should be someone different than the design professional.

Architects, professional engineers, and land surveyors ("design professionals") have obtained statutory protections. A public agency can only mandate the design professional to indemnify the agency for claims resulting from negligence, recklessness or willful misconduct.[73] Liability is typically based on failure to follow industry standards. Negligence, recklessness or willful misconduct seldom occurs. Consequently, this statute virtually prevents indemnity by design professionals.

The engineer's importance to the management team requires the selected consultant be highly qualified for the proposed assignment, have a reputation for integrity and honesty, and be able to successfully complete the assignment within the schedule and budget. A first step is to create a clear definition of why a consultant is needed, whether for a specific short-term assignment, a long-term consulting relationship, a routine design project or a complex state-of-the-art research project. Quality is the single characteristic common to a consultant's selection for any assignment. The commitment to quality based selection will save money, time and resources in the long run because the consulting engineer's recommendations can save significantly more than its fees.

Consulting engineers are very specialized and firms range in size from small sole practitioners to firms with thousands of employees. A key to evaluating the quality and technical expertise of a consulting engineer is the *key personnel* who will be working for you. A large firm experience is not important if key personnel are not available. The knowledge and expertise of the project manager and key staff proposed to work on your assignment should be examined carefully.

The process of selecting a consultant is varied. Referral from other agencies, advertisement for services, statements of qualifications and brochures, and directories of engineering firms can be used to develop a list of potentially qualified firms. Often, small firms present small fixes to problems and large firms present large solutions.

Many different forms of fee can be used – hourly rates, fixed fees, cost plus fixed fees, etc. Occasionally, a district feels it lacks the knowledge to negotiate an appropriate fee. At such time, communications with other districts with similar projects, review of Standard Manuals of Practice such as ASCE Manual 45 or use of a special consultant to assist in the negotiations can alleviate this anxiety. When negotiating fees, be open and straightforward about your budget and availability of funds for the engineering assignment.

The public increasingly demands access to the decision-making process. Effective communications between the public and public agencies must be a two-way street. The public must present their concerns to the agency. The agency must explain their policies to the public. More than ever, a public relations employee (or consultant) is needed to provide communication expertise.

Selection of a public relations expert must be based above all on ability to communicate. The interview process is critical to the task.

Enter the 21st century. Communication with the public is no longer just a matter of dealing with print media. The internet has changed other areas of modern life and it has changed "public outreach." Many agencies have websites. A few will podcast meetings and important presentations. The blogosphere is, as yet, free from local agency discoveries. Few traditional, public relations consultants can offer advice on internet services. A specialist in internet services is usually needed.

CHAPTER 3

EMPLOYEES

Nowhere is state interference with local initiatives greater than with employee relations. Legislatures routinely dictate benefits employees can not gain at the bargaining table.

The role of employees is often overlooked. The governing board and CEO want to tell employees what to do because employees are having all the fun. They actually are doing something – not just talking about it. The board conjures up programs, management orders implementation of programs, and employees implement. Have you ever run across an employee who wants to butt in on management decisions or tell the governing board what to do? Employees know their place on the organizational chart; they have the best seat in the house.

The process for hiring employees is fundamentally different than the process for hiring management or consultants. Intangible skills, such as ability to communicate, remain important for employees, but they are not of paramount importance. Let's put it this way. The president of General Motors must understand fuel injection systems are important for vehicles but the president must not spend time learning how to design the fuel injection components. The employees of General Motors must understand how to manufacture fuel injection systems but it is not important for the employees to understand why fuel injection systems are preferred. Written tests are normally adaptable for specific job skills needed for employees.

Typically, the CEO or Human Resources/Personnel Officer is responsible for hiring employees. In very small organizations, the governing body may want to become involved in the hiring of employees. This is a bad idea. Directors should never be involved in the decision to hire or the decision to fire anyone other than the CEO. (Of course, the board can be available to review employee discipline as an appeal tribunal.) Other than the mandatory loyalty oath and discrimination prohibitions, state law does not mandate the process for hiring employees.[74]

Two statutes apply <u>exclusively</u> to *public* agency *hiring* practices. One statute says:

> No local agency shall, as a part of its hiring practices or promotional practices, employ any educational prerequisites or testing or evaluation methods which are not job-related unless there is no adverse effect.[75]

Further,

> Each local agency's hiring practices and promotional practices shall conform to the Federal Civil Rights Act of 1964.[76]

Most hiring laws apply to the public and private sector alike. These laws prohibit discrimination based on gender, creed, color, national origin, ancestry, physical disability, medical condition, and marital status.[77] Discrimination based on pregnancy, childbirth, or related conditions is prohibited.[78] Age discrimination is prohibited. Sexual preference has protected status. Employers also cannot discriminate on the basis of military status, residency, use of workers' compensation benefits, or political activity. Discrimination based on gender preference (cross-dressing) is prohibited.

The First Amendment and statutes prohibit government from interfering with the "free" exercise of religious beliefs.[79] An employer who refuses to hire because of the religious beliefs violates the Constitution and statutes. The "establishment clause" of the First Amendment prohibits government from forcing citizens to participate in religious activities. Employers cannot require religious belief as a condition of hiring.

The Federal Americans With Disabilities Act ("ADA") prohibits discrimination against the disabled.[80] Under the federal law, a private employer of 12 or more employees and *all* public employers must hire without regard to physical or mental disability.[81] Further, public facilities must be accessible so disabled employees can work. Disability discrimination can be difficult to detect. To reduce opportunities for disability bias, federal regulations require employers to not ask about the applicant's disabilities. Pre-hire physicals are forbidden. An employer may not refuse to hire an applicant with a preexisting condition because the person might be injured on the job.[82] Because disabilities cannot disqualify an applicant, the employer may only ask the ultimate questions: "Can you perform the job?" or "Is accommodation necessary?" Physicals can be given after an applicant is hired because an employer will be careful about rejecting a person already offered a job based on the subsequent physical.

Most Californians have a passable understanding of the Federal ADA. Until recently, compliance with the Federal ADA meant compliance with California's Disability Act. This is no longer true. The California version is significantly broader than the Federal ADA. The California Law says the Federal ADA is "a floor of protection."[83] If the State law is silent or provides less benefits, the Federal ADA applies. The California statute is not limited to actual disabilities. Californians are protected if an employer "perceives" a disability or if the employee has a potentially disabling condition.[84] The California statute is not limited to disability which "substantially" limits "major life activities."[85] A disability exists in California when a life activity is more difficult.[86]

Discrimination based on a medical condition is prohibited only if the condition is cancer, pregnancy, or a genetic characteristic associated with symptoms of disease or disorder or associated with a statistically increased risk of development of a disease or disorder.[87] This can be a subset of the broader prohibition of discrimination on the basis of physical disability.

Employers cannot insist on hiring married or single applicants.[88] Persons <u>over</u> the age of 40 are protected from age discrimination.[89] However, an employer can impose "bona fide requirements for the job" based on fitness (or promotion based on seniority, training or prior service).[90] Unlike most other types of discrimination, the burden of proving this violation is on the victim.[91] An employer can discriminate based on age against a person <u>under</u> 40!

The prohibition against discrimination based on sexual preference was introduced in a backhand way. The California Supreme Court outlawed such discrimination in *Gay Law Students v. Pacific Telephone and Telegraph*.[92] A later Court of Appeals decision followed suit.[93] From this, the legislature concluded a statute was needed to codify the court decisions.[94] Of course, two court decisions do not establish law in a complex, controversial area, particularly when neither decision involved public employees. Ironically, even though the Legislature found the courts resolved the issue on constitutional principles (meaning the legislature was not free to act), lawmakers created an exemption for businesses employing five or fewer employees and certain religious or nonprofit corporations.[95]

The prohibition against gender preference (cross-dressing) was introduced without fanfare – no examples of egregious conduct were presented.[96]

The prohibition against discriminating against those in the military is longstanding.[97] The prohibition includes protections against changing employment status while on military leave.[98]

Public agencies cannot discriminate in hiring based on residency.[99] However, the courts will uphold a residency requirement if the agency demonstrates a rational basis.[100]

Employees cannot be discriminated against for the use of workers' compensation benefits. An employer cannot refuse to hire a person with a history of receiving workers' compensation benefits. (Discrimination on this basis may also violate disability laws.)

No serious person advocates discrimination. Modern discrimination is subtle. The proof of bias is difficult because discrimination is disguised. As a result, special rules of proof have developed. These rules of evidence account for much of the controversy in the area and force agencies to stockpile data. A person claiming to be the victim has the initial burden of establishing discrimination. This can be accomplished by presenting statistics showing the workforce does not reflect the diversity of the community. The employer then has the burden of showing neutral reasons for the statistical disparity. If the employer introduces enough evidence, the burden of proof shifts back to the job applicant to show the employer's reasons are a pretext.

The California Legislature has been virtually silent on the subject of hiring preferences by local agencies.[101] Only one statute applies to local agencies:

> Every local agency shall provide to the Fair Employment and Housing Commission a copy of any affirmative action plan and subsequent amendment to such plan adopted by the local agency.[102]

For decades, the courts mandated or approved affirmative action plans. Cases arise in employment and contracting for goods or services in the state and the federal courts. The U. S. Supreme Court addressed affirmative action hiring in a series of cases under the equal protection clause. In an early case, the Court found the layoff of non-minority teachers under a labor agreement designed to preserve affirmative hiring policy violated equal protection.[103] The Court invoked the "compelling interest" test to hold:

> ...[A] public employer...must ensure that, before it embarks on an affirmative-action program, it has convincing evidence that remedial action is warranted. That is, it must have evidence to justify the conclusion that there has been prior discrimination.[104]

In a later case, the Court affirmed a court order imposing a one-black for one-white promotion requirement for state troopers in Alabama.[105] Here, the Court said:

> In determining whether race-conscious remedies are appropriate, we look to several factors, including the necessity for the relief and the efficacy of alternative remedies; the flexibility and duration of the relief, including the availability of waiver provisions of the relationship of the numerical goals to the relevant labor market, and the impact of the relief on the rights of third parties.[106]

Finally, the Court examined hiring practices of the Santa Clara County Transportation Agency.[107] The Agency had adopted a plan that considered gender "as one factor" when evaluating employees for promotion in a field that traditionally under-represented females. The Court concluded an employer need not rely on its own past or present discriminatory practices to justify affirmative action as long as the work force fails to reflect the countywide labor pool and the plan does not necessarily adversely affect the rights of male employees.[108] Taken together, these cases seem to permit affirmative action to remedy historical racial discrimination or to make the work force similar to the labor pool.

State courts relied entirely on these federal cases until Proposition 209, adopted by the voters in November 1996, created a new set of issues for the *California* Courts. The measure states:

> The state shall not discriminate against, or grant preferential treatment to, any individual or group on the basis of race, sex, color, ethnicity or national origin in the operation of public employment, public education, or public contracting.[109]

The measure does not ban all affirmative action programs. Only race-based programs are targeted. Some race-based programs may survive Proposition 209. For example, a program setting goals and mandating a good faith effort to achieve the same diversity in the work force as the community may still be legal.[110] Further, the federal court can still order affirmative action to remedy past discrimination.

Affirmative action is still mandated in cases other than "race, sex, color, ethnicity, or national origin." Public employers must affirmatively hire disabled persons by making a good faith effort to "reasonably accommodate" the hiring of the disabled. The accommodation varies from case-to-case depending on the circumstances. A small employer might not be expected to pay for expensive machinery to accommodate a sight-impaired typist but a large federal agency can be required to hire readers to accommodate blind job applicants.[111] Accommodations reflect social values. Employees who are hypersensitive to tobacco smoke are considered physically disabled and entitled to reasonable accommodation.[112] Agencies have been required to make a "minor reassignment" to accommodate an asthmatic.[113] The courts seem to have distinguished "good" mental illness from "bad" mental illness when describing the extent of the required accommodation. A person suffering from apraxia will be too distracted to work unless placed in isolation; an isolated workroom is mandated.[114] On the other hand, employers have not been required to accommodate a kleptomaniac.[115] The burden of proof in a disability case is similar to the burden in a discrimination case. A handicapped person is not required to show ability to perform the job.[116] The disabled applicant need only make a "facile" showing accommodation is possible for the burden to shift to the agency to demonstrate accommodation is not required.[117] Failure to accommodate can result in the employer being mandated to make the accommodation and employers may be required to reinstate the employee with back pay.[118]

The preferences for veterans are usually overlooked in the affirmative action debate. Public agencies may give veterans priority in employment without fear of a reverse discrimination lawsuit.[119] Further, veterans returning from service in the military have the same workplace rights as they would have accrued if they had not been absent.[120] This includes most seniority rights and may include the right to take a promotional exam before the eligibility date.

Just as some "good" affirmative action programs have survived, the courts and legislature promote some "good" discrimination. Agencies must avoid hiring smokers, drug users and illegal aliens. The State Legislature introduced a widespread smoking ban as an amendment to the California Occupational "Safety and Health Act of 1973 ("OSHA").[121] The statute forces employers to discriminate against smokers. Can an agency screen out smokers from the pool of job applicants? Remember, the law prohibits discrimination on the basis of physical disability, but the basis of the OSHA ban is public health. The employer must take "reasonable steps" to carry out this ban, including posting signs and consulting employees.[122] An employer of five or fewer individuals may permit smoking only if:

(1) smoking areas are not accessible to minors;

(2) employees who enter the area consent and no one is required to work in a smoking area;

(3) air from the smoking area is exhausted outside; and

(4) ventilation complies with Cal OSHA and EPA standards.[123]

Employer *may* set aside a break room where smoking is permitted but the room must meet the following standards:

(1) air from the room shall not be circulated to other parts of the building;

(2) ventilation standards established by Cal OSHA or EPA shall be satisfied;

(3) the room must be in a non-work area; and

(4) there must be sufficient break rooms to satisfy non-smokers.[124]

Most employers and employees have little reason to disobey smoking laws. Unfortunately, the "smoke police" are occasionally heavy handed in their approach to enforcement and this promises to make this law controversial.

Drug abuse is in the scourge of modern America. An agency using federal funds must promise to implement "drug free workplace" rules.[125] The Federal Drug Free Workplace law mandates employers to abate drug use among employees consistent with privacy rights.[126] "Safety sensate position" must be subject to drug testing pursuant to Federal Department of Transportation Regulations.[127] Courts have not consistently supported programs to combat drug abuse by workers. Under State law, employers risk violation of privacy rights if drug testing is too aggressive.[128] For example,

> ...off duty drug or alcohol use with no on-the-job impairment is not work connected unless the employee works in a safety-sensitive position or the employee's position is such that his conduct will undermine public trust and damage the employer's reputation or the drug test is part of a federally imposed safety program.[129]

The same court said:

> A generalized interest in the integrity of the work force has not been found sufficient to overcome privacy interests in drug testing cases.[130]

Even an interest in safety at a nuclear power plant is not sufficient to justify drug testing of employees not in safety-sensitive positions.[131] Similarly, an employer cannot use a contractual agreement to circumvent the public policy favoring privacy, nor enforce such an agreement if it intrudes on an employee's right to privacy.[132]

The Fourth Amendment to the U. S. Constitution prohibits government from "unreasonable" search and seizure. The courts applied the Fourth Amendment to all types of government activities, not just the pursuit of criminals.[133] Hence, governmental employers – expected to set an example for the rest of society – have a greater burden than private employers. For government workers, the criterion for drug testing is whether it is reasonable under the circumstances of the case.[135] The reasonableness test involves a balancing of the employer's interest against the employee's interest in Fourth Amendment protections.

> [I]n limited circumstances, where privacy interests implicated by the search are minimal, and where an important governmental interest furthered by the intrusion would be placed in jeopardy by a requirement of individualized suspicion, a search may be reasonable despite the absence of suspicion.[135]

The government's interest is greater in some cases than others. There is more reason to discover drug use among customs agents charged with interdicting a drug smuggler than customs agents who maintain unclassified records.[136] The invasion is also relative. Office workers may be more embarrassed by having to provide urine samples than high school athletes who routinely share locker rooms.[137]

The Fourth Amendment is not the only constitutional barrier to employee drug testing. The California Constitution guarantees citizens the right of privacy.[138] Public and private employers are held to the same privacy standard.[139] A slightly different balancing test is employed to determine if the testing program violates privacy rights under the California Constitution. The question is whether the employer's legitimate interests outweigh the employee's reasonable expectations of privacy. Employer interest analysis seems the same under the search and seizure and privacy amendments. In the case of privacy, the employee's expectations to be free from unreasonable search changes to expectation of privacy. On this basis, the courts upheld testing of college athletes who would share lockers and showers.[140]

So much for the theory. Now apply it to the workplace:

- Employers may require job applicants to submit to reliable, professional drug testing as a condition of employment.

- Employers may <u>not</u> require employees to submit to reliable, professional drug testing as a condition of promotion, unless the employee will occupy a "drug sensitive" position.

- Employers may require employees to submit to reliable, professional drug testing when there is reasonable suspicion that drug use has affected job performance.

The law sometimes evolves slowly when it is difficult to know whether old-fashioned values should be protected in light of modern threats to society. More specifically, is drug abuse so great a threat as to merit relaxation of Constitution protections from unreasonable search and seizure? The answer to this question will ultimately determine the scope of employee drug testing. With few significant exceptions, the courts have provided search and seizure and privacy protections. As of now, the courts fear government more than courts fear drugs and drug dealers. Time will tell if this judgment is correct.

Citizenship is also addressed in specific statutes. A person is not eligible to hold county or district "office" unless at the time of election or appointment the person is a citizen of the state.[141] An officer and the officer's deputies are considered one and the same.[142] The courts have framed a two-prong test for determining what is an office: the office cannot be transient, occasional or incidental, and some portion of the sovereign's power must be exercised.[143]

The Meyers-Milias-Brown Act directs local agencies to engage in "consultation" and "negotiation" with representative of "employee organizations." Terms such as "union" and "collective bargaining" are notable by their absence from this statute but the Meyers-Milias-Brown Act amounts to collective bargaining mandates for local government. Agencies must coordinate employee relations laws with civil service laws. The courts interpreted the Meyers-Milias-Brown Act, the Winton Act and succeeding acts to apply many of the National Labor Relations Act principles to public employees.[144] Traditional notions of civil service employment are cast aside when in conflict with the public employer-employee relations statements.

The public employee may join or refuse to join in an employee organization.[145] Employee organizations represent their members in their employment relations with public agencies.[146] The scope of representation includes matters relating to employment conditions, including but not limited to wages, hours and other terms and conditions of employment.[147] Theoretically, agencies need not bargain over management rights but courts have adopted a balancing test to determine what is outside the scope of bargaining. "Balancing" is a nice way of saying the court will decide and typically, the decision will favor employee bargaining rights. Public agencies must meet and confer in good faith with the recognized employee organizations representing agency employees.[148] If an agreement is reached during such consultations, a memorandum of agreement is prepared and submitted to the governing body for approval or disapproval.[149]

Before the employer-employee bargaining can begin, it is necessary to determine who represents what. Employees can perform widely different work. Employees in one department may have little in common with employees in another department. An engineering department will face different employment issues than a clerical department. The first step is the grouping of employees within various "bargaining units," each of which represents a community of interest. Smaller agencies typically determine bargaining units following informal consultation with the employee organizations that potentially represent the employees within the units. In larger local agencies, an independent commission can determine bargaining units.

Once the representational unit is created, it is necessary to determine which, if any, employee organization will represent the unit. The Meyers-Milias-Brown Act provides the public agency may adopt reasonable rules and regulations affecting the administration of employer-employee relations. Under this authority, most local agencies adopt rules describing how the employee organization representing the unit is to be identified (certified and decertified). Larger agencies often have an independent commission to oversee the process.[150]

After the unit is determined and the employee organization recognized, the employee organization and the agency's representatives must meet and confer in good faith (negotiate) concerning matters within the scope of representation. An agreement is set forth in a document called a "memorandum of understanding" presented by labor and management to the governing board for approval.

The process is designed to eliminate discord and generate agreement between the employer and the employee but negotiations are not always successful. When negotiations fail, the impasse can lead to impasse resolution. In the private sector, impasse resolution has developed to a fine art. These procedures are imported to the public sector. Mediation or conciliation is a relatively mild form of impasse resolution where a neutral third party, i.e. mediator or conciliator, obtains the views of each party in confidence to discover whether a common ground may exist. This procedure is based upon the presumption each party has a final position and is unwilling to express the position to the other party but is willing to express to a neutral third party. Fact-finding is a more rigorous method of impasse resolution. A neutral fact-finder hears evidence presented by each party and issues a report indicating which party's facts are true.[151] The fact-finder's decision is limited to the determination of the facts; the fact-finder does not decide which party is correct. Fact-finding is based upon the premise that the promise of public disclosure of unreasonable positions will spur agreement. Arbitration is similar to fact finding. The arbitrator receives evidence from each party concerning the issues. The arbitrator decides which party is correct. Arbitration may be binding or nonbinding. Nonbinding arbitration means the arbitrator's decision is advisory. Binding arbitration means the parties agree in advance to accept and implement the arbitrator's decision.

Public agencies and public employee organizations are not required to engage in impasse resolution. This helps to insure that impasse procedures will be invoked only if there is a legitimate chance for success. However, this also means disputes can remain unsettled. When the failure of the parties to agree is a result of bad faith bargaining, the other party can claim an unfair employer-employee relations practice. The Legislature has eliminated many local prerogatives with respect to unfair practice charges by giving the State Public Employees Relations Board jurisdiction to resolve such disputes.[152] PERB jurisdiction can be avoided if a fair arbitration agreement is signed by employees.[153]

For employee organizations, the ultimate tool for impasse resolution is a strike. The courts once held strikes are not permitted unless authorized by statutes, and the statutes do not give public employees the right to strike. Until 1985, no matter the context, the courts consistently declined to give public employees the right to strike.[154] This was brought to an abrupt halt when the California Supreme Court shocked the state with its decision in *County Sanitation District No. 2 of Los Angeles County v. Los Angeles County Employees Association, Local 660*.[155] In this case, the agency sought damages from the union because of a strike. The court could have concluded damages were not available without further comment. Instead, the court went the extra distance and decided damages were not available because strikes are legal.

Disagreement over salary and benefits seems to be the primary cause of work stoppages. However, other issues sometimes produce unexpected confrontations. The law requires agencies to make certain types of deductions from payroll. The ability of the union to demand access to the payroll deduction mechanism is often critical to the union's survival. Employees may authorize deductions.[156] Employers may establish procedures to insure the orderly administration of the system.[157] The rules may limit union dues deductions to unions having at least 10 employees or one percent of the employees in a particular unit.[158] Further, the union must be a "bona fide organization" representing employees; a mere shell created to collect dues deductions does not qualify. Because of the importance of payroll deductions to the credibility of the union, the subject is almost always part of the "package" negotiated by the union. Often, a union will attempt to obtain union dues deductions from employees who are not members of the union under the "agency shop" theory that all employees benefit from representation so all employees should pay. Agency shop is required under many circumstances if the union follows proper procedures.[159] There is some merit to this position because unions have the duty to fairly represent all members of a bargaining unit, not just union members.[160]

Unions often bypass the negotiating table in favor of sympathetic legislators. A raft of statutes have created mandatory employee benefits because business will tolerate mandatory benefits if competitors are similarly affected. The dynamics of the public sector are different – there are no competitors in the usual sense. Public agencies will tolerate mandatory benefits if enough money remains to pay for programs the voters demand.

The terms and conditions of employment may be unilaterally established by the governing board in the absence of a bargaining unit, or may be negotiated with employees. Regardless of how the terms of employment are established, some benefits are mandated.[161] The legislature has been largely unwilling to mandate local agency salaries but state legislature has been willing to mandate benefits.

The Federal Fair Labor Standards Act (FLSA) regulates hours of work and requires premium (overtime) pay for employees working more than 40 hours in a week.[162] The FLSA contains a partial exemption for some public officers and for employees traditionally expected to work unusually long hours. Firefighters, police and some utility operators can be denied overtime compensation if they are given time off ("compensatory time-off") within a reasonable period after the overtime accrues.[163] State law cannot vary the terms of the FLSA, but state law can impose more stringent overtime requirements. Persons who work more than 40 hours per week are entitled to overtime under federal law and persons who work more than 8 hours per day are entitled to overtime pay under State law.[164] For the present, the eight-hour workday does not apply to special districts or cities.

The Family Leave Act applies to private employers of 50 or more and *all* public employers.[165] To be eligible, employees must have completed a training period of up to 3 months.[166] Employers must allow eligible employees to take off work without pay for up to 4 months to provide for:

(1) the birth, adoption, serious health condition or to "bond" with the employee's child;

(2) the care of a parent or spouse who has a serious health condition; or

(3) the care of the employee who has a serious health condition.[167]

Employers may mandate reasonable advance notice and require the use of paid leave before allowing the use of unpaid leave under this statute.[168] At the end of the leave, the employee must be allowed to return the same or, as nearly as practical, equivalent job.[169] Reinstatement is not required if:

(1) the employee is among the highest paid 10 percent of the workforce within a 75-mile radius of the workplace;

(2) refusal is necessary to prevent substantial and grievous economic injury to the employer's operations; and

(3)   the employer promptly notifies the employee of intent not to reinstate before the leave starts or gives the employee the opportunity to return if the leave has already started.[170]

Leave under the California Family Leave Act can run concurrently with leave under the Federal Family and Medical Leave Act of 1993.[171]

Local agencies must participate in the State Unemployment Compensation Insurance Fund.[172] Private sectors often contest these benefits. Most public employers do not actively manage or contest unemployment claims.

Local agencies are permitted to provide a number of benefits. (Special districts cannot provide benefits in the absence of legislation authorizing the benefit.) Agencies may provide health coverage.[173] The Agency may pay for group coverage for active directors, officers, employees and dependants or retired officers, employees, certain retired directors (elected before January 1, 1995) and their dependants.[174] The statute requires a "plan" but it is generally believed self-administered groups are authorized. (This is particularly important for dental or visual health services for which a group plan is not always available or economical.) The health plan provider must offer coverage consistent with statutory limits on coverage. The law authorizing agencies to provide health plan coverage includes a definition of "dependents." Agencies cannot enroll employees in a health plan using a different definition.

Employees can be offered a pension plan.[175] The plan need not be administered by the Public Employees Retirement System (PERS). But PERS is common among local entities. PERS also offers a "cafeteria" criteria-style group health plan. Under the PERS medical plan, each employee can select a privately administered group health plan on an approved list.

Local agencies may provide disability insurance.[176] Some agencies provide incentives for employees not to use sick leave benefits by agreeing to purchase a portion of unused benefits. Sometimes, permissive benefits become mandatory. Agencies are not required to provide sick leave. When sick leave is provided, employees must be permitted to use it to attend to the illness of a child, spouse or parent.[177] Conditions on the use of sick leave continue to apply.[178] Sick leave benefits used under these circumstances will apply against the benefits afforded by the Family and Medical Leave Act.[179]

A public agency can revise or eliminate permissive benefits if the benefits are not "vested." There is no firm rule on when benefits vest. In general, a benefit vests when an employee has performed everything necessary to earn the benefit. If an employee earns one day of vacation for each month of service, after three months, three vacation days have vested. Unvested benefits can be curtailed. In the example just given, the employer could eliminate vacation accrual during the fourth and following months but the employee must still be given three days off for vested vacation. Vesting issues become complicated when a benefit requires years to accrue, such as a pension. The courts will often find a benefit to have vested before the right has completely accrued. When this happens, the Court may construct an elaborate rationale when in fact "fairness" is the criteria.

An important tenet of pension law is provisions are liberally construed in favor of the employee.[180] Under California pension law, rights acquired by public employees under legislated pension plans become vested as to each employee at least on the happening of the contingency upon which the pension becomes payable.[181] Vesting prior to the happening of the contingency is less settled. Prior to retirement, pension benefits can be altered. However, the alteration cannot be significant enough to be a substantial detriment to the employee. In a case of first impression, a court ruled an employer can institute a prospective pay reduction for an at-will employee without breach of an employment contract.[182]

Many principal acts allow employees to be hired "at-will." At-will employees have the same protections as an at-will executive: very little. They can be disciplined for no reason but they cannot be disciplined for bad reasons and they are entitled to a name clearing hearing if even good reasons are given for the termination. Many agencies provide employees with assurances they can only be disciplined or fired "for cause," regardless of whether the Principal Act compels such a result. A complete list of "cause" is not possible because what would be cause for termination for one job would not necessarily be cause for termination for another. Because of this, the <u>process</u> for discipline is as important as the substance.

Courts have created an awkward process for public employee discipline. If the manager feels the discipline is appropriate, the manager must provide the employee with a pre-discipline notice ("*Skelly* letter" – after the case which created the rule) outlining the potential discipline, reasons for the action and giving the employee an opportunity to meet and argue. (This process makes a lot of sense in large organizations but doesn't make much sense when the department head is the CEO.) After hearing from the employee, the manager may modify the discipline as appropriate. The letter is then sent to the employee as an official act.

Skelly rights have been extended to various kinds of disciplinary proceedings and to some non-permanent employees.[183] Employees may be disciplined without receiving *Skelly* rights when necessary to protect the public or in an emergency. *Skelly* is based on "property" or "vested" interests. When an agency can establish the lack of vested rights, *Skelly* does not apply.[184] The implementation of *Skelly* depends in part on the size of the agency. In most smaller agencies, a short waiting period during the appeal to the chief executive officer will satisfy the law.

Though less heralded, *Lubey v. San Francisco* is another court rule profoundly impacting traditional civil service laws.[185] In *Lubey*, several probational police officers were fired because of alleged criminal activity. The reasons for the discharges were widely publicized. Because they were probationary employee, they were denied *Skelly* rights and a civil service hearing. The appellate court nonetheless ordered the city to conduct a "liberty hearing" to give the fired officers the opportunity to clear their name by presenting their side of the story. The court was careful to point out the city would <u>not</u> be required to reinstate the officers. The purpose of the hearing was to give the officers the opportunity to remove a cloud from their ability to gain employment elsewhere.

Together, *Skelly* and *Lubey* create a dilemma: Under *Skelly*, certain employees are entitled to notice of the reasons for disciplinary action *before* the discipline is imposed. Under *Lubey*, employers should be silent on the reasons for discipline. These cases force the agency to determine whether an employee enjoys *Skelly* rights or *Lubey* rights.

An independent administrative process for reviewing for-cause discipline will make it less likely that a court will overturn the decision. Anyone <u>not</u> involved in the disciplinary process can sit as the appeals board. Often, the governing body will sit as the *ex officio* personnel board. Regardless of how the review board is constituted, it is important for the hearing officers to not have any prior contact with the matter because employees are entitled to due process. Due process means employees:

- Are informed of the nature of the charges in writing;
- Are given an opportunity to respond to those charges (at the *Skelly* letter stage and thereafter);
- Have response heard by a *neutral* party; and
- Can confront accusers and evidence at the hearing.

The neutral party will make the decision only on evidence actually presented at an administrative hearing. The personnel board can deliberate in a closed session and the decision should be written. The personnel board should make a finding on each separate charge, both as to the truthfulness of the charge and as to whether the charge is sufficient, alone, or in combination with the other charges to sustain the progress level of discipline. Just as the decision of the personnel director is final unless appealed to the personnel board, the decision of the personnel board is final unless appealed to the court.

Highly specific and specialized rules have evolved for court review of public employee discipline. In court, the record is everything. A personnel review board which compiles a complete record detailing a basis for concluding the discipline was correct will find its decisions sustained by the court in most cases. The fact the employee is able to present contrary evidence on the record is not supposed to sway the court.

Even when a public employee can be fired for no reason, the discharge cannot be for an improper reason. An at-will employee cannot be terminated for the exercise of free speech.[186] Similarly, a public agency cannot dismiss at-will employees on the basis of race, color, creed, sex, national origin, religion, "gender identity" or disability.[187] In other words, some discipline is barred by public policy.[188] For example, the "Whistle Blower" statute states "no local agency officer, manager or supervisor" shall take "a reprisal action" against an employee or applicant for employee who files a complaint of "gross mismanagement or significant waste of funds, abuse of authority, or substantial and specific damage to public health or safety."[189] Violation carries criminal and civil penalties.[190] A violation will *not* occur if:

(1)   the employee's complaint was knowingly false;

(2)   the complaint is based on confidential records;

(3)   the complaint discloses confidential information;

(4)   the employee was the subject of an investigation before the complaint;

(5)   the employee violated other rules; or,

(6)   the disciplining supervisor did not know of the
        complaint.

Employers must maintain a discrimination free workplace. Employers must use neutral methods to evaluate employees for promotion and discipline, and must prevent harassment of employees in protected classes. Harassment of a protected class can take many forms. Unwanted solicitation of sexual favors is an obvious extreme example of gender based harassment. Treating females as second class employees is a more subtle form of gender discrimination. A member of a protected class (female or other) cannot be "harassed" by the employer or person empowered by the employer. Harassment can take many forms. Physical harassment includes unwanted touching or physical interference. Visual harassment occurs when derogatory or suggestive posters or drawings are set out in the workplace. Verbal harassment includes slurs, epithets and suggestive comments.[191]

Harassment can result in a constructive discharge. This means the employee can act as if wrongfully terminated and seek damages because the termination is based on protected class discrimination. California law defines workplace harassment:

> [H]ostile work environment sexual harassment is established where there is unwelcome sexual conduct that a reasonable person of the same gender as the complainant would consider sufficiently severe or pervasive to alter the conditions of employment and create an abusive working environment.[192]

In other words, sexual harassment can be established by showing the average, reasonable woman would be offended by the conduct in question. Perhaps no feature of sexual harassment law engenders more hostility by males than the idea something not offensive to men can be the basis for complaint by females.

The concept originated in a federal court decision.[193] The facts in the case are too lengthy to repeat but an experiment illustrates the problem. The facts reported by the court were read to a group of male and female professionals by this author. When questioned, the men in the audience described the conduct of the male in the case as boorish, stupid, heavy handed or crass. But the females in the audience described the defendant's conduct as highly offensive, criminal or worse. Thus the problem: men and women have different views on what is sexually offensive. The law recognizes this difference by examining female harassment complaints from the point of view of the woman. This may seem unfair to men but the differences between men and woman are obvious (despite objection by extremists) and no other standard seems capable of ensuring women a hospitable workplace.

The law on sexual harassment is difficult to explain because men and women have difficulty separating legitimate concerns from illegitimate opportunism. Honest males will condemn predatory conduct by those in positions of power and may find it difficult to believe such conduct occurs. Honest females will tolerate flirtations but may find it difficult to believe males are innocent. Perception is more important than reality. If an employee reasonably believes a person can affect employment status if sexual advances are rejected, the employee will be forced to choose between job and privacy. This is a choice the law allows the employee to avoid.

Employers and employees cannot agree in advance how to resolve all harassment claims. But a process for handling harassment clients can enable an employer to discover and act on valid claims. An aggressive program to combat harassment should include at least the following elements:

- The governing board, general manager and department heads must publicly affirm their written commitment to preventing harassment in the work place.

- This commitment must be regularly restated.

- If this commitment cannot honestly be given, training should be provided to establish and to explain the legal requirements and why the law is necessary.

- The Agency should establish a written procedure for discovering, investigating, and acting on harassment complaints.

- Finally, employees who do not "get it" despite training, must be disciplined.[194]

Any law as sweeping as a law on gender discrimination will yield abuses. The courts are beginning to deal with such abuse. Some employees accuse everyone in the chain of command to improve their bargaining position. A court has held this terror tactic cannot be used against a personnel officer just because they were in the wrong place in the organization chart.[195]

Discrimination on the basis of disability became especially important with the adoption of the Federal Americans with Disabilities Act ("ADA") and its state analog. Employers must do more than avoid discriminating against employees with physical or mental disabilities. Public employers must make a good faith effort to "reasonably accommodate" an employee with a disability.[196] The ADA does not apply every time a person with a medical condition is affected by an employment decision. An employee is not considered disabled under ADA unless generally unable to work.[197] ADA does not apply if the medical condition is mitigated by treatment.[198] "Reasonable accommodation" does not mandate the creation of a new job.[199] California's Disability Act is similar to the federal ADA. However, the State Act uses a different definition of mental disability. For example, the State Act applies to persons who are "regarded" as disabled even if they are not disabled.[200]

Unless based on a bona fide occupational qualification, no employer can refuse to promote or refuse to train because of "pregnancy, childbirth, or related medical condition of any female employee."[201] Employers must treat pregnancy, childbirth and related medical conditions the same as any other medical condition but the employer must offer up to four months leave under this statute.[202] Employers must make reasonable accommodations by transferring pregnant employees to less strenuous duty on request.[203]

Discrimination based on political speech is prohibited by case law. This usually arises in the context of criticism of agency policies.[204] Insubordinate or disrespectful employees can be disciplined. But employees exercising their First Amendment rights to petition government cannot be disciplined.[205] The difference between insubordination and free speech is vague. Objections to how the policy of an employer affects the speaker are not considered free speech.[206]

One of the most difficult decisions facing an employer is deciding when to discharge an employee absent after an illness or injury. Often, an injured employee has no intention of returning to work but refuses to resign so as to continue receiving benefits such as health plan coverage. The decision to discharge an injured employee suspected of malingering is difficult on humanitarian grounds and because of conflicting demands by disability and Workers' Compensation laws. An employee injured on the job is entitled to medical treatment and rehabilitation under Workers' Compensation laws and reasonable accommodation must be made under the Americans with Disabilities Act if the worker is disabled and not rehabilitated. Punishment is severe when an employer discriminates against an employee due to the filing of a Workers' Compensation or accommodation claim. As a result, an employee on leave due to an industrial injury usually cannot be dismissed. Further, there is no penalty to an employee who abuses the process by malingering. In fact, the law seems designed to protect malingerers.

The employer must proceed methodically to dismiss an employee who abuses the system. The following suggests a path to follow:

- Determine if the injury is "industrial." If the injury is not industrial, i.e., there is no worker's compensation claim, determine if accommodation is necessary under ADA. If the injury is non-industrial and there is no disability under ADA, proceed with the dismissal process.

- If the injury is industrial, do not attempt to change job status until the employee's condition is "permanent and stable" and the employee is able to return to work or the employee is able to return but refuses.[207]

- When the industrial injury is permanent and stable, determine whether vocational rehabilitation is appropriate. Rehabilitation must be completed under Workers' Compensation laws before the employee can be treated like other employees.

- When the injury is permanent and stable and rehabilitation is complete, determine whether accommodation is necessary under ADA. If accommodation is not necessary, the employee may be disciplined for not returning to work in the same manner as an employee who is excessively absent. If accommodation is offered and the employee still fails to return to work, the employee may be disciplined in the same manner as an employee who is insubordinate.

The process seems simple. Unfortunately, an employee who knows how to "work the system" can avoid returning to work for years. When this happens, the employer cannot lose patience. Employee discipline is possible only in the absence of retaliation and after Workers' Compensation and disability benefits are provided. The relationship between workers compensation benefits and the Americans with Disabilities Act (ADA) was examined in a recent case which held an employee who is permanently disabled from performing work under Workers' Compensation Act is not an "eligible person" for ADA benefits.[208]

PART 2
ADMINISTRATIVE REGULATIONS

A public agency needs rules to describe how the agency team deals with each other and works for the agency. These rules should cover ethics, meetings, financial process, and how to conduct an environmental review. These rules can be contained in an administrative code. This part discusses the essential elements of an administrative code. (This part does not discuss regulations for dealing with customers or taxpayers. The "external" regulations are described later.)

CHAPTER 4
"ETHICS"

In 2006, the California Legislature adopted a statute mandating ethics training for <u>local</u> officials. Not surprisingly, ethics is not one of the mandated subjects. The mandatory list is nonetheless a useful summation of laws governing personal conduct of public officials.

Real ethical standards are more important than laws. More than one official has ousted an unethical predecessor for conduct short of actually violating the law. The official – not the attorney – must judge whether the conduct is ethical. Directors employ the ethics developed throughout life. Officials must be alert for ethical challenges unique to officeholders. Public office is important to the person and to the community. People seek office because they believe their leadership skills are better than others are. Officials naturally believe their proposals are more deserving than opponents are and important for the good of the community. Confidence is a step away from arrogance. An ends-justifies-the-means standard is always just around the corner. Such a standard is no standard at all. This is the source of more ethical failures by elected officials than anything else. Public officials must be as skeptical about their own opinions as they are about their neighbors.

Elected officials have something many people want: the power that attends public office and the opportunity to manage large sums of money. The law deals fairly well with the opportunity for financial gain. The law has little to say about the pursuit of power. Public officials should erect the same barriers against those seeking to tap into the agency's power as they erect for those seeking to tap into the agency's treasury.

It has been fashionable to intellectualize and quibble over what is ethical. Our institutions have largely avoided the subject. The need to demand ethical behavior can no longer be avoided. The need for debate on fine points cannot be the excuse for failure to immediately articulate well-established, widely accepted ethical principles.

The existence of universal ethical principles may be a surprise to some. But those who have devoted careful attention to the subject can identify an impressive list of basic principles. The Josephson Institute of Ethics has developed useful suggestions for making ethical decisions:

(1) "The decisions must take into account and reflect a concern for the interest and well-being of all stakeholders.

(2) Ethical values and principles always take precedence over non-ethical ones.

(3) It is ethically proper to violate an ethical principle only when it is clearly necessary to advance another true ethical principle, which, according to the decision maker's conscience, will produce the greatest balance of good in the long run."

The next thing that comes to mind when discussing ethics is usually conflicts of interest. Conflicts of interest fall into two categories: contractual and non-contractual. Contractual conflicts of interest have been regulated since shortly after California became part of the Union. (Before that, this law was part of the common law of England.) The statute is brief; no government official can participate in the formation of a contract if the official has a financial interest in the contract:

- This law covers elected or appointed officials, whether they be officers, employees, and some independent contractors, full-time or part-time.
- Actual or potential financial gain is prohibited. Social or family advantage is not against this law.
- It covers all steps leading to contract formation, including decisions on whether to bid or negotiate.

There are two types of exceptions to the contractual conflicts of interest laws. Some financial interests are excluded as a matter of public policy ("non-interest exception"). Some interests are excluded if the official discloses the interest and abstains from participating in the decision-making process ("remote interest exception").

Nothing needs to be done to invoke the non-interest exception exemption. Notice how specifically the law describes the non-interests:

(a) An officer or employee shall not be deemed to be interested in a contract if his or her interest is any of the following:

(1) The ownership of less than 3 percent of the shares of a corporation for profit, provided that the total annual income to him or her from dividends, including the value of stock dividends, from the corporation does not exceed 5 percent of his or her total annual income, and any other payments made to him or her by the corporation do not exceed 5 percent of his or her total annual income.

(2)   That of an officer in being reimbursed for his or her actual and necessary expenses incurred in the performance of official duties.

(3)   That of a recipient of public services generally provided by the public body or board of which he or she is a member, on the same terms and conditions as if he or she were not a member of the body or board.

(4)   That of a landlord or tenant of the contracting party if the contracting party is the federal government or any federal department or agency, this state or an adjoining state, any department or agency of this state or an adjoining state, any county or city of this state or an adjoining state, or any public corporation or special, judicial, or other public district of this state or an adjoining state unless the subject matter of the contract is the property in which the officer or employee has the interest as landlord or tenant in which event his or her interest shall be deemed a remote interest within the meaning of, and subject to, the provisions of Section 1091.

(5)   That of a tenant in a public housing authority created pursuant to Part 2 (commencing with Section 34200) of Division 24 of the Health and Safety Code in which he or she serves as a member of the board of commissioners of the authority or of a community development commission created pursuant to Part 1.7 (commencing with Section 34100) of Division 24 of the Health and Safety Code.

(6)   That of a spouse of an officer or employee of a public agency in his or her spouse's employment or office-holding if his or her spouse's employment

or office-holding has existed for at least one year prior to his or her election or appointment.

(7) That of a non-salaried member of a nonprofit corporation, provided that this interest is disclosed to the body or board at the time of the first consideration of the contract, and provided further that this interest is noted in its official records.

(8) That of a non-compensated officer of a nonprofit, tax-exempt corporation, which, as one of its primary purposes, supports the functions of the body or board or to which the body or board has a legal obligation to give particular consideration, and provided further that this interest is noted in its official records. For purposes of this paragraph, an officer is "non-compensated" even though he or she receives reimbursement from the nonprofit, tax-exempt corporation for necessary travel and other actual expenses incurred in performing the duties of his or her office.

(9) That of a person receiving salary, per diem, or reimbursement for expenses from a government entity, unless the contract directly involves the department of the government entity that employs the officer or employee, provided that the interest is disclosed to the body or board at the time of consideration of the contract, and provided further that the interest is noted in its official record.

(10) That of an attorney of the contracting party or that of an owner, officer, employee, or agent of a firm which renders, or has rendered, service to the contracting party in the capacity of stockbroker, insurance agent, insurance broker,

real estate agent, or real estate broker, if these individuals have not received and will not receive remuneration, consideration, or a commission as a result of the contract and if these individuals have an ownership interest of less than 10 percent in the law practice or firm, stock brokerage firm, insurance firm, or real estate firm.

(11) Except as provided in subdivision (b), that of an officer or employee of, or a person having less than a 10-percent ownership interest in, a bank, bank holding company, or savings and loan association with which a party to the contract has a relationship of borrower, depositor, debtor, or creditor.

(12) That of (A) a bona fide nonprofit, tax-exempt corporation having among its primary purposes the conservation, preservation, or restoration of park and natural lands or historical resources for public benefit, which corporation enters into an agreement with a public agency to provide services related to park and natural lands or historical resources and which services are found by the public agency, prior to entering into the agreement or as part of the agreement, to be necessary to the public interest to plan for, acquire, protect, conserve, improve, or restore park and natural lands or historical resources for public purposes and (B) any officer, director, or employee acting pursuant to the agreement on behalf of the nonprofit corporation. For purposes of this paragraph, "agreement" includes contracts and grants, and "park," "natural lands," and "historical resources" shall have the meanings set forth in subdivisions (d), (g), and (i) of Section 5902 of the

Public Resources Code. Services to be provided to the public agency may include those studies and related services, acquisitions of property and property interests, and any activities related to those studies and acquisitions necessary for the conservation, preservation, improvement, or restoration of park and natural lands or historical resources.

(13) That of an officer, employee, or member of the Board of Directors of the California Housing Finance Agency with respect to a loan product or programs if the officer, employee, or member participated in the planning, discussions, development, or approval of the loan product or program and both of the following two conditions exist:

(A) The loan product or program is or may be originated by any lender approved by the agency.

(B) The loan product or program is generally available to qualifying borrowers on terms and conditions that are substantially the same for all qualifying borrowers at the time the loan is made.

(b) An officer or employee shall not be deemed to be interested in a contract made pursuant to competitive bidding under a procedure established by law if his or her sole interest is that of an officer, director, or employee of a bank or savings and loan association with which a party to the contract has the relationship of borrower or depositor, debtor or creditor.[209]

To invoke the remote interest exception, the official must abstain from participating in the decision-making process and announce the reason for the abstention. The remote interest exceptions are also very specific:

(b) As used in this article, "remote interest" means any of the following: (1) That of an officer or employee of a nonprofit entity exempt from taxation pursuant to Section 501(c)(3) of the Internal Revenue Code (26 U.S.C. Sec. 501(c)(3)) or a nonprofit corporation, except as provided in paragraph (8) of subdivision (a) of Section 1091.5.

(2) That of an employee or agent of the contracting party, if the contracting party has 10 or more other employees and if the officer was an employee or agent of that contracting party for at least three years prior to the officer initially accepting his or her office and the officer owns less than 3 percent of the shares of stock of the contracting party; and the employee or agent is not an officer or director of the contracting party and did not directly participate in formulating the bid of the contracting party. For purposes of this paragraph, time of employment with the contracting party by the officer shall be counted in computing the three-year period specified in this paragraph even though the contracting party has been converted from one form of business organization to a different form of business organization within three years of the initial taking of office by the officer. Time of employment in that case shall be counted only if, after the transfer or change in organization, the real or ultimate ownership of the contracting party is the same or substantially similar to that which existed before the transfer or change in organization. For purposes of this paragraph, stockholders, bondholders, partners, or other persons holding an interest in the

contracting party are regarded as having the "real or ultimate ownership" of the contracting party.

(3)   That of an employee or agent of the contracting party, if all of the following conditions are met:

(A)   The agency of which the person is an officer is a local public agency located in a county with a population of less than 4,000,000.

(B)   The contract is competitively bid and is not for personal services.

(C)   The employee or agent is not in a primary management capacity with the contracting party, is not an officer or director of the contracting party, and holds no ownership interest in the contracting party.

(D)   The contracting party has 10 or more other employees.

(E)   The employee or agent did not directly participate in formulating the bid of the contracting party.

(F)   The contracting party is the lowest responsible bidder.

(4)   That of a parent in the earnings of his or her minor child for personal services.

(5)   That of a landlord or tenant of the contracting party.

(6)   That of an attorney of the contracting party or that of an owner, officer, employee, or agent of a firm that renders, or has rendered, service to the contracting party in the capacity of stockbroker, insurance agent, insurance broker, real estate agent, or real estate broker, if these individuals have not received and will not receive remuneration, consideration, or a commission as a result of the contract and if these individuals

have an ownership interest of 10 percent or more in the law practice or firm, stock brokerage firm, insurance firm, or real estate firm.

(7) That of a member of a nonprofit corporation formed under the Food and Agricultural Code or a nonprofit corporation formed under the Corporations Code for the sole purpose of engaging in the merchandising of agricultural products or the supplying of water.

(8) That of a supplier of goods or services when those goods or services have been supplied to the contracting party by the officer for at least five years prior to his or her election or appointment to office. (9) That of a person subject to the provisions of Section 1090 in any contract or agreement entered into pursuant to the provisions of the California Land Conservation Act of 1965.

(10) Except as provided in subdivision (b) of Section 1091.5, that of a director of or a person having an ownership interest of 10 percent or more in a bank, bank holding company, or savings and loan association with which a party to the contract has a relationship of borrower or depositor, debtor or creditor.

(11) That of an engineer, geologist, or architect employed by a consulting engineering or architectural firm. This paragraph applies only to an employee of a consulting firm who does not serve in a primary management capacity, and does not apply to an officer or director of a consulting firm.

(12) That of an elected officer otherwise subject to Section 1090, in any housing assistance payment

contract entered into pursuant to Section 8 of the United States Housing Act of 1937 (42 U.S.C. Sec. 1437f) as amended, provided that the housing assistance payment contract was in existence before Section 1090 became applicable to the officer and will be renewed or extended only as to the existing tenant, or, in a jurisdiction in which the rental vacancy rate is less than 5 percent, as to new tenants in a unit previously under a Section 8 contract. This section applies to any person who became a public official on or after November 1, 1986.

(13) That of a person receiving salary, per diem, or reimbursement for expenses from a government entity.

(14) That of a person owning less than 3 percent of the shares of a contracting party that is a for-profit corporation, provided that the ownership of the shares derived from the person's employment with that corporation.[210]

The courts have added "rule of necessity" exception to allow a conflicted official to participate in a contract formation if the official's participation is necessary for the body to have a quorum to act and action is required.

Board members, other than the official with the conflict, can void a contract made in violation of this law.[211] For example, the successful bidder on a public works project can be required to forfeit all compensation and leave the job in place as a result of bribing the official responsible for reviewing the bids.[212] In the absence of one of the exceptions, contracts can be void even if the official with the conflict refrains from participation. The district attorney enforces contractual conflicts of interest laws. (The Fair Political Practices Commission (FPPC) is conducting an experiment to determine whether it should and could also administer contractual conflicts of interest.) The official who violates this provision can be: barred from holding office; fined up to $5,000; and sentenced to as long as six months in prison.[213]

In 1973, the Legislature adopted a comprehensive statute prohibiting non-contractual conflicts. The statute was declared unconstitutional. The voters then adopted an Initiative known as the Political Reform Act of 1974. The Political Reform Act deals with non-contractual conflicts of interest in terms similar to the prohibitions against contractual conflicts:

> No public official at any level of state or local government shall make, participate in making or in any way attempt to use his official position to influence a governmental decision in which he knows or has reason to know he has a financial interest.[214]

Violation is a misdemeanor and can result in the loss of office.[215] Unlike contractual conflicts, it is always possible to avoid a violation by refraining from participation. Many key terms for non-contractual conflicts are defined by the Act:

> A public official has a financial interest in a decision within the meaning of Section 87100 if it is reasonably foreseeable that the decision will have a material financial effect, distinguishable from its effect on the public generally, on the official, a member of his or her immediate family, or on any of the following:
>
> (a) Any business entity in which the public official has a direct or indirect investment worth one thousand dollars ($1,000) or more.
>
> (b) Any real property in which the public official has a direct or indirect interest worth one thousand dollars ($1,000) or more.

(c)   Any *source of income* other than gifts and other than loans by a commercial lending institution in the regular course of business on terms available to the public without regard to official status, aggregating two hundred fifty dollars ($250) or more in value provided to, received by or promised to the public official within 12 months prior to the time when the decision is made.[216]

(d)   Any business entity in which the public official is a director, officer, partner, trustee, employee or holds any *position of management*.

(e)   Any donor of, or any intermediary or agent for a donor of, a gift or gifts aggregating two hundred fifty dollars ($250) or more in value provided to, received by, or promised to the public official within 12 months prior to the time when the decision is made…

> For the purposes of this section, indirect investment or interest means any investment or interest owned by the spouse or dependent child of a public official, by an agent on behalf of a public official, or by a business entity or trust in which the official, the official's agents, spouse, and dependent children own directly, indirectly, or beneficially a 10-percent interest or greater. (Emphasis added.)[217]

In short, there is a four-pronged test for non-contractual conflicts. The proposed decision must have a (1) reasonably foreseeable, (2) material financial effect on (3) an owned business entity, real property, a source of income, or a managed business entity (4) distinguished from the effect on the public generally.[218]

The Act established the FPPC to adopt regulations on non-contractual conflicts.[219] For complexity and obtuse language, these regulations are close to the federal tax code.[220] The regulations explain the statutory language in great detail.

First, the exceptions. A public official can participate in a non-contractual decision even if the decision affects material financial interest if:

(1)   the official's participation in the decision is legally required (rule of necessity); or

(2)   the impact on the official is the same as the impact on the public generally.

A public official's participation is "legally required" if there is no "alternative source of decision consistent with the purposes and terms of the statute authorizing the decision."[221] Participation is not legally required to break a tie or if a quorum can be convened later in time to make the decision without the disqualified official.[222] If participation is legally required, a participant is selected at random from the pool of conflicted officials. The chosen official must disclose the conflict, state the reason why there is no alternative source of decision and participate only at an official meeting.[223] The exception does not apply if one or more of the disqualified board members refuse to participate in the random selection process.[224] The exception also does not apply if the necessity arises because other directors abstain for reasons unrelated to conflicts.

The impact of a decision on the official's financial interest is the same as the "public generally" if the decision affects the official "in substantially the same manner as it will affect all members of the public or a significant segment of the public."[225] An industry, trade or profession does not constitute a "significant segment" of the general public unless the industry, trade or profession is a predominant industry, trade or profession in the area represented by the official.[226] In jurisdictions with a population of 25,000 or less covering 10 square miles or less, a decision affecting the official's principal residence does not disqualify the official if:

- The official is required to reside within the jurisdiction;
- The official is elected at-large;
- The decision does not have a direct effect on the residence;
- The residence is more than 300 feet from the property which is the subject of the decisions; and
- The residence is on a parcel not more than ¼ acre or not larger than 125% of the median lot size in the jurisdiction.[227]

Retail customers are considered part of the public generally and not a disqualifying source of income if the customers during the preceding 12 months are at least 10 percent of the population or households of the jurisdiction or number at least 10,000.[228] The "public generally" exception requires a case by case analysis. For example, a director may vote to change water rates if all customers are similarly affected but may not vote on a water conservation measure with disproportionate impact on the director.[229] A noteworthy exception to the public generally exception applies to rate setting:

> The financial effect of a governmental decision on the official's economic interest is indistinguishable from the decision's effect on the public generally if any of the following apply:
>
> (1)   The decision is to establish or to adjust assessments, taxes, fees, charges, or rates or other similar

decisions which are applied on a proportional basis on the official's economic interest and on a significant segment of the jurisdiction as defined in subdivision (a)(1) above.

(2) The decision is made by the governing board of a landowner voting district and affects the official's economic interests and a significant segment of the landowners or water users subject to the jurisdiction of the district (using the thresholds set forth in subdivision (a)(1) above) in proportion to their real property interests or by the same percentage or on an 'across-the-board' basis for all classes.

(3) The decision is made by the governing board of a water, irrigation, or similar district to establish or to adjust assessments, taxes, fees, charges, or rates or other similar decisions, such as the allocation of services, which are applied on a proportional or 'across-the-board' basis on the official's economic interests and a significant segment of the property owners or other persons receiving services from the official's agency using the thresholds set forth in subdivision (a)(1) above.[230]

Unless the foregoing exceptions apply, the FPPC Regulations require abstention when the decision may have a material financial effect on the official.

Second, financial effect. The FPPC regulations contain "general" and "specific" descriptions of "financial effect." The general rules apply when specific rules do not cover an issue.[231] Under the general rule:

The financial effect of a governmental decision is material if the decision will have a significant effect on the official or a member of the official's immediate family, or on the source of income, the source of gifts, the business entity, or the real property, which is an economic interest of the official.

The specific regulations are divided into two categories: "direct" and "indirect" effects. A decision has a direct effect on a financial interest if the decision affects:

(1) A person who has been a "source of income" of $250 or more during the preceding 12 months (other than a governmental agency) or there is a nexus between the decision and the purpose for which the income is received.[232]

(2) A small "business entity" in which the official has an investment of $2,000 or more or a large business in which the official has an investment of $10,000 or more, or any business entity in which the official holds a management position.[233]

(3) "Real Property" worth $2,000 or more owned by the official.[234]

(4) "Personal expenses, income, assets or liabilities" of the official or the official's immediate family increasing or decreasing by at least $250.[235]

(5) The official, or her agent, initiates the proceeding by filing an application, claim, appeal or similar request.[236]

(6) The official is a named party in or the subject of the proceedings.[237]

(7) The issuance, renewal, approval, demand or revocation of a license, permit or other entitlement to or contract with the official.[238]

A decision may have an "indirect" effect on three types of interests: "business entities," "real property" or "income." A decision has an indirect affect on an official's interest in a business entity when it involves:

(1)　A business listed on the New York or American Stock Exchange if the decision increases or decreases the "gross revenue" of the business by $250,000 or more per fiscal year (or $1,000,000 or more if the business is a Fortune 500 company), the *expenses* of the business by $100,000 or more (or $250,000 if Fortune 500), or "assets or liabilities" of the business by $250,000 or more (or $1,000,000 if Fortune 500).[239]

(2)　A business listed on the National Association of Securities Dealers National Market List if the decision increases or decreases: the "gross revenues" of the business by $150,000 or more per fiscal year; the expenses of the business by $50,000 or more; or the "assets or liabilities" of the business by $150,000 or more.[240]

(3)　A business listed on the Pacific Stock Exchange or on the Eligible Securities List maintained by the California Department of Corporations if the decision increases or decreases: the "gross revenues" of the business by $30,000 or more; the expenses of the business by $7,500 or more or "assets or liabilities" by $30,000 or more.[241]

(4)　Any other type of business if the decision increases or decreases the "gross revenues" of the business by $10,000 or more; the expenses of the business by $2,500 or more; or "assets or liabilities" of the business by $10,000 or more.[242]

A decision has an indirect affect on an official's "ownership" of real property when it involves:

(1)   Property within 300 feet of the property owned by the official.[243]

(2)   Capital improvements and the official's property will receive improved services.[244]

(3)   Property more than 300 feet but within 2,500 feet of the property owned by the official and the fair market value of the official's property is reasonably expected to increase or decrease by $10,000 or more or the rental value by $1,000 or more per year.[245]

(4)   Property more than 2,500 feet from the property of the official and reasonably foreseeable to be affected as above and the effect is different from the effect on at least twenty-five percent of the property within the 2,500 foot radius or the official owns ten or more properties within 2,500 feet.[246]

A decision has an indirect affect on an official's "leasehold interest in real property" if:

(1)   The decision will change the legally allowable use and the lessee has the right to sublease.[247]

(2)   It is reasonably foreseeable the lessee will change actual uses because of the decision. [248]

(3)   It is reasonably foreseeable the decision will change actual use of property within 300 feet of the leased property and the changed use will significantly enhance or decrease the use or enjoyment of the leased property.[249]

(4)   The decision will affect rent by $250 or 5 percent, whichever is greater during the 12 months following the decision.[250]

(5)   The decision will change the termination date of the lease.[251]

A decision has an indirect affect on an official's income or gifts from a non-profit entity, if it involves:

(1) An entity with gross annual receipts are $400,000,000 or more and the decision increases or decreases: the "receipts" of the entity by $1,000,000 or more; the "expenses" by $250,000 or more or "assets or liabilities" by $1,000,000 or more.[252]

(2) An entity with gross annual receipts between $100,000,000 and $400,000,000 and the decision increases or decreases: the "receipts" of the entity by $400,000 or more; the "expenses" by $100,000 or more or "assets or liabilities" by $400,000 or more.[253]

(3) An entity with gross receipts between $10,000,000 and $100,000,000 and the entity's "receipts" are increased or decreased by $200,000 or more, "expenses" by $50,000 or more, "assets or liabilities" by $200,000 or more.[254]

(4) An entity with gross receipts between $1,000,000 and $10,000,000 and the entity's "receipts" are increased or decreased: by $100,000 or more, "expenses" by $25,000 or more, "assets or liabilities" by $100,000 or more.[255]

(5) An entity with gross receipts between $100,000 and $1,000,000 and the entity's "receipts" are increased or decreased: by $50,000 or more, "expenses" by $12,500 or more, "assets or liabilities" by $50,000 or more.[256]

(6) An entity with gross receipts between $100,000 and $10,000 and the entity's "receipts" are increased or decreased: by $2,500 or more, "expenses" by $10,000 or more, "assets or liabilities" by $25,000 or more.[257]

The income from individual retail customers is not disqualifying if the amount spent on the preceding twelve months is less than one percent of gross sales for the preceding fiscal year.[258] Income consisting of "commissions" for services rendered as an insurance broker or agent, a real estate broker or agent, a travel agent or salesperson, a stockbroker or a retail or wholesale salesperson has a material financial interest if it exceeds $250 for a self-employed individual official or $10,000 for a business entity which employs the official.[259] The interest in the commission can disqualify the official from participating in a decision involving:

(1) an insurance carrier providing a policy, the person purchasing the policy, or the brokerage firm;

(2) the person represented by the real estate agent including property owners, brokers or finders;

(3) airlines, hotels, tour operators, traveler, or travel agency;

(4) stock brokerage or stock trader;

(5) retail or wholesale stores or customers.[260]

A "former" employer can be a source of income unless: all income was received or accrued prior to taking office; income was paid in normal course and there was no expectation of renewed employment when the official took office.[261]

The question frequently arises whether conflicts laws are violated if a director or director's spouse is employed by the agency. As to non-contractual decisions, the FPPC has concluded mere election of an employee to the board does not violate the Political Reform Act.[262] Employment of a director's spouse does not violate the Political Reform Act unless the director participates in a decision concerning the employment status or salary for the spouse.[263] But an employee who is elected to the board must resign employment.[264]

Cases and FPPC regulations on non-contractual matters make further fine distinctions. In some instances, the governing board is uniquely affected. For example, when an agency and officers are sued, the governing board must decide which officers will be defended. A director can vote to provide herself a defense if the lawsuit alleges the director acted within the scope of the office, but the director cannot vote to defend punitive damage claims.[265] In another case, a director was permitted to vote on contracts affecting his utility company because the district he served provided public services.[266] On the other hand, the FPPC ruled a director who has a pending application for a water connection cannot vote on connection fees because a significant segment of the public is not affected.[267] A director is not liable for violations by other directors.[268]

The legislature occasionally adopts conflict statutes covering fine points of law. A public officer or employee cannot disclose confidential information for pecuniary gain.[269] Violation of this statute is a misdemeanor. The Statute applies if disclosure is prohibited by another statute or rule, including a rule adopted by the agency.

The doctrine of incompatibility of offices has nothing to do with conflicts of interest but the conflict laws are never discussed without mentioning the incompatibility doctrine. The incompatibility doctrine depends on the potential for a clash between the two offices. The doctrine has nothing to do with the opportunity for personal gain.

The doctrine of incompatibility of offices finds its origin in the English common law and the Bible (no man can serve two masters). The doctrine is narrow: it applies to dual *office* holding. It does not apply to employment. It applies if one of the offices has the power over the other. The doctrine is broadly interpreted. For example, the attorney general concluded the office of school district trustee is incompatible with the office of a director of a water district even though the school district does not receive service from the water district because the school district could ask for service.

When offices are incompatible, the first office is forfeited, but forfeiture is not automatic. An office is forfeited only as the result of a court order (known as a *quo warranto* decree). The Attorney General is the only person authorized to file a *quo warranto* petition. When an incompatible challenge arises, the Attorney General has three choices: (1) find incompatibility exists and do nothing; (2) find incompatibility exists and bring *quo warranto* action; or (3) find incompatibility exists and authorize a private party to bring *quo warranto* action.[270]

The incompatibility doctrine is a common law doctrine. Local agencies can adopt statutes on subjects not "fully occupied" by state legislation. State legislation deals with many of the qualifications for a local office holding but state legislation does not deal with incompatibility. (A recent state statute on incompatibility of offices merely says the common-law incompatibility doctrine is adopted.) Local agencies can adopt ordinances to permit dual office holding. (Because only the first office is forfeited under the incompatibility doctrine, only the first agency need adopt an ordinance.)

Because the Attorney General has a key role in the pursuit of incompatibility violations, the Attorney General opinions are particularly important. The Attorney General has a broad view of the doctrine.[271]

Bribery is illegal but enforcement is difficult because guilty parties can characterize a bribe as an innocent transaction. Throughout history, honoraria, gifts or loans have been disguised as bribes. The Political Reform Act ("Act") says local, elected officials cannot accept "honoraria."[272] Honoraria are payments for appearances, speeches and other abstract services.[273] Local officials cannot accept a "gift" from a single source in the amount of $290 or more.[274] This amount is adjusted annually to reflect inflation. Elected officials cannot accept personal loans of $250 or more from employees or contractors of the agency or $500 or more from anyone unless in writing.[275]

Elected officials have used public money to pay for campaign mailings disguised as information about their agency. The Political Reform Act deals with this by stating elected officials cannot be featured in a "mass mailing" financed at public expense.[276] FPPC regulations on mass mailings are also detailed:

- A mass-mailing is a tangible item, "such as a videotape, record, button or written document" prepared or sent at agency expense to at least 200 persons in a single calendar month at the recipient's residence, place of employment or business, or post office box.[277]

- An official is "featured" if his or her photograph or signature is shown or the item singles out the official by manner of display of name or office in the layout such as by headlines, captions, type size, typeface or type color.

- A mass-mailing cannot include the name, office, photograph or other reference to elected officers if the item is prepared or sent in cooperation or concert with the officer.[278]

The mass-mailing regulations do not apply to:

- Responses to unsolicited requests;[279]

- Press releases;

- A mailing which requires an elected officer's signature essential to the functioning of a governmental program;

- A legal notice;

- A telephone directory or similar roster;

- Mailings to another agency;[280]

- A meeting announcement (if the official's name is only mentioned once without photograph or signature) or meeting agenda.[281]

An official's name can appear in the letterhead or logo of the stationary if the elected officials appear in the same type size, type face, type color and location and does not include the officer's photograph, signature or similar reference.[282] The regulations are designed to prevent disguised campaigns at public expense. Thus, all organizations supported by public money are subject to mass mailing regulation.[283]

Generally, campaign contributions are not considered a source of income covered by the conflicts laws. However, officers cannot act in a quasi-judicial capacity, especially as a hearing officer, on matters affecting a campaign contributor.[284] Officers cannot accept campaign contributions from a person appointed by the officer to a board or commission.[285] A public official cannot solicit campaign contributions from persons on the agency's employment lists unless the solicitation is directed to a significant segment of the public.[286] A public official cannot increase the salary of public agency employees who are campaign contributors.[287]

The statute mandating ethics training says public access and competitive bidding must be covered. These subject are handled below.

CHAPTER 5

PUBLIC ACCESS

From the public's perspective, the most important laws affecting agencies mandate access to agency meetings and documents. Even accidental violations of these laws cause acute embarrassment because the local press is particularly vigilant in guarding public access.

There are times when an agency should make decisions in private, but mostly, privacy is sought merely to avoid embarrassment. In any event, agencies have no choice. The Ralph M. Brown Act mandates <u>public</u> meetings for decision makers:

> All meetings of the legislative body of a local agency shall be open and public, and all persons shall be permitted to attend any meeting of the legislative body of a local agency... [288]

Most of the terms in this statute have special meanings. "Local agency" includes political subdivisions, boards, commissions and agencies of a political subdivision.[289] The term also includes private nonprofit organization appointed by the local agency as a financing vehicle or created to administer public funds.[290] "Legislative body" includes the governing board and other bodies where officers of an agency serve in official capacity supported with funds provided by the agency.[291] Advisory commissions, committees or bodies of agencies created by formal action of the board or by a member of the board are legislative bodies.[292] Permanent boards or commissions are also legislative bodies.[293] *Ad hoc* committees composed of less than a quorum of the governing board are not legislative bodies if the committees are not compensated.[294] A "meeting" is broadly defined as an event where the legislative body deliberates action:

> Any congregation of a quorum of the legislative body or advisory body at the same time and place to hear, discuss or deliberate on any ruling within the jurisdiction of the City; and any use of direct communication, personal intermediaries or technological devices by a quorum of the legislative body or advisory body to develop a collective concurrence to action by the legislative body or advisory body.[295]

Sometimes a meeting can occur by accident. For example, a committee meeting can become an unlawful board meeting if a quorum of the governing body is present at the committee meeting.[296] For this reason, members of the governing board who are not committee members may attend meetings of a standing committee, but may not ask questions or make statements.[297]

"Action taken" is the actual vote by a majority of the members sitting as a body or a collective commitment or promise by a majority to take a position or a negative action.[298] A straw poll violates the Brown Act if it leads to a commitment.

The Brown Act excludes from the definition of meeting:

- Individual contracts between members and other persons;

- Attendance at a conference or similar gathering open to the public involving discussions of issues of interest to the public generally and public agencies specifically;

- Attendance at open and publicized meetings addressing topics of community concern by someone not associated with the agency, or

- Attendance at social or ceremonial events. [299]

These exceptions apply only if the members do not discuss agency business.

The Brown Act requires decisions of the governing body and standing committees of the governing board be made during public meetings. The Brown Act is frustrating to executives who are conscientious and want to keep their board fully advised on the affairs of the agency. The public meeting law makes communication with directors difficult for the CEO. The CEO cannot negotiate policy decisions with the board except during public meetings. Because of the expansive interpretation given to the Brown Act, the CEO cannot even fall just short of a decision by the board. This does not mean the CEO is unable to communicate with board members under any circumstance. CEOs can and frequently do provide oral and written reports to board members outside the boardroom on the status of important projects and programs. The CEO can advise on potential controversial items which may arise before the next board meeting. The executive can even meet with less than a quorum of the board outside of the boardroom to learn the directors' views on important matters. "What do you think of …?" is always a proper question. "Will you vote for this if I can get other directors to vote for it?" is never a proper question outside the boardroom.

The agency can call four types of meetings: "regular," "special," "adjourned" (regular or special) and "emergency." The legislative body establishes the time and place for regular meetings by ordinance or resolution.[300] (A regular meeting falling on a holiday is automatically conducted on the next business day.[301])

A special meeting may be called by the presiding officer or a majority of the legislative body by delivering a written notice personally or by mail to each member of the legislative body and to each local newspaper of general circulation, radio or television station requesting such notice in writing.[302] The notice must be delivered and actually <u>received</u> at least 24 hours before the time of the meeting. The call and notice of a special meeting must specify the time and place of the meeting and the business to be transacted. No other business may be considered.[303]

If an emergency makes it unsafe to meet at a regular meeting place, meetings may be held for the duration of the emergency at a place designated by the presiding officer. An emergency "involving matters upon which prompt action is necessary due to the disruption or threatened disruption of public facilities" can justify a meeting without complying with the 24-hour notice requirement.[304] Other special meeting requirements, except for the 24-hour notice requirement, must be observed. The minutes of an emergency meeting must list the persons who were attempted to be notified. A roll call vote on actions taken at such a meeting must be posted for a minimum of 10 days in a public place as soon after the meeting as possible. A closed session cannot be conducted at an emergency meeting.

Regular, adjourned regular, special or adjourned special meetings may be adjourned to a time and place specified in the order of adjournment.[305] Less than a quorum may order adjournment or, if all members are absent from the meeting, the clerk or secretary may declare the meeting adjourned to a stated time and place, then cause written notice to be given in the same manner as provided for special meetings. A copy of the order or notice of adjournment must be conspicuously posted on or near the door of the place where the meeting was held within 24 hours after the time of adjournment.

The agency must mail notice of regular meetings at least one week prior to the meeting (unless one week's notice is impracticable) to property owners within the agency who have filed requests.[306] Requests for notice are valid for one year unless renewal is requested. The legislative body may establish a reasonable annual charge for sending such notices.

An agenda must be posted for regular and adjourned meetings at least 72 hours before the meeting.[307] A legislative body cannot act on matters not on the posted agenda unless an emergency exists or unless the need to take action arises after the 72-hour deadline.[308] A majority vote of the body is necessary to find that an emergency exists.[309] A four-fifths vote (unanimous if less than 5 are present) is necessary to find the need to take action on an issue that arose after the deadline.[310] The agenda for the regular meeting can serve as the agenda for the adjourned meeting if the adjournment does not exceed five days.[311] The 72-hour agenda rule does not apply to special meetings.[312] An agenda must be posted 24 hours before special meetings and each director must receive <u>actual</u> notice of the meeting 24 hours in advance.[313] The agenda for a regular or adjourned regular meeting must include opportunity for public comment.[314] However, the legislative body may not act on public's comments on matters not on the agenda until the subject is placed on the agenda in compliance with the 72-hour rule.[315] The public must be given the opportunity to comment on each item before action is taken.[316]

Meetings must be held within the District, except:

- To comply with state or federal law or court order;
- To inspect real property or personal property which cannot be moved;
- To meet with another public agency on multi-agency matters;

- To discuss legislative or regulatory matters with state or federal officials;

- To discuss matters relating to a facility in the facility; and

- To visit legal counsel's office if so doing will reduce legal fees relating to the meeting.[317]

Despite common practice, there is no authority for one or two board members to demand an item be placed on the agenda. The preparation of the agenda should follow the same protocol for calling a meeting. The president or three board members may call a special meeting; the president or three board members may create the agenda. If a dispute arises, a board member can request the item to be placed on a future agenda by motion at a meeting.[318]

Teleconferencing has been possible for about a decade but is not often practiced despite miraculous, technological advances. Teleconferencing may be "used for all purposes in connection with any meeting."[319] The statute includes several requirements:

- Votes shall be by roll call;

- Agenda shall be posted at each teleconference location;

- Teleconference locations shall be identified in the notice of the meeting;

- The locations shall be accessible to the public; and

- The public must be allowed to address the agency at each location.

Teleconferenced meetings must be conducted in a manner that "protects the statutory and constitutional rights of the parties and the public." At least a quorum shall participate from locations within the agency boundaries. Requiring at least a quorum within the agency infers: teleconferencing may be used to obtain a quorum, if at least a quorum is present within the agency. Teleconferencing is an opportunity for public agencies to expand participation by members of the legislative body who would otherwise be unable to attend, and to permit public participation at remote locations throughout the area. However, the practice cannot be implemented without some effort. An experiment should be conducted during a routine meeting.

E-mail is not mentioned in the Brown Act, but the use of e-mail is regulated. A legislative body cannot make a decision or make collective progress in making a decision except during a public meeting. This general rule applies to e-mail communication. Members of a legislative body can make their views known to other members without violating the Act, only if the receiving member does not convert a monologue into a dialogue. E-mail and chat rooms must be used carefully because the technology makes dialogue too easy.

There are exceptions to the requirement for meeting in public. A closed session may consider the employment or dismissal of an employee or to hear charges against an employee by another person or employee, unless the employee requests a public hearing.[320] A report of any action taken in a closed session and any roll call vote thereon must be presented at the public meeting during which the closed session is held, or at the next public meeting if a public employee is appointed or dismissed because of action taken during a closed session.[321] The Brown Act does not authorize a closed session to consider the appointment of a person to fill a board vacancy nor does this exception apply to the appointment of independent contractors unless the contractor performs work normally performed by an employee.[322]

A closed session may be convened to meet with designated representatives of the agency during negotiations with employee organizations to review the agency's position and to instruct agency representatives.[323]

A closed session may be held on matters posing a threat to the security of public buildings or a threat to the public's right of access to public services or facilities.[324] A closed session may be held when a group interrupts a meeting and order cannot be restored by removing the individuals interrupting the meeting.[325] Under these circumstances, only matters appearing on the agenda may be considered and duly accredited representatives of the press or other news media, excepting those who are participating in the disturbance, must be allowed to attend the session.[326] The legislative body may establish a procedure for readmitting individuals not responsible for the disturbance.[327]

A public agency may meet with its attorneys in closed sessions when the attorney-client privilege associated with litigation would otherwise apply. There are limits to the attorney-client privilege:

> ...a legislative body of the local agency, based on advice of its legal counsel,... (may hold) a closed session to confer with, or receive advice from, its legal counsel regarding pending litigation when discussion in open session concerning those matters would prejudice the position of the local agency in the litigation.[329]

Litigation includes *potential* litigation "if there is a significant exposure to litigation against the local agency." No other attorney-client closed session is permitted. This exception does not justify a closed session for other matters which could be covered by the attorney-client privilege. This exception does not apply to legal advice in the absence of litigation or a real threat of litigation.

A closed session can be held to discuss acquisition or sale of real property;[330] to determine whether to issue a permit or license;[331] to analyze liability claims;[332] or to discuss security threats.[333]

Prior to holding a closed session, the legislative body must state the general reason for the closed session and may state the legal authority for the session.[334] The Act lists language that will satisfy this notice requirement. This language will satisfy the statute; it is a "safe harbor" but the language is not mandatory:

(1)   For a closed session under Government Code Section 54956.7: "License/Permit Determination;"

(2)   For a closed session under Government Code Section 54956.8: "Conferences with Real Property Negotiator [also identify property];"

(3)   For a closed session under Government Code Section 54956.9: "Conferences with Legal Counsel - Existing Litigation [name of case unless disclosure would jeopardize service or settlement];" or "Conference with Legal Counsel - Anticipated Litigation [potential case name]" "Liability Claims (name of claimant);"

(4)   For a closed session under Government Code Section 54956.94: "Liability Claims [name of claimant];"

(5)   For a closed session under Government Code Section 54957: "Threats to Public Services or Facilities [name of law enforcement agency and title of officer];" or "Public Employee [specify position];" or "Public Employee Performance Evaluation [specify position];" or "Public Employee Discipline/Dismissal/Release;" and

(6)   For a closed session under Government Code Section 54957.6: "Conferences with Labor Negotiator [name of agency representative and employee organization or an unrepresented employee]."[335]

Once in the closed session, the legislative body may consider only those matters covered in the statement.[336] Action may be taken in a closed session, but the action must be reported as soon as it can without prejudicing the agency:

(1)   Approval of an agreement concluding real estate negotiations should be reported after the agreement is final. The Board shall report approval and the substance of the agreement in an open session at the public meeting when the closed session is held if the Board's approval closes the deal. The District must disclose the approval and the substance of the agreement when the other party accepts the District's offer if final approval rests with the other party.

(2)   Authorization for counsel to defend or seek judicial relief shall be reported in an open session at the public meeting when the closed session is held. The report should identify the adverse parties and substance of the litigation. In the case of approval to initiate or to intervene in an action, the announcement need not identify the action, the defendants, or other particulars. But the announcement shall specify direction to initiate or to intervene in an action has been given and the action, the defendants, and the other particulars shall be disclosed when the action has commenced. The announcement can be withheld if it would jeopardize service of process or ability to conclude settlement negotiations.

(3)   Approval for counsel to settle pending litigation shall be reported after the settlement is final. The Board reports acceptance and identifies the substance of the agreement in an open session when the Board accepts the offer. If final approval

rests with the other party or with the court, the District must disclose the approval and the substance of the agreement when the settlement becomes final. A settlement cannot be approved in closed session if substantive law otherwise requires a public hearing.[337]

(4) Disposition of claims discussed in a closed session must be reported in the same manner as the settlement of litigation.

(5) Action to appoint, employ, dismiss, accept the resignation, or otherwise affect the employment status of a public employee shall be reported at the public meeting when the closed session is held. The reports shall identify the title of the position and specify changes in compensation. However, a report of dismissal or of non-renewal of an employment contract shall be deferred until the first public meeting following the exhaustion of the employee's administrative remedies. A rejected dismissal proposal need not be disclosed.[338]

(6) Approval of an agreement concluding labor negotiations shall be reported after the agreement is final and accepted or ratified by the other party. The report shall identify the item approved and the other party or parties to the negotiation.[339]

Employees and consultants can be disciplined for disclosing what happens in a closed session. Except in very limited circumstances, elected officials cannot be punished for disclosing confidential information obtained in a closed session. Disclosure of confidential information by directors is usually a political issue. However, the disclosure can result in misdemeanor liability if an elected official uses the confidential session for personal gain.[340] Further, an elected official who attends a closed session affecting the officer's financial interests violates conflicts of interest laws.[341] Finally, disclosure could constitute an "improper condition" which exposes the official to impeachment.

The legislative body may designate a person to attend closed sessions and keep a record of the topics discussed and decisions.[342] This record is not open to public inspection pursuant to the California Public Records Act and must be kept confidential. This book is available only to members of the legislative body or to a Court, if a violation of law is alleged to have occurred at the closed session. Closed sessions are not held unless confidentiality is important, and most public agencies do not create records of closed sessions. However, a brief record is helpful to answer charges of a Brown Act violation. Counsel should prepare a brief memorandum summarizing the date of the closed session, attendance and action taken.

The Brown Act encourages public attendance and participation at agency meetings. During regular meetings, the public must be given the opportunity to ask questions or offer comments on district business not appearing on the agenda.[343] During every meeting, the public must have the opportunity to address the board before action is taken.[344] The board may address "reasonable regulations" including limiting the time allocation for public testimony on a particular item and for each speaker.[345] Remember, the First Amendment to the U. S. Constitution guarantees the right to petition government for redress of grievances so any restriction on public testimony must be carefully drafted. No one can be required to register her name or provide other information or fulfill a condition precedent to attendance.[346] A person attending a public meeting may record the proceeding on a tape or video recorder unless such action would disrupt the meeting.[347] The agency must permit meetings to be broadcast unless the agency finds the broadcast equipment will disrupt the meeting.[348] No fee may be charged for carrying out the Act except as authorized by the Act.[349] Finally, the meeting or function cannot be held in a facility prohibiting admittance on the basis of race, religion, creed, color, national origin, ancestry or sex.[350] The agency must make "reasonable accommodation" to facilitate access by disabled persons. This includes physical access (ramps and doors) and a range of services for the hearing impaired.

Agenda material distributed to a majority of the members of the legislative body for discussion at a public meeting are public records as soon as distributed and shall be made available prior to the meeting.[351] Documents distributed during the meeting must be available prior to the discussion. Other writings discussed at the meeting must be made available as soon as practicable. Fees may be established by the agency to cover the cost of copying the documents. No fee shall be charged for merely inspecting the documents.

The Brown Act has not subsumed every nook and cranny of public meetings. Reasonable, nondiscriminatory restrictions can be imposed on the length of public comments at meetings.[352] Meetings can be opened with an invocation without violating the Brown Act or Constitution.[353]

If a member of the legislative body attends a meeting that violates the Brown Act *with knowledge of the fact,* the member is guilty of a misdemeanor.[354] Although the misdemeanor penalty should be a powerful reason to avoid violations of the Act, reliance on advice of agency counsel with respect to the lawfulness of the meeting will avoid prosecution in most cases. The most powerful inducement for compliance remains the risk of public embarrassment.

A court action can be brought to declare the legislative body's action null and void for violating the rules on special meetings, open meetings and posting of agenda.[355] This remedy is limited. First, a court action cannot be brought unless the plaintiff demands within 30 days to rescind the action or to cure the defect. The lawsuit must be commenced within 15 days of the agency's response, or within 15 days of the expiration of the demand or 75 days from the action, whichever is earlier.[356]

Not all agency actions can be attacked in this manner. This procedure does not apply if:

(1)   the action was in "substantial compliance" of the Act;

(2)   the action was in connection with the sale or issuance of notes, bonds or other debt instruments;

(3)   the rights of innocent contractors would be impaired; or

(4)   the action was in connection with the collection of a tax.[357]

The Brown Act is designed to protect the public's right to participate in the business of local agencies. This praiseworthy goal has been largely accomplished but at an increasingly steep price because of the direct and subtle implications of the Act.[358] The most pervasive reason for small agencies to have legal counsel attend meetings is to assure compliance with the Brown Act. The Brown Act occupies a significant part of each bureaucrat's day. The public's business is becoming subservient to Brown-Act-Bureaucracy.

The Brown Act began as a relatively simple prescription. Recalcitrant local agencies and reluctant state agencies took advantage of the generalities of first statutes. These "abuses" were attacked not at the ballot box but by the adoption of loophole closing laws. It may be overly cynical to suggest the impossibility of drafting a statute without loopholes. But at least concede: an agency represented by competent counsel has a better than even chance of finding a new loophole to replace the old. The Brown Act evolved into a complicated mess. These statutes are becoming a legal subspecialty, a tax code of government etiquette.

Inevitably, complicated laws round up innocent parties. Consider some of the quirks of current statutes. A committee created by formal action of the governing board is subject to the Brown Act even if it has no decision making power; however, less than the quorum of the governing board can meet and discuss policy issues, if no formal appointment is made. Committee meetings are minefields. The governing board has acted if two separate committees comprising a quorum of the board act. If the second committee meeting is noticed as a board meeting to avoid this trap, non-committee members must be invited to attend.[359] If non-committee members are invited to attend, why bother with the committee? No less authority than the Attorney General has opined that governing boards of opposing public agencies cannot meet in closed session to settle a lawsuit.[360] Amendments may eliminate these problems. But people of good will still have to confront other problems in this law.

Because of the Brown Act, public agencies cannot call meetings, conduct meetings or make decisions without a lawyer present. Before applauding this state of affairs, remember opinionated lawyers are not trained in the art of governance. Lawyers are not representatives of the voters. The best lawyers temper legal advice with an understanding of practical consequences but most lawyers are not equipped to facilitate the work of policy makers. The popular complaint is true: we are becoming a nation directed by lawyers more concerned with what cannot be done than what should be done. The Brown Act is not the only law contributing to the problem, but it is an important expression of this mistaken philosophy.

Some argue a bad law is better than no law. The unexamined question is whether the public would be deprived of opportunity to participate in public decisions in the absence of the Brown Act. Elected officials can be expected to promote their ideas in public. Why else run for office? The tenure of elected officials who avoid public scrutiny is usually short. State and federal Legislatures regularly meet in closed session, yet there is no outcry the public is being deprived of their right to know about what is going on in Sacramento or Washington D.C. The need for the Brown Act is ambiguous.

If the Brown Act is not needed to implement the policy of open government, does it accomplish another worthy goal? Government usually sets policy with fanfare but grows silent when forced to admit a policy or project has failed. Policy failure fills time on the airways and consumes newsprint. Failed policy sells advertising and newspapers. The Brown Act constituency, the news media, puts the proposition more delicately: the public has a right to know when their elected officials are failures.

Perhaps the public's right to know about bad decisions can be preserved without making the business of governing a legal quagmire. The Public Records Act insures access to virtually all government documents.[361] Replace everything in the Brown Act except the statement of purpose with a clear statement on how government decisions are made and recorded. The statement could include the following:

- The governing board establishes policy and supervises the implementation of policy by management. If policy is unwise or management fails to carry out policy, the board shall be held accountable.

- The governing board shall compile a written record of policy decisions. Management shall provide written reports on the implementation of policy decisions. These reports are public records.

- The governing body shall prepare an annual report showing the status of each policy decision including policies that have been abandoned.

Finally, those who proclaim the dire consequences of government secrecy would do well to remember the finest moment in the history of government occurred in secret. The Second Continental Congress drafted the U.S. Constitution without public participation.

Ironically, the public frequently demands government to act efficiently, like the private sector. Yet, the public places demands on public agencies not placed on the private sector. Records handling is one area where the public sector is treated radically different than the private sector. It is questionable whether the public gains anything by having access to virtually every record of a public agency. It is certain that public agencies must increase their bureaucratic oversight to comply with public records laws. There are major differences between the public and the private sector when it comes to handling of records. The public has access virtually to every paper and electronic record of a public agency. Nothing like this would be tolerated in the private sector. Granted, public agencies perform the public's business but even shareholders do not have access to the types of records the public has access to in a public sector.

There are three aspects to records' handling in the public sector: records must be available for inspection and copying, records must be retained for a specified period, and records may be destroyed only in specific circumstances.

In a nutshell, every written and electronic record in the possession of an agency is available for public inspection (and copying) unless one of a handful of specific exemptions applies. Public Records Act applies to "writings." A "writing" is broadly defined to include not only tangible documents but also documents stored in electronic form on computer disks. This means agencies must comply with the Public Records Act with respect to computer maintenance programs. Most agencies do not realize that e-mail can be a public record. E-mail can not be routinely erased from public agency computers.

The Public Records Act carries costly and embarrassing penalties. Agencies are well advised to assign responsibility for compliance to a single well-trained person – the custodian of records. (The well-trained custodian of records is also important for the management of records during litigation.) The custodian must be trained to contact agency counsel because questions are inevitable.

The exemptions from disclosure are narrow. The most common exemptions are for preliminary drafts and attorney-client privilege documents involving litigation. (Not every letter from agency counsel involves pending litigation privilege.) The complete exemption list is:

(a)   Preliminary drafts, notes, or interagency or intra-agency memoranda that are not retained by the public agency in the ordinary course of business, if the public interest in withholding those records clearly outweighs the public interest in disclosure.

(b)   Records pertaining to pending litigation to which the public agency is a party, or to claims made pursuant to Division 3.6 (commencing with Section 810), until the pending litigation or claim has been finally adjudicated or otherwise settled.

(c)   Personnel, medical, or similar files, the disclosure of which would constitute an unwarranted invasion of personal privacy.

(d)   Contained in or related to any of the following:

(1) Applications filed with any state agency responsible for the regulation or supervision of the issuance of securities or of financial institutions, including, but not limited to, banks, savings and loan associations, industrial loan companies, credit unions, and insurance companies.

(2) Examination, operating, or condition reports prepared by, on behalf of, or for the use of, any state agency referred to in paragraph (1).

(3) Preliminary drafts, notes, or interagency or intra-agency communications prepared by, on

behalf of, or for the use of, any state agency referred to in paragraph (1).

(4) Information received in confidence by any state agency referred to in paragraph (1).

(e)   Geological and geophysical data, plant production data, and similar information relating to utility systems development, or market or crop reports, that are obtained in confidence from any person.

(f)   Records of complaints to, or investigations conducted by, or records of intelligence information or security procedures of, the office of the Attorney General and the Department of Justice, and any state or local police agency, or any investigatory or security files compiled by any other state or local police agency, or any investigatory or security files compiled by any other state or local agency for correctional, law enforcement, or licensing purposes. However, state and local law enforcement agencies shall disclose the names and addresses of persons involved in, or witnesses other than confidential informants to, the incident, the description of any property involved, the date, time, and location of the incident, all diagrams, statements of the parties involved in the incident, the statements of all witnesses, other than confidential informants, to the victims of an incident, or an authorized representative thereof, an insurance carrier against which a claim has been or might be made, and any person suffering bodily injury or property damage or loss, as the result of the incident caused by arson, burglary, fire, explosion, larceny, robbery, carjacking, vandalism, vehicle theft, or a crime as defined by subdivision (b) of Section

13951, unless the disclosure would endanger the safety of a witness or other person involved in the investigation, or unless disclosure would endanger the successful completion of the investigation or a related investigation. However, nothing in this division shall require the disclosure of that portion of those investigative files that reflects the analysis or conclusions of the investigating officer. Customer lists provided to a state or local police agency by an alarm or security company at the request of the agency shall be construed to be records subject to this subdivision. Notwithstanding any other provision of this subdivision, state and local law enforcement agencies shall make public the following information, except to the extent that disclosure of a particular item of information would endanger the safety of a person involved in an investigation or would endanger the successful completion of the investigation or a related investigation:

(1) The full name and occupation of every individual arrested by the agency, the individual's physical description including date of birth, color of eyes and hair, sex, height and weight, the time and date of arrest, the time and date of booking, the location of the arrest, the factual circumstances surrounding the arrest, the amount of bail set, the time and manner of release or the location where the individual is currently being held, and all charges the individual is being held upon, including any outstanding warrants from other jurisdictions and parole or probation holds.

(2) Subject to the restrictions imposed by Section 841.5 of the Penal Code, the time, substance,

and location of all complaints or requests for assistance received by the agency and the time and nature of the response thereto, including, to the extent the information regarding crimes alleged or committed or any other incident investigated is recorded, the time, date, and location of occurrence, the time and date of the report, the name and age of the victim, the factual circumstances surrounding the crime or incident, and a general description of any injuries, property, or weapons involved. The name of a victim of any crime defined by Section 220, 261, 261.5, 262, 264, 264.1, 273a, 273d, 273.5, 286, 288, 288a, 289, 422.6, 422.7, 422.75, or 646.9 of the Penal Code may be withheld at the victim's request, or at the request of the victim's parent or guardian if the victim is a minor. When a person is the victim of more than one crime, information disclosing that the person is a victim of a crime defined by Section 220, 261, 261.5, 262, 264, 264.1, 273a, 273d, 286, 288, 288a, 289, 422.6, 422.7, 422.75, or 646.9 of the Penal Code may be deleted at the request of the victim, or the victim's parent or guardian if the victim is a minor, in making the report of the crime, or of any crime or incident accompanying the crime, available to the public in compliance with the requirements of this paragraph.

(3) Subject to the restrictions of Section 841.5 of the Penal Code and this subdivision, the current address of every individual arrested by the agency and the current address of the victim of a crime, where the requester declares under penalty of perjury that the request is made for a scholarly, journalistic, political, or governmental purpose, or that the request is made for investigation

purposes by a licensed private investigator as described in Chapter 11.3 (commencing with Section 7512) of Division 3 of the Business and Professions Code. However, the address of the victim of any crime defined by Section 220, 261, 261.5, 262, 264, 264.1, 273a, 273d, 273.5, 286, 288, 288a, 289, 422.6, 422.7, 422.75, or 646.9 of the Penal Code shall remain confidential. Address information obtained pursuant to this paragraph may not be used directly or indirectly, or furnished to another, to sell a product or service to any individual or group of individuals, and the requester shall execute a declaration to that effect under penalty of perjury. Nothing in this paragraph shall be construed to prohibit or limit a scholarly, journalistic, political, or government use of address information obtained pursuant to this paragraph.

(g) Test questions, scoring keys, and other examination data used to administer a licensing examination, examination for employment, or academic examination, except as provided for in Chapter 3 (commencing with Section 99150) of Part 65 of the Education Code.

(h) The contents of real estate appraisals or engineering or feasibility estimates and evaluations made for or by the state or local agency relative to the acquisition of property, or to prospective public supply and construction contracts, until all of the property has been acquired or all of the contract agreement obtained. However, the law of eminent domain shall not be affected by this provision.

(i) Information required from any taxpayer in connection with the collection of local taxes that is received in confidence and the disclosure of the information to other persons would result in unfair competitive disadvantage to the person supplying the information.

(j) Library circulation records kept for the purpose of identifying the borrower of items available in libraries, and library and museum materials made or acquired and presented solely for reference or exhibition purposes. The exemption in this subdivision shall not apply to records of fines imposed on the borrowers.

(k) Records, the disclosure of which is exempted or prohibited pursuant to federal or state law, including, but not limited to, provisions of the Evidence Code relating to privilege.

(l) Correspondence of and to the Governor or employees of the Governor's office or in the custody of or maintained by the Governor's Legal Affairs Secretary. However, public records shall not be transferred to the custody of the Governor's Legal Affairs Secretary to evade the disclosure provisions of this chapter.

(m) In the custody of or maintained by the Legislative Counsel, except those records in the public database maintained by the Legislative Counsel that are described in Section 10248.

(n) Statements of personal worth or personal financial data required by a licensing agency and filed by an applicant with the licensing agency to establish his or her personal qualification for the license, certificate, or permit applied for.

(o) Financial data contained in applications for financing under Division 27 (commencing with Section 44500) of the Health and Safety Code, where an authorized officer of the California Pollution Control Financing Authority determines that disclosure of the financial data would be competitively injurious to the applicant and the data is required in order to obtain guarantees from the United States Small Business Administration. The California Pollution Control Financing Authority shall adopt rules for review of individual requests for confidentiality under this section and for making available to the public those portions of an application that are subject to disclosure under this chapter.

(p)   Records of state agencies related to activities governed by Chapter 10.3 (commencing with Section 3512), Chapter 10.5 (commencing with Section 3525), and Chapter 12 (commencing with Section 3560) of Division 4 of Title 1, that reveal a state agency's deliberative processes, impressions, evaluations, opinions, recommendations, meeting minutes, research, work products, theories, or strategy, or that provide instruction, advice, or training to employees who do not have full collective bargaining and representation rights under these chapters. Nothing in this subdivision shall be construed to limit the disclosure duties of a state agency with respect to any other records relating to the activities governed by the employee relations acts referred to in this subdivision.

(q)   Records of state agencies related to activities governed by Article 2.6 (commencing with Section 14081), Article 2.8 (commencing with Section 14087.5), and Article 2.91 (commencing with Section 14089) of Chapter 7 of Part 3 of

Division 9 of the Welfare and Institutions Code, that reveal the special negotiator's deliberative processes, discussions, communications, or any other portion of the negotiations with providers of health care services, impressions, opinions, recommendations, meeting minutes, research, work product, theories, or strategy, or that provide instruction, advice, or training to employees.

Except for the portion of a contract containing the rates of payment, contracts for inpatient services entered into pursuant to these articles, on or after April 1, 1984, shall be open to inspection one year after they are fully executed. If a contract for inpatient services that is entered into prior to April 1, 1984, is amended on or after April 1, 1984, the amendment, except for any portion containing the rates of payment, shall be open to inspection one year after it is fully executed. If the California Medical Assistance Commission enters into contracts with health care providers for other than inpatient hospital services, those contracts shall be open to inspection one year after they are fully executed. Three years after a contract or amendment is open to inspection under this subdivision, the portion of the contract or amendment containing the rates of payment shall be open to inspection.

Notwithstanding any other provision of law, the entire contract or amendment shall be open to inspection by the Joint Legislative Audit Committee and the Legislative Analyst's Office. The committee and that office shall maintain the confidentiality of the contracts and amendments until the time a contract or amendment is fully open to inspection by the public.

(r) Records of Native American graves, cemeteries, and sacred places and records of Native American places, features, and objects described in Sections 5097.9 and 5097.993 of the Public Resources Code maintained by, or in the possession of, the Native American Heritage Commission, another state agency, or a local agency.

(s) A final accreditation report of the Joint Commission on Accreditation of Hospitals that has been transmitted to the State Department of Health Services pursuant to subdivision (b) of Section 1282 of the Health and Safety Code.

(t) Records of a local hospital district, formed pursuant to Division 23 (commencing with Section 32000) of the Health and Safety Code, or the records of a municipal hospital, formed pursuant to Article 7 (commencing with Section 37600) or Article 8 (commencing with Section 37650) of Chapter 5 of Division 3 of Title 4 of this code, that relate to any contract with an insurer or nonprofit hospital service plan for inpatient or outpatient services for alternative rates pursuant to Section 10133 or 11512 of the Insurance Code. However, the record shall be open to inspection within one year after the contract is fully executed.

(u) (1) Information contained in applications for licenses to carry firearms issued pursuant to Section 12050 of the Penal Code by the sheriff of a county or the chief or other head of a municipal police department that indicates when or where the applicant is vulnerable to attack or that concerns the applicant's medical or psychological history or that of members of his or her family.

(2) The home address and telephone number of peace officers, judges, court commissioners,

and magistrates that are set forth in applications for licenses to carry firearms issued pursuant to Section 12050 of the Penal Code by the sheriff of a county or the chief or other head of a municipal police department.

(3) The home address and telephone number of peace officers, judges, court commissioners, and magistrates that are set forth in licenses to carry firearms issued pursuant to Section 12050 of the Penal Code by the sheriff of a county or the chief or other head of a municipal police department.

(v) (1) Records of the Major Risk Medical Insurance Program related to activities governed by Part 6.3 (commencing with Section 12695) and Part 6.5 (commencing with Section 12700) of Division 2 of the Insurance Code, and that reveal the deliberative processes, discussions, communications, or any other portion of the negotiations with health plans, or the impressions, opinions, recommendations, meeting minutes, research, work product, theories, or strategy of the board or its staff, or records that provide instructions, advice, or training to employees.

(2) (A) Except for the portion of a contract that contains the rates of payment, contracts for health coverage entered into pursuant to Part 6.3 (commencing with Section 12695) or Part 6.5 (commencing with Section 12700) of Division 2 of the Insurance Code, on or after July 1, 1991, shall be open to inspection one year after they have been fully executed.

(B) If a contract for health coverage that is entered into prior to July 1, 1991, is amended on or after July 1, 1991, the amendment, except for any portion containing the rates of payment, shall be open to inspection one year after the amendment has been fully executed.

(3) Three years after a contract or amendment is open to inspection pursuant to this subdivision, the portion of the contract or amendment containing the rates of payment shall be open to inspection.

(4) Notwithstanding any other provision of law, the entire contract or amendments to a contract shall be open to inspection by the Joint Legislative Audit Committee. The committee shall maintain the confidentiality of the contracts and amendments thereto, until the contract or amendments to a contract is open to inspection pursuant to paragraph (3).

(w) (1) Records of the Major Risk Medical Insurance Program related to activities governed by Chapter 14 (commencing with Section 10700) of Part 2 of Division 2 of the Insurance Code, and that reveal the deliberative processes, discussions, communications, or any other portion of the negotiations with health plans, or the impressions, opinions, recommendations, meeting minutes, research, work product, theories, or strategy of the board or its staff, or records that provide instructions, advice, or training to employees.

(2) Except for the portion of a contract that contains the rates of payment, contracts for health coverage entered into pursuant to Chapter 14 (commencing with Section 10700) of Part 2 of Division 2 of the Insurance Code, on or after January 1, 1993, shall be open to inspection one year after they have been fully executed.

(3) Notwithstanding any other provision of law, the entire contract or amendments to a contract shall be open to inspection by the Joint Legislative Audit Committee. The committee shall maintain the confidentiality of the contracts and amendments thereto, until the contract or amendments to a contract is open to inspection pursuant to paragraph (2).

(x) Financial data contained in applications for registration, or registration renewal, as a service contractor filed with the Director of Consumer Affairs pursuant to Chapter 20 (commencing with Section 9800) of Division 3 of the Business and Professions Code, for the purpose of establishing the service contractor's net worth, or financial data regarding the funded accounts held in escrow for service contracts held in force in this state by a service contractor.

(y) (1) Records of the Managed Risk Medical Insurance Board related to activities governed by Part 6.2 (commencing with Section 12693) or Part 6.4 (commencing with Section 12699.50) of Division 2 of the Insurance Code, and that reveal the deliberative processes, discussions, communications, or any other portion of the negotiations with health plans, or the impressions, opinions, recommendations, meeting minutes, research, work product, theories, or strategy of the board or its staff, or records that provide instructions, advice, or training to employees.

(2) (A) Except for the portion of a contract that contains the rates of payment, contracts entered into pursuant to Part 6.2 (commencing with Section 12693) or Part 6.4 (commencing with Section

12699.50) of Division 2 of the Insurance Code, on or after January 1, 1998, shall be open to inspection one year after they have been fully executed.

(B) In the event that a contract entered into pursuant to Part 6.2 (commencing with Section 12693) or Part 6.4 (commencing with Section 12699.50) of Division 2 of the Insurance Code is amended, the amendment shall be open to inspection one year after the amendment has been fully executed.

(3) Three years after a contract or amendment is open to inspection pursuant to this subdivision, the portion of the contract or amendment containing the rates of payment shall be open to inspection.

(4) Notwithstanding any other provision of law, the entire contract or amendments to a contract shall be open to inspection by the Joint Legislative Audit Committee. The committee shall maintain the confidentiality of the contracts and amendments thereto until the contract or amendments to a contract are open to inspection pursuant to paragraph (2) or (3).

(5) The exemption from disclosure provided pursuant to this subdivision for the contracts, deliberative processes, discussions, communications, negotiations with health plans, impressions, opinions, recommendations, meeting minutes, research, work product, theories, or strategy of the board or its staff shall also apply to the contracts, deliberative processes, discussions, communications, negotiations with health plans, impressions, opinions, recommendations, meeting minutes, research, work product, theories, or strategy of applicants pursuant to Part 6.4 (commencing with Section

12699.50) of Division 2 of the Insurance Code.

(z) Records obtained pursuant to paragraph (2) of subdivision (c) of Section 2891.1 of the Public Utilities Code.

(aa) A document prepared by or for a state or local agency that assesses its vulnerability to terrorist attack or other criminal acts intended to disrupt the public agency's operations and that is for distribution or consideration in a closed session.

(bb) Critical infrastructure information, as defined in Section 131(3) of Title 6 of the United States Code, that is voluntarily submitted to the California Office of Homeland Security for use by that office, including the identity of the person who or entity that voluntarily submitted the information. As used in this subdivision, "voluntarily submitted" means submitted in the absence of the office exercising any legal authority to compel access to or submission of critical infrastructure information. This subdivision shall not affect the status of information in the possession of any other state or local governmental agency.

(cc) All information provided to the Secretary of State by a person for the purpose of registration in the Advance Health Care Directive Registry, except that those records shall be released at the request of a health care provider, a public guardian, or the registrant's legal representative.

Nothing in this section prevents any agency from opening its records concerning the administration of the agency to public inspection, unless disclosure is otherwise prohibited by law. Nothing in this section prevents any health facility from disclosing to a certified bargaining agent relevant financing information pursuant to Section 8 of the National Labor Relations Act (29 U.S.C. Sec. 158).[362]

The Public Records Act contains one general exception. Under this provision, an agency may withhold a record if the need for privacy is more important than the need for disclosure. The courts will apply a strong presumption against the need for privacy. This makes it a general exception almost impossible to invoke.

The agency must provide copies of identified records. Any person – including persons employed by other public agencies and other public agencies – may request a record.[363] The reasonable costs of the copies may be covered but a fee for research in locating and setting aside of the records cannot be charged. An agency should have a procedure for handling requests for inspection and copying. The agency should require the request to be written so the requester cannot later claim the request has not been satisfied. The custodian should respond to the request in writing for the same reason.

Contrary to popular belief, the Public Records Act does not mandate records be provided within a specific period of time. The Act requires the custodian to respond to the request within ten days by explaining whether or not the records which will be provided. Records must then be provided within a reasonable time, taking into consideration the nature of the request. For example, a voluminous request for very old records should take longer to satisfy than a request for a single page of a current document. The response should include the estimated cost of copying the records and request a deposit be made before the copy work takes place. (Sometimes the public requests voluminous records in the belief they can be obtained for free. Once the modest charge is made known, the request may become more focused.)

Not many laws include attorney fees for agency victories. The Public Records Act contains such a provision. The agency can be forced to pay attorney fees but this statute is one of the few that allows public agencies to recover attorney fees if the agency is successful.

Even at home, it is hard to avoid being drowned in a sea of paper. Imagine the problems for public agencies with the Public Records Act providing stiff penalties for not making public records available. Statutes require the retention of writings for specified times. Compliance with records retention laws is another opportunity for records management if the custodian is careful and skilled.

First, *"duplicate"* records may be destroyed *"at any time,"* if:

(1) The board of directors authorizes the destruction, and

(2) The original or a photographic record is on file with the agency.[364]

This provision is useful only to clean files replete with copies.

Second, "original" documents may be destroyed and need not be photocopied, nor is any copy required to be retained, if:

(1) The board of directors authorizes the destruction,

(2) The documents are more than two years old, and

(3) The documents were not prepared or received pursuant to statute.[365]

The problem of the obscure statutes plagues this provision. Proving the negative, i.e., no statute exists, is almost impossible. Consequently, this provision is difficult to use.

Third, "unacceptable bids" for construction or installation of facility or public work may be destroyed, if:

(1) The board of directors authorizes the destruction, and

(2)   The documents are more than two years old.[366]

Fourth, routine video monitoring tapes can be destroyed after one year.[367] Finally, a straightforward rule. Of course, even these records should not be destroyed if there is litigation concerning contract award.

Fifth, *"Original"* records may be destroyed *"at any time,"* provided:

(1)   The board of directors authorizes the destruction,

(2)   The document was not required by law to be filed and preserved, and

(3)   Accurate reproductions are maintained on file.[368]

This provision is a variation of the rule for destruction of two-year-old originals.

Sixth, unless the law "expressly" requires the original to be preserved, the "original" may be destroyed if:

(1)   The record is reproduced by a medium that does not permit alterations and that complies with the minimum standards of the National Institute of Standards and Technology.

(2)   The device that is used to make the reproduction is accurate in all respects.

(3)   The reproduction is readily accessible.[369]

The problem of discovering no statute expressly requires the original to be preserved is repeated here. At least, this provision offers hope modern devices such as optical disks can be used to create the reproductions in lieu of paper files.

These brief provisions are helpful but do not dispose of all questions, particularly in light of the Public Records Act. The laws relating to destruction of "city" records may be of guidance even to the special districts.[370] A city record, other than those listed below, may be destroyed by a department head, without making a copy thereof, when the record is no longer required, if:

(1) The city council approves the destruction by resolution,

(2) The city attorney consents in writing to the destruction,

(3) The records are more than five years old,

(4) The records are not required to be kept by statute,

(5) The records do not affect title to real property or liens thereon, and are not minutes, ordinances or resolutions of the city council or its commissions.[371]

A city record may be destroyed, without the consent or authorization of the city council or city attorney, if a legible copy thereof is maintained.[372]

The state codes occupy about 20 feet of shelf space. It is impossible to determine without exhaustive review whether a particular record is kept by statutory mandate. The following are some examples of records received by an agency pursuant to state statute. The list is illustrative only:

(1) Certificate of incorporation of the agency.

(2) Documents received pursuant to eminent domain proceedings brought by the agency.

(3) Ballot arguments *pro* or *contra* a bond issue.

(4) Results of bond propositions received from the canvassing body.

(5) Certificate of assessed valuation prepared by the auditor of each county in which property taxable by the agency lies.

(6) Documents received from tax assessors detailing agency taxes collected.

(7) Statement of boundary line change.

(8) Resolution ordering annexation of territory to the agency along with legal description and map.

(9) Certificate of Secretary of State reciting the filing of annexation papers by the agency in his office.

(10) Documents received relating to claims brought against the agency under the provisions of Government Code Section 900, *et seq.*

(11) Documents received relating to claims brought against the agency under the provisions of Government Code Section 940.

(12) Securities acquired with surplus agency monies.

(13) Receipt for securities deposited in bank.

No record should be destroyed pursuant to a destruction program if the record must be open for inspection under the Public Records Act. In light of the potential for severe punishment for failure to comply with the Public Records Act, a bias should exist favoring retention of the records for public inspection in any case where the slightest doubt may exist.

In analyzing a records question, use a two-step approach: first, determine whether the record must be open for public scrutiny pursuant to the Public Records Act; and second, if it is not subject to the Public Records Act, determine when the document may be destroyed.

If the document is subject to the Public Records Act, at least a microfilm copy should be maintained for a reasonable period of time. The "reasonableness" of the retention must be judged on a case-by-case basis after examining all the facts involved. For example, an item relating to a major personal injury claim for which no suit has been filed probably will be "stale" within two years, inasmuch as the Statute of Limitations will have run out by that time. On the other hand, an item relating to a contractor, should be maintained as long as there are dealings under the contract and at least four years thereafter.

A methodical records maintenance policy takes these three categories into consideration. Technology permits easy search of records once they are in digital format. An agency which has the financial and technical wherewithal can digitally archive most records. Once a digital copy is made of all records, an agency can wait five years, then destroy all records which need not be maintained in perpetuity.

Agencies can reduce their paper load by aggressively using digital technology in the first place. For example, minutes must be maintained for meetings but the law does not state the minutes must be in writing. (The Public Records Act treats digital recordings as if they are writings.) Hence, it is possible to videotape meetings and have the recording constitute the minutes of the meeting. The Secretary's role is merely to index the video recordings during and after the meetings.

CHAPTER 6

FINANCIAL

There was a time when public agency finance was the job of amateurs. Mistakes were corrected by increasing a tax. Planning was child's play. That changed in 1978 when the voters enacted the first in a series of increasingly stringent initiatives limiting taxes. As a result, government finance now demands a level of skill rivaling the most sophisticated private sector business.

Financial planning is an annual event. The budget is the plan by showing anticipated revenues, anticipated expenditures, and changes in reserves.[373] Developing the budget is an iterative process.

On the expenditure side, management suggests projects consistent with the mission of the agency; the directors consider management's recommendations and add their own. The next draft of the budget includes estimates for the revised projects, and so on, until the board is satisfied the budget shows the projects for the upcoming year. Estimating the cost of programs and projects is only half the job. Management must locate revenues from fees, taxes, and other sources. The board must decide whether enough revenues will be generated and reduce expenditures if revenues are not adequate.

The budget must be filed with the county board of supervisors by September 1 of each year. (Districts may file a statement of anticipated receipts and expenditures instead of a budget.) The approved budget must be examined regularly to confirm expectations. Some variations are to be expected, but the manager must advise the board immediately when significant deviations are projected.

The annual audit report must be filed with the county and the state controller's office by September 1 of each year. An annual audit will show for the prior year whether the budget projections were successful. The audit is a report card. An agency which consistently fails to meet budget projections is a financial failure even if it remains solvent because the failure shows inability to plan for even a short term. The annual audit can be performed by the county auditor or, more typically, by an independent auditor engaged by the local agency.

Every business has several sources of revenue, but businesses cannot obtain taxes, and assessments. There are several types of taxes: *ad valorem* property taxes, non-*ad valorem* property taxes, excise taxes and income taxes.[374] Local government cannot levy *ad valorem* taxes. Each county levies an *ad valorem* tax equal to 1% of market value of real and personal property located within the county and this tax is allocated among taxing agencies, based on taxes levied by agencies in 1978.[375]

Non-*ad valorem* taxes can take any form as long as the tax is not based on the value of the property to be taxed. Parcel or flat taxes are not based on the value of property. Parcel tax may be based on size of the parcel, land use, or other factors. Two types of the non-*ad valorem* taxes are possible: special taxes and general taxes. A special tax is a tax levied for specific governmental purpose. Special districts levy special taxes but cities and counties can levy special taxes if the proceeds are spent for specific purposes. A general tax is a tax levied for general governmental purposes. Cities and counties can levy general taxes. Special districts cannot levy general taxes. A special tax requires two-thirds approval of those voting, and a general tax requires a majority approval.[376]

One of the many tax initiatives introduced Article XIII B to the State Constitution. This article prohibits an agency from expending taxes in excess of an "appropriation limit" without voter approval which can have a maximum term of four years. (The appropriate limit consists of taxes received in 1978 adjusted to reflect changes in the cost of living and population.) Thus, the voters can approve a general tax (by majority vote) or special tax (by 2/3's vote) but the approval is effective for only four years once the appropriation limit is reached.

An assessment is like a tax. It is imposed regardless of the wishes of the owner of the property to be assessed. An assessment is different than a tax. An assessment must be proportional to the benefits conferred by the agency on the property to be assessed.

Many agencies providing water and sanitation service have levied "standby charges" against property, regardless of whether the services were actually provided. A standby charge is a special type of assessment. Proposition 218 says new standby charges levied for the first time after 1998 must be approved in the same manner as other assessments. Water and sanitation charges which existed as of 1998 may be continued to be levied without regard to the protest criteria.

After the adoption of Proposition 13 in 1978, agency fees could not exceed the reasonable costs of service for which the fee or charge is imposed. ("Reasonable costs" includes reasonable reserves.) Before the adoption of Proposition 218 in 1998, a person challenging the fee had the burden of establishing the fee exceeded the reasonable cost of service. Because reasonable has an eye-of-the-beholder quality, successful challenges were extremely rare. Proposition 218 changed the process for adopting many fees and the burden of proof. Agencies must compile a "record" showing the cost of the program for which the fee is charged, and how the cost is fairly spread among the ratepayers.

The reasonable cost of service rule presents many challenges. A fee charged for one type of service, say water rate, cannot be used for an unrelated service, say police service, because the part of the water rate used for police service is – by definition – not a cost of water service. This does not mean every dollar of every fee must stay in the same department. The characterization of the fee by the agency and, ultimately, the court, matters. For example, an agency can transfer part of a building permit fee from the building department to the planning department because the planning department provides some "new construction" services and the fee is related to new construction.[377]

Proposition 218's procedural changes affect "property related fees." The agency must conduct a duly-noticed public hearing before it can adopt a property related fee. "Property related" must be difficult to define because the California Supreme Court has wrongly decided two cases on the subject. In the first case, the Supreme Court decided a water connection fee is not a property related fee because it was paid before property was connected to the water system.[378] The court overlooked the fact service had to be connected to something and the something is always real property. In the second case, the California Supreme Court said the water rates were property related fees because the water had to be delivered to property.[379] The court overlooked the fact service is often provided to non-property owners, i.e., renters. The court should have reached the opposite result in both cases.

The hearing required by Proposition 218 is not much different than the hearing agencies conduct to establish the record on cost of service. Written notice must be given to the person who requests and receives service and is liable for the fee at least 45 days before the hearing.[380]

The Legislature adopted a statute dealing with "capital facilities charges" which presaged Proposition 218. Under this statute, capital facilities' charges cannot be imposed unless the agency first conducts a duly-noticed public hearing to receive evidence concerning the reasonable cost of the service for which the charge is collected. Proceeds from capital facilities' charges must be placed in a segregated account and spent only for the purposes announced during a hearing. Capital facilities' fees unspent after five years must be refunded.

Capital facilities' charges have also received special treatment by the California Supreme Court. In 1985, the Court ruled a capital facilities' charge imposed on a public school was an assessment. Because the Constitution prohibits a local agency from assessing another local agency, the Court held the school district could not be forced to pay water connection fees. The Legislature subsequently enacted a statute allowing school districts to pay capital facilities' charges when the water agency and the school district have negotiated in good faith. What is missing from the court's analysis and from the statute is the obvious.[381] A water agency does not have to serve a school district which refuses to pay.

California Constitution Article XIII B was added during the first wave of tax reform initiatives. This initiative contained a requirement for the state to reimburse local agencies for the costs of programs mandated by the state (and imposed an appropriations limit).[382] Under this article, the state must reimburse local government for the costs of services which the state forces local government to provide. The provision contained a few sensible exceptions to the reimbursement mandate, e.g., federal mandates compelling action do not force the state to pick up the cost. The courts have assumed the role of protector of the State Treasury and have upheld virtually every statute or interpretation created by the state to avoid its responsibility under the Constitution.[383] Local agencies have largely ignored the opportunity to claim reimbursement. A recent decision may signal a change. Costly conditions on permits issued by the Regional Water Quality Control Board for storm water runoff are subject to cost reimbursement.[384]

The voters continue to demand government act more like business when it comes to financial decisions.[385] Companies in the private sector can be aggressive investors. Investment earnings can be an important source of agency revenues. Investment earnings must be protected by a clear and conservative investment policy. Unfortunately, the array of permitted investments gives agencies the latitude to adopt foolish investment policies.

When establishing an investment policy, the agency must continually ask: what is our mission, what is our goal, what is our purpose. An investment policy which furthers the mission, goals and purpose of an agency (to provide service to taxpayers and customers) will not pursue high investment yield. This is a good thing. The agency must have a clear and concise investment policy and a process to ensure the policy is being followed.

The treasurer (or financial officer) must submit an investment policy for the governing body's approval.[386] The policy can simply state investments must be prudent, taking into account safety, yield and the need for liquidity, or can specify the investments and investment ratios.[387] The minimum investment policy is stated in the law:

> When investing, reinvesting, purchasing, acquiring, exchanging, selling or managing public funds, the primary objective of a trustee shall be to safeguard the principal of the funds under its control. The secondary objective shall be to meet the liquidity needs

of the depositor. The third objective shall be to achieve a return on the funds under its control.[388]

State law lists permitted types of investment. The policy should specify a maximum percentage for each category of the investment portfolio and maximum duration for each type of investment. For example, the policy could say not more than 80 percent of the portfolio will be invested in treasury bills, or not more than 50 percent of the treasury bills shall be for a duration of longer than one year.

The policy should require the treasurer or chief fiscal officer to render quarterly compliance reports in accordance with generally accepted accounting methods to the CEO, internal auditor, and governing body within 30 days after the end of each quarter.[389] For investments managed by an outsider, the report should include current value and method of determining current value.[390] The report should explain whether the next six months cash flow requirements can be met.[391] The agency must file copies of the investment policy, no later than 60 days after the close of the second quarter of each calendar year, and 60 days after subsequent amendments thereto, shall provide the statement of investment policy to the California Debt and Investment Advisory Commission.[392]

Most investment policies contain high-sounding statements of what an agency hopes to achieve. While these statements are useful, they are usually open to interpretation. Because the list of permitted investments is relatively short, ambiguities can be avoided by specifying permitted investment. The policy should also create a process for reviewing certain investments. For example, the policy could permit purchases of "treasury bills" without further board action but could require approval of the board before investing in a "diversified management fund."

The list of permitted investments have grown over the years. Initially, agency investments were limited to notes, bonds and other indebtedness of the United States, California, or local agencies of this state.[393] Later, debt instruments guaranteed by the federal government were added.[394] Certain types of "paper" were made eligible for investment, including bills of exchange, i.e., bankers' acceptances, certificates of deposit, repurchase or reverse repurchase agreements and "prime" commercial paper.[395] The diversified management fund is a way for public agencies to invest in a mutual fund. Up to 15 percent of the agency's surplus may be invested in such a fund. Such funds enable investment in "pools" of Treasury bills, Treasury bonds, or Fannie Mae or Ginnie Mae mortgages. Notes, bonds or other obligations secured by collateral of the same type that secures public agency deposits are permitted.

The length (term) of an investment depends on the needs of the agency. When reserves are small and likely to be needed, long-term investments are unwise. Money set aside to pay a note cannot be invested for longer than the term of the note.[396] Conversely, an agency with large reserves may wish to avoid short-term investments to maximize yields. Investments for a term longer than five years must be specifically approved by the governing board.[397]

Smaller agencies or agencies outside the regional financial centers may be unable to actively manage investments. The trust department of a major bank can help in such cases or the agency can participate in a common investment fund such as maintained by most county treasurers or by the state treasurer, i.e. the Local Agency Investment Fund.[398]

Custody of the debt instrument is an important consideration when using the services of an investment broker or advisor. Some agencies permit the investment broker to hold instruments in the broker's name so the instruments may be quickly sold when a better investment appears or just because it is easier. The portfolio can be wiped out if the broker becomes insolvent when investments are held in the broker's name. Further, brokers have been known to (illegally) pledge instruments held in their name for others as collateral for the margin of the broker's personal investments. In such a case, the agencies' instruments can be called when the broker's investment fails. <u>The broker should not hold securities for safekeeping, except in limited circumstances.</u>[399] The securities should be held in the agency's vault or in a depository, not in the broker's vault. The broker will protest. A separate depository will be inconvenient and may result in missed investment opportunities. However, most brokers are located near an independent depository and inconvenience should be minor. More importantly, if the investment policy is dependent upon quick transactions, the agency is probably taking too many risks in the first place.

The treasurer must submit reports on investments to the chief executive officer, internal auditor and governing body within 30 days after the end of each quarter.[400] The report must describe each current investment, its yield, the issuer, dollar amount invested and maturity date. The treasurer must certify investments have been in accordance with the approved investment policy. The report must also describe investments managed by others for the agency. <u>The Treasurer can be liable for bad investments which violate the investment policy</u>.

Dramatic investment losses were reported during the 1980s and 1990s by California agencies. Since ridicule attends bad investment decision, the problem is probably more widespread than publicly reported. Some losses may be attributed to volatile financial markets. But inattention is often the culprit. The investment policy is ineffective unless the governing board monitors compliance. Warning signs will disclose the need for full-scale investigation:

- **Boasting about high earnings is a sure sign something is amiss**. An agency should be slightly embarrassed if return on investments is lower than neighboring agencies. An agency should be terrified if return on investments is appreciably greater than neighboring agencies. Some finance officers believe their job is to earn as much money as possible. A stated policy against speculation is no guarantee the finance officer will take a conservative approach. *Listen for boasting.*

- **Watch for churning.** There is opportunity for quick profit if a finance officer buys and sells an investment on the same day. Unfortunately, same day trading shows willingness to take risks and usually demonstrates the program is profit oriented. This is also a sign investment brokers may be taking advantage of the finance officer to engage in a practice known as "churning." Churning occurs when investments are bought and sold with high frequency without substantial advantage to the investor. Churning creates commissions for brokers and risks for agencies. *Watch for same day transactions.*

- **Watch for margin investments.** A trade is leveraged when only a part of the investment is paid when the trade is made. There is opportunity for high profits by selling before the balance is due. There is also risk of catastrophic loss if the sale does not occur. Some margin transactions are difficult to expose. For example, an agency may order $1 million worth of banker's acceptances. Instead of buying $1 million worth of banker's acceptances, the broker uses the $1 million to buy $10 million on margin. If banker's acceptances appreciate before the investment is delivered, the broker pockets the balance. If the value of the investment goes down, the broker cannot return the principal and may attempt to hold the agency liable for a margin call. *Do not permit margin transactions.*

Many losses are due to bad advice or predatory practices by investment advisors. Agencies must establish rigorous procedures for selecting and using advisors, including:

- <u>The brokers or advisors must understand the agency's investment policy and affirm whether the policy will be followed</u>. The investment policy must require persons wishing to deal with the agency make an application. Essential information, including the agency's investment philosophy, will be disclosed during the process. The agency must **not** deal with the investment broker who comes "off the street" with a "hot" deal.

- <u>Do not use the services of a broker not qualified through screening, even if the broker appears to provide a better rate of return.</u>

- <u>The fees and commissions should depend upon the amount and frequency of transactions</u>. If the agency is paying more than $300.00 commission on $1 million investment, it might be overcharged.

- <u>The broker must disclose "principal" transactions</u>. When an agency places an order to purchase a security, and the broker purchases the security in the open market, the broker is acting as an agent. For this, the broker earns a commission. If the broker sells a security the broker already owns, the broker is acting as a principal. Principal transactions can produce huge profits for the broker. The agency is entitled to know what the broker paid for the security sold to the agency as a principal. Broker profits on principal transactions should not be appreciably greater than the commissions earned as an agent.

- <u>The broker must execute an agreement to work within the confines of the investment policy</u>, including margin prohibitions, churning restrictions, a fee schedule and other understandings on principal or agent trading.

The law distinguishes surplus and non-surplus money. Non-surplus money is money needed for the current fiscal year and cannot be "invested." Non-surplus money may only be "deposited." [401] The governing board must determine the surplus. The bank (or savings and loan) that accepts a deposit must have sufficient collateral to insure repayment.[402] The collateral may be in the form of specified securities held in a "pool" or may be in the form of federal deposit insurance if the *treasurer* of the agency agrees to waive other security requirements.[403]

Agencies have a one-time opportunity to obtain revenue from the sale of surplus property. State law says little about the sale of personal property except local agencies should have a policy. The procedure for the sale of surplus personal property is usually based on the value of the property. For example, when property has only nominal value, donation to a local charity is often the best course. The policy on disposition of personal property should include the following:

(1) A declaration the property is surplus by someone with authority (the board or chief executive officer);

(2) Donation of valueless property to a local charity; and

(3) Sale of property with value pursuant to sealed bids or an auction.

One problem frequently encountered by agencies is what to do about useful but worthless goods. Old computers fall in this category. One solution is to donate the goods to another public agency. The only difficult part of a decision is how to determine whether the goods are truly worthless. Failed bidding can supply evidence of worthlessness as will an informal appraisal by an expert in the field.

Agencies may sell surplus *real* property with a few constraints by state law. Every year, each local agency must inventory lands and make a public record of the inventory.[404] A public hearing must be conducted before property is transferred.[405] Surplus real property must be offered to other public agencies to further statewide policies concerning: education, affordable housing, open space, parks and recreation, and enterprise zones. [406] If a fair market offer is made by one of these agencies, the property must be conveyed to the agency. (The law does not deal with competitive proposals from these agencies nor is the law clear regarding whether offers for less than market value by these other agencies must be accepted.) An agency can follow the following procedure for disposing of surplus real property:

(1) Declare the property surplus, i.e., no longer necessary for the District's use of purposes.[407]

(2) Offer the property to the appropriate agency for developing low- and moderate-income housing.[408]

(3) Offer to sell or lease the property for park and recreational purposes or open-space purposes to: any park or recreation department of a city, county, district or agency within which the land may be situated and State Resources Agency.[409]

(4) Offer to sell or lease land suitable for school facilities construction to the school district where the land is located.[410]

(5) Offer to sell or lease to any enterprise zone if the property is in an area designated as an enterprise zone.[411]

(6) Offer to sell or lease the property if it is located in a designated redevelopment program area.[412]

The agencies interested in purchasing the property must notify the seller agency within 60 days after receipt of the offer.[413]

The agencies must then negotiate in good faith for at least 60 days, and if a deal cannot be reached, the land can be sold on the open market.[414] This procedure need not be followed if the property is "exempt surplus property," including:

(1) Less than 5,000 square feet; or

(2) Less than the minimum legal residential building lot size; or

(3) No record access and is less than 10,000 square feet in size and is not contiguous to existing publicly owned land used for parks, recreational, open-space, affordable housing purposes, or to land in an enterprise zone, or a designated area. (If the surplus property is not sold to the contiguous owner, then it is not "exempt surplus property.")[415]

But exempt surplus property is <u>not</u> the following:

(1) Property located within 1,000 yards of an historical unit of the State Parks System; or

(2) Property within 1,000 yards of property which is on or may be eligible for the National Register of Historic Places.

When real property is initially acquired by eminent domain, the eminent domain judgment may have established severance damages because of the project's impact on the other landowners' property by the use of the project "in the manner proposed." The agency can incur additional liability if a subsequent sale causes the property to be used in a different manner. Property acquired by eminent domain can only be used for the purposes stated in the eminent domain acquisition documents. This can mean the property must be sold to the former owner if it becomes surplus. Similarly, property acquired by dedication carries the potential for hidden liability when sold because the former property owner can argue the "nexus" for the dedication was false.

State law prohibits public employees from purchasing surplus real or personal property from their employer:

> Nor shall…officers or employees be purchasers at any sale or vendors at any purchase made by them in their official capacity.[416]

This could mean public officers and employees cannot purchase any surplus goods from their agency. However, such an interpretation interferes with the rights of employees to be treated equally with other citizens. A better view is the officer or employee cannot purchase surplus goods if the officer or employee has "inside knowledge" about the goods or has anything to do with declaring the goods surplus. Since the general manager and directors are supposed to know all, the general manager and directors cannot purchase surplus property from the agency.

State and federal grants are important sources of revenue for many local agencies. Some programs and projects can be funded almost entirely from state and federal assistance. Grants do not always save money. An airport district needed to construct security fencing estimated to cost $60,000 and estimated to take two months to complete. The district sought a federal grant. The district had to redesign the fence to federal standards, making the final cost $250,000. It took six months to complete. The district's matching share was $60,000. The district obtained a higher quality fence for the same investment. But the original fence design was adequate at one point. The same tale plays out over and over again when small districts seek federal or state assistance for their projects. The lesson is: the agency should avoid grants if the agency can obtain what it needs without state and federal assistance.

Securing a state grant should not result in many new operational requirements. The same cannot be said for the federal government. The following federal laws are applicable upon receipt of federal grant funds. A local agency using federal funds must comply with a variety of federal procurement laws. Each federal agency has its own set of regulations. Most include the following mandates:

(1) *Prevailing wages* must be paid for public works projects, but the rate is not determined by the state prevailing wage law. The rate is determined by the federal *Davis-Brown Act*.[417]

(2) Certify compliance with the *Copeland Anti-Kickback* law.[418]

(3) Provide *equal employment* opportunities.[419]

(4) Actively solicit *minority and women-owned small business* participation.[420]

(5) Actively solicit *Vietnam Era Veterans*. [421]

(6) Actively solicit *handicapped workers*. [422]

(7) Disclose *lobbying activities*. [423]

(8) Certify compliance with *Clean Air* and *Clean Water* laws.[424]

(9) Maintain *financial* records.[425]

This list is illustrative. The federal agency providing money may have added requirements.

The Davis-Bacon Act is the federal version of the state prevailing wage law. A local agency receiving a federal grant must comply with both state and federal wage laws. The two laws use different wage scales in some instances. The local agency must pay the higher wage dictated by the state prevailing wage statute or Davis-Bacon Act.

Often, the federal government will mandate disadvantaged business hiring quotas. Proposition 209 prohibits hiring quotas (and affirmative action) throughout the state unless mandated by the federal government. Agencies may not impose affirmative action requirements except to the extent required by federal law federal affirmative action requirements. Federal affirmative action requirements are often less than they appear to be. Federal grant conditions must be carefully studied before an affirmative action program is adopted by a state or local agency.

One of the problems with dealing with large entities, such as the state of California or the federal government, is that time has no meaning. Grant conditions say funded programs are subject to audit years after completion. Local agencies will be exposed to possible refund demands for years and even decades. To make matters worse, state and federal employees routinely disavow the decisions of their predecessors. When dealing with the federal or state bureaucracy on grant funds, demand written instructions and determine whether the person has authority to issue the order.

Even the most stable local agencies occasionally find themselves "cash poor." When this happens, they may need to borrow or, in government parlance, obtain revenue through the sale of debt instruments.

For decades, "bonds" were the preferred debt instruments of local agencies for converting long-term cash flow into cash. The many initiative measures restricting a taxing authority of public agencies have made it difficult to repay long-term debt with taxes and have created an opportunity for financial consultants to create debt instruments to compete in the marketplace.

Agencies must have a clear idea of what they hope to accomplish through the issuance of debt instruments because the agency can be hamstrung for years by unwise borrowings. An agency should ask what a lender can legitimately expect as security for the loan. In some cases, new taxes will provide the cash flow necessary to retire long-term debt but taxes usually will not provide security for debt. In most cases, security comes from "revenue stream." Long-term borrowing is most feasible when a project will produce revenues. An agency which cannot show revenues to fund the debt, is wasting its time.

Agencies "dip into" reserves when revenue does not match expenditures. The question is not whether reserves will be used but whether they must be replenished and whether an appropriate level of reserves is maintained. The agency should have a written policy on reserves to satisfy the inquiries of customers and to ensure continuity. Deciding the appropriate level for a reserve is difficult. Everyone has an opinion. The agency must decide the purpose for which a reserve is maintained to establish the amount. Sometimes an agency will establish several reserves.

Just as at home, money is easier to spend than obtain. Public agencies must acquire goods and services with an attention to a process – some dictated by state statute and some homegrown. The agency's administrative code must include purchasing procedures.

State law says little or nothing about acquisition of personal property. To be sure, there are statutes prohibiting public officials from obtaining property for their personal use. Public agencies should establish procedures for purchasing goods, services and supplies. The process can consist of a series of progressively more stringent requirements dependent on the estimated cost. The purchasing procedures can authorize the chief executive officer (or purchasing officer) to obtain goods or services estimated to cost less than $500 or $1,000 without bidding and without a formal contract. (Even here, however, a purchasing order should be used.) Midrange purchases, say between $500 and $2,000, should not be made in the absence of a formal solicitation. The agency will specify in writing what it hopes to acquire and interested vendors will respond in writing. This avoids misunderstandings between the agency and vendor over what is to be supplied. The personality of the agency will dictate whether this written interchange should be part of a bidding process. More expensive items, say between $2,000 and $5,000, can be acquired through informal bidding. Once again, written requests and responses are expected but the purchasing agent will also be required to solicit a minimum number of proposals, say three to five. Finally, the most expensive acquisitions, say in excess of $5,000, should be acquired through a formal bidding process. Written statement of what the agency expects to acquire will be met by written responses. Instead of soliciting proposals from a select group, the agency will solicit proposals by a general call broadcast to the public such as in newspaper.

The purchasing process should also deal with who is allowed to accept the proposals. Often, the chief executive officer or purchasing agent can accept proposals for lesser amounts if reports are provided to the board. The board's approval can be required when informal or formal bids are solicited.

The acquisition of real property is several degrees different than the acquisition of personal property. Real property transactions must be written. Agencies often overlook the use of eminent domain in acquiring property. Many believe eminent domain is an antagonistic process. It need not be. A "friendly" eminent domain action can accomplish much for both the buyer and seller. For the buyer (agency), the eminent domain case can create a new parcel without a parcel map or subdivision map. For the seller, eminent domain offers tax advantages.

Not every sale is voluntary. Sometimes public agencies must acquire a parcel (or part of a parcel), notwithstanding the desires of the property owner. When this happens, eminent domain is the agency's only resort. The eminent domain process is lengthy but not particularly complicated. It begins with the acquisition of information. The agency must identify the property by legal description, obtain an estimate of the value of the property, and a title report. With this information, the agency must approach the owners of the property and make a fair market value offer.

Assuming the owners reject the offer, the owners of the property will be given notice of the consideration of a "resolution of necessity" by the governing board. The resolution of necessity will identify the property, describe the public use to which the property is to be put, and explain why the property is necessary to fulfill that public use. The agency is not required to demonstrate the property is the "best suited" parcel for a particular public use. The agency need only show the property is suited for the stated purposes. The owners can contest whether the property is truly needed for a public purpose and whether a good-faith offer has been made.[426] Typically, the resolution of necessity will also authorize counsel to file an eminent domain case to acquire the property.[427]

The eminent domain complaint will identify the property and restate the contents of the resolution of necessity. The court can be asked to allow the agency to take the property before the eminent domain trial commences if the resolution of necessity states "immediate possession" of the property is necessary. A court will allow immediate possession if the agency shows a pressing need and deposits the amount of "probable" just compensation. The property owner can contest the agency's showing of necessity and the amount of the deposit.

Prior to trial, the agency and the property owner will exchange appraisal reports. Most eminent domain cases do not involve a contest over the agency's need to acquire the property. However, national publicity for the *Elho* case may have changed that. A typical eminent domain case is heard by a jury which decides which appraiser makes the most sense. The agency deposits the amount of the jury award with the court. The court authorizes a final order of condemnation to be entered. The agency records the final order of condemnation. This constitutes documentation of the agency's title.

A couple of things about eminent domain can be confusing. Three different property valuations can occur during the typical eminent domain process. An initial evaluation will precede the resolution of necessity. A second evaluation will precede the order of possession. A final appraisal will be presented at trial. The appraisals need not be exactly the same because each appraisal will be progressively more formal.

Severance damages can be confusing. Most understand the concept of valuing property. "Market value" of real property is the amount a willing buyer will pay a willing seller when the property is exposed to the market for a reasonable period of time. There will be differences of opinion on what constitutes fair market value, but usually, a range of values will be presented by the appraisers. A more difficult question is whether the taking of a part of a larger parcel has created incidental damages ("severance damages"). For example, suppose the agency acquires 4/10 of a one-acre parcel. The property owner can claim 6/10 "remainder" has no further value. If the property owner succeeds, the agency must also pay for lost value of the 6/10 acre remainder. This will be something less than 100% but it can be substantial. Appraisers frequently differ greatly on severance damages.

Property acquired by eminent domain is for specific public use; it must be put to that use. Agencies cannot acquire property for roadway purposes and use it for a City Hall. Agencies are permitted to change their mind. If a project is canceled, the agency must return the property.[428]

The law also directs how public agencies expend monies for public works projects. These laws fall into two categories. Many (not all) agencies must secure competitive bids for works of improvement. Even agencies not required to secure bids must adhere to mandatory contract provisions.

Historical, public works projects presented a great opportunity for graft and corruption. As a result, reform minded legislators created public bidding requirements. Despite the importance of public bidding requirements, not all public works jobs have to be bid. Further, public administrators who believe bidding generates costly overhead often attempt to avoid bidding by new strategies.

Most competitive bidding statutes are contained in the Public Contracts Code. This Code does not cover all local agencies. For example, airport districts and county water districts are not required to use competitive bidding for their public works projects. The Code also imposes competitive bidding requirements for different activities. For example, a municipal water district must solicit competitive bids for "works of improvement" expected to cost $25,000 or more, but community services districts must solicit competitive bids for "public works projects" expected to cost $10,000 or more. Some types of agencies have special bidding requirements. General law cities must solicit competitive bids for the installation of carpet. The law does not designate how the bid solicitation is to be done. Most agencies advertise in a newspaper of general circulation or in the "green sheet" – an industrial trade journal. Most agency ads run for at least ten days. Proposals can be solicited in any way which fosters competition.

Competitive bidding is <u>not</u> required when it is "impracticable" or when an emergency exists which requires immediate action. The impracticality exception is based on a case arising at the beginning of the 20th century which found it was not practical to draft specifications for something as complicated as a parking meter. Obviously, impracticality changes with the times. The emergency exemption can arise only when health and welfare of the community is at stake. For example, a broken water main can be repaired without first soliciting bids, but bidding cannot be avoided because of an imminent price increase.

A contract awarded in violation of bidding requirements is void.[429] The rationale for voiding a contract let in violation of bidding requirements in the bidding mode is a measure of the agency's power.[430] When a public works contract is void, the contractor cannot recover the value of the work even after the work is completed.[431] The agency can escape payment for the work even though the failure is the agency's responsibility:

(1)   Failure to award the contract following open competitive bidding unless the failure is the agency's fault;[432]

(2)   Conflict of interest violation, including any "extracurricular" payments by the contractor to an agency official;[433] and

(3)   Failure to require the filing of a payment bond.[434]

Even though compliance with these laws can be easily verified, few, if any, contractors make the necessary effort.[435]

Anyone who makes the rounds of industry conferences is bound to hear a panel discussing the merits of design-build contracting. The benefits of design-build contracting are often illusory. Most agencies can do better with aggressive competitive bidding. The law allows design-build contracts in lieu of competitive bidding in the following circumstances:

(1)   The project is financed by bonds;

(2)   The project will produce revenue; and

(3)   The project involves utility service.

Every year there are efforts to expand the scope of the design-build exception, but unless something drastic happens, the exception will remain just that, an exception to the rule.

The proponents of design-build contracts say the process saves time and money. No data is offered because "it is obvious." Actually, "it" is not obvious. When competitive bidding is employed, most of the time is spent designing the project and evaluating proposals. The period for the notice inviting bids can be as short as two weeks. The design-build process eliminates the period for soliciting bids, but requires more effort in the design of the project and the evaluation of the prospective design-builders. In most cases, design-build contracting is slower than competitive bidding. But, is it cheaper? The firm awarded the design-build contract will tell you the agency is saving money and every unsuccessful bidder will say the opposite. Are negotiated contracts more likely to produce lower prices than bid contracts? This argument has raged for years without a clear winner. Design-build exposes agencies to the abuses competitive bidding is meant to avoid. Sugar-coat the design-build selection process how you want, but you cannot eliminate the opportunity contracts will be awarded to "favorites."

Criticism of design-build contracting is not praise for competitive bidding. The process needs reform. Fortunately, the reform can take place without "throwing the baby out with the bath water." The reform does not require more statutes or regulations. Aggressive competitive bidding can satisfy the policy goals and legal requirements and accomplish everything design-build contracting purports to accomplish. Aggressive competitive bidding breaks down the process of finding the (1) lowest, (2) responsible bidder into two steps. During step one, the agency seeks out "responsible" bidders. The design engineer can even question bidders about what it would take to make the contract most efficient (one of the alleged efficiencies for design-build contracts). At the end of the phase, the agency identifies a short list of responsible bidders who have expressed special interest in the project and who may have even helped smooth out the edges of the design. The collaboration between potential bidders and the agency is important to the formulation of the bid package. The bidders then offer prices for a variety of bidding options. The selection of the lowest bidders becomes an arithmetical exercise. Design-build versus aggressive competitive bidding? One has limited application under the law and opens the process for abuse, the other is legal and effective There is no reason to use design-build contracting when aggressive competitive bidding is possible.

Agencies may be able to "pre-qualify" bidders when the exceptions to competitive bidding do not apply.[436] The agency can adopt a policy on prequalification for projects requiring "specialized skills' or which are expected to cost more than $5 million. The policy must incorporate regulations issued by the Department of Industrial Relations. The regulations include a uniform rating system, notice to disqualified bidders, and opportunity to protest. The policy can apply to specific projects or a class of projects. The policy can include subcontractors.

State law commands local agencies to include many provisions in every public works contract even in the absence of competitive bidding. This is worth repeating because it is frequently misunderstood: agencies must include statutory provisions in every public works contract even when bidding is not required. The most controversial mandatory provision for local contracting is the requirement to pay "prevailing wages." Generally, the prevailing wage is equal to the wages negotiated by the Association of General Contractors with the building trades' unions. Prevailing wages are mandated on every public works job expected to cost $1,000 or more. The purpose of this law is to ensure that contractors employing union labor are not put at a disadvantage on public works jobs. The definition of "public works" in the statute is broad; it includes structures constructed by private parties to be dedicated to an agency. Enforcement of the prevailing wage law is usually at the insistence of unions. Because unions can not obtain information directly from the contractor, the statute allows "interested parties" to request information on wage payments from the agency which must obtain the information from the contractor. The consequence for failure to pay prevailing wages can be severe. The contractor can be fined $25/day for each worker who is not paid the prevailing wage. The agency is not responsible for this payment but the agency can be required to reimburse the contractor if the agency fails to mandate the contractor to pay prevailing wages.

Payment bonds are to protect workers and material suppliers. A payment bond is mandatory for a public works contract valued at $25,000 or more. (The amount of the bond can be less than 100% for higher value contracts.) The Attorney General has opined a contractor who fails to provide payment bonds cannot be paid even if the agency failed to demand payment bonds.

The agency can not pay more than 95% of the contract price until the job is complete. (The statute is slightly more complicated. An agency may withhold 10% of the contract price until 50% of the job is complete and thereafter may make payments in full.) The contractor can mitigate the financial impacts of this retention by requiring the agency to enter into a deposit agreement. With the deposit agreement, the agency pays the withheld amount into an interest-bearing escrow account which is released to the contractor when the job is completed.

Public property can not be liened or attached. Laborers and material suppliers cannot establish a "mechanics lien" on public jobs. The payment bond and retention schedule are efforts to place workers and material suppliers in the same position on public jobs as on private jobs. Under the stop-notice statute, a subcontractor can request the agency to withhold payment of the retained amount if the contractor fails to pay the subcontractor. Stop-notice claims must be filed within 180 days of cessation of labor or within 30 days after the filing of a "notice of completion," provided the notice is recorded within ten days of the finding of completion by the governing body. The stop-notice provisions should be taken into account when establishing a schedule for contract payments. The contract should say the retained amount will be paid 45 days (more than 30 days) after the recordation of the notice of completion. This way, the agency will know if claims are filed before releasing the retention. When a claim is filed, the agency should act quickly to a position of neutrality. The agency should file a stop-notice bond or deposit the retained amount in a neutral fund.

Other mandatory provisions include:

(1) The contractor must observe normal *working hours* and pay overtime.[437] The normal hours are determined by reference to union agreements. Holidays are determined by statute.[438]

(2) The contractor must employ *apprentices* in a certain number and type.[439]

(3) The contractor must provide a *workers' compensation certificate*.[440]

(4) Delays resulting from calamities caused by *acts of God* must be excused. [441]

(5) Responsibility for *relocation of underground utilities* must be allocated in accordance with state law.[442] This statutory requirement is similar to court-made law dealing generally with payment for unanticipated work.

(6) Public works contract must deal with *excavation safety*.[443] The contractor must submit a separate bid for all shoring involved in excavations 5 feet or more in depth and either prepare a separate plan for excavation safety or confirm compliance with standard specifications promulgated by the Division of Industrial Relations.

(7) Contractors must *assign rights accruing under anti-trust laws* to the agency.[444]

(8) A document prepared by a *consultant* costing $5,000 or more, usually the case when a consultant prepares plans and specifications, must contain a statement the document was prepared by a non-employee.[445]

(9) The contractor shall *list subcontractors* who perform more than one half of 1% of the work in the bid documents.[446] The contractor cannot "substitute" a subcontractor except in limited circumstances. (The list provides important information when it comes to stop notices.)

(10) The contract must provide for *mandatory arbitration* of disputes of less than $375,000.[447] The law details the process for the exchange of demands between the agency and the contractor prior to arbitration and delegates authority to the arbitrator.

(11) Contracts must deal with the discovery of *hazardous waste* during construction.[448] The contractor must be paid for waste removal and the contractor cannot be held liable except for contractor negligence.

(12) A *non-collision certificate* or declaration must attest each bidder is acting independently from other bidders.[449] If the certificate is an affidavit, the contractor's signature must be notarized. Many agencies permit the certificate to be a declaration under penalty of perjury because a notarization is unnecessary.

(13) *Native soil* must be used to backfill unless special conditions exist.[450]

Of course, agencies can not rely on mandatory provisions for all the protection that is needed. There are many industry sources for other "standard provisions." The Green Book of Public Works Contract Specifications is widely used. The additional provisions which should be included in every public works contracts deal with insurance, indemnification and defense, employee safety, change orders, time for performance, liquidated damages and early termination.

Often, public works contracts are administered by a staff member or engineer who has designed the project. This may be satisfactory for smaller jobs but is a recipe for disaster for larger jobs. Contractors often request additional compensation by arguing the design of the work was defective or the field conditions were not as advertised. The contractor can not be expected to make unbiased reports on field conditions, so an independent consultant will be needed to evaluate the contractor's claims. There will be a natural tendency to paper over design flaws if the design engineer is responsible for contract administration. Large jobs should be administered by someone other than the design engineer. (Pre-bid activities, such as site inspection, should be part of contract administration meetings but the design professionals should also attend these meetings.)

Not every design failure should result in payments by the design professional. A perfect design is infinitely expensive to create. The question is whether the design is so defective as to entitle the contractor to extra payment. When the design is flawed enough to allow the contractor to obtain additional compensation, the agency should obtain compensation from the engineer for the extra costs resulting from the bad design. The extra cost is not always 100% of the additional amounts paid to contractor. If, for example, the design failed to describe some work necessary to the project and the contractor is paid for the extra work, the design consultant will argue the extra cost would have been incurred, even if specifications were correct because the agency would have awarded the contract anyway. Some design flaws are so great and costs so significant, the agency would not undertake a project.

Contract disputes are easier to resolve when the evidence is clear. Technology is making the job of gathering evidence easier. Material sampling has been a routine part of contract administration for decades. Digital videotape can provide powerful evidence when methods rather than materials are called into question.

Every business must reduce exposure to liability through safety programs. A risk management team must create the safety program. The "risk management team" should include someone familiar with operations and someone familiar with liability issues. Often, someone on the management team will provide expertise in operations and general counsel will provide expertise for liability issues. The risk management team must make recommendations to the board on the scope, type and amount of insurance coverage. An insurance carrier is an important member of the risk management team to deal with casualties which occur, despite the safety programs.

Selecting coverage is an important decision and requires judgment. Every entity needs coverage for: workers' compensation, automobile hazards, and general liability. Coverage for workers' compensation and automobile hazards is self-explanatory; the only real question is the amount of coverage and amount of deductible. Basic general liability insurance is fairly well standardized. However, insurance companies must offer optional coverage for "terrorism." Public entities will want to consider optional coverage for inverse condemnation and civil rights violations. Entities operating reservoirs must address potential flood damage.

The amount of coverage is never easy to determine. Risk adverse professionals, such as lawyers, will say you can never have too much coverage or too small a deductible. Managers would rather spend premium dollars on operations by having lower coverage amounts and higher deductibles. ("SIR" or "self-insured retention" is the insurance industry's way of describing a deductible.) Both approaches are somewhat correct. Both approaches are somewhat wrong. The governing board must make a policy decision about how much risk should be incurred and how much risk should be covered by insurance. (At the least, insurance amounts should be enough to cover the cost of defending possible lawsuits.)

Three basic types of coverage are available to public agencies: traditional insurance, pooled insurance, and self insurance. In every case, the "carriers" financial capacity should be a primary concern. The capacity of an insurance company can be determined by the use of insurance rating services. ("Best rating" is a common service.) Several joint powers insurance authorities represent local agencies. Once again, the financial capacity of the entity providing the insurance is a key factor. A joint powers insurance authority does not technically "insure" anything. The members of the authority "pool" their risks. An authority made up of well managed, solvent entities is more attractive than an entity authority made up of potentially insolvent and poorly managed entities. There is no rating service available to help judge the quality of members of the pool. For this reason, public entities are well advised to only join pools involving entities of the same type so local knowledge of the pool participants is available. Because the authority is not an insurance carrier, the courts do not apply in the usual rules of insurance carriers to coverage issues. When dealing with an insurance carrier, any ambiguity in coverage is interpreted against the carrier. When dealing with an authority, coverage ambiguities are resolved in accordance with traditional laws of contract interpretation.

The public sector has a few disadvantages over the private sector, which should be recognized when purchasing insurance. Public agencies can be sued for violating a person's civil rights or for taking a person's property without payment of just compensation. Civil rights and inverse condemnation coverage should be purchased. Unfortunately, these coverages can be difficult to find and expensive. The public sector also has advantages. There can be no liability in the absence of statute. These good and bad differences should be taken into account when purchasing insurance.

Many carriers resist informing insureds of the right to separate, independent counsel when a lawsuit seeks damages for causes of action not covered by the policy.[451] The right to separate counsel was explained in a court case with *Cumis* in the name. Separate counsel is often called "*Cumis* counsel." The Rules of Professional Conduct were the basis of the *Cumis* decision.[452] The insured was sued for wrongful interference with an inducing breach of contract and intentional infliction of emotional distress. The adjuster for the insurer selected a law firm to represent the interests of the insured. The adjuster never asked the law firm for an opinion of coverage, nor did the law firm give coverage advice to the insured or the insurer. The adjuster reserved the right to deny coverage if the award was based on willful conduct, breach of contract, or punitive damages. The law firm selected by the insurer told the adjuster, "it did not see a conflict of interest."

The trial court saw the conflict:

> The carrier is required to hire independent counsel because an attorney in an actual trial would be tempted to develop the facts to help his real client, the Carrier Company, as opposed to the Insured, for whom he will never likely work again. In such a case as this the insured is placed in an impossible position; on the one hand the carrier says it will be happy to defend him and on the other it says it may dispute paying any judgment, but trust us. …Insurance companies hire relatively few lawyers and concentrate their business. A lawyer who does not look out for the carrier's best interest might soon find himself out of work.[453]

The court continued:

> Here, it is uncontested the basis for liability, if any, might rest on conduct excluded by the terms of the insurance policy. Goebel &

Monaghan ['insurance company counsel'] will have to make certain decisions at the trial of the *Eisenmann* ['insured'] action which may either benefit or harm the insureds. For example, it will have to seek or oppose special verdicts, the answers to which may benefit the insureds by finding non-excluded conduct and harm either *Cumis'* [the 'insurer'] position on coverage or the insureds by finding excluded conduct. These decisions are numerous and varied. Each time one of them must be made, the lawyer is placed in the dilemma of helping one of his clients concerning an insurance company and harming the other.

The conflict may appear before trial. Goebel and Monaghan represented the insureds in the...underlying action settlement conference and the case did not settle although a demand was made within policy limits. Before and during the settlement conference, ...insurance company counsel was in contact with Cumis but had no contact with the insureds about settlement until after the conference ended. The insureds then wrote a letter to counsel: 'You should know that the credit union desires the lawsuit to be settled without trial. Our insurance coverages, duly paid and contracted for, are precisely for such cases and any settlement liability that may arise therefrom. Your confidence in the defensibility of the case is appreciated. Should trial prove you wrong, however, and the jury awards damages, the insurance may no longer cover the credit union's possible losses. As you know, such losses would considerably exceed any possible settlement amount. It is clear that trial in lieu of settlement in this case subjects the credit union to a considerably additional risk while possibly lowering or eliminating a claim payout by Cumis [insured]. Such is not the basic premise upon which we contracted for insurance with Cumis.'... [454]

The court continued:

The potential problems may develop during pretrial discovery which must go beyond simple preparation for a favorable verdict to develop alternate strategies minimizing exposure... Insurance company counsel was bound to investigate all conceivable bases on which liability might attach. These investigations and client communications may provide information relating directly to the coverage issue. Furthermore, counsel may form an opinion about the insureds' credibility. As between counsel's two clients, there is no confidentiality regarding communications intended to promote common goals. (Evidence Code §962.) But confidentiality is essential where communication can affect coverage. (See Footnote 92.) Thus, the lawyer is forced to walk an ethical tightrope, and not communicate relevant information which is beneficial to one or the other of his clients.[455]

The court's rationale was clear:

The lawyer's duties in the conflict of interest situation presented here are correlative to the law insurer's contractual duty to pay for an

independent lawyer when it reserves its rights
to deny coverage under the policy. [456]

The final paragraph in *Cumis* sums up the decision:

> We conclude the Canons of Ethics impose
> upon lawyers hired by the insurer an obligation
> to explain to the insured and the insurer the
> full implications of joint representation in
> situations where the insurer has reserved its
> rights to deny coverage. If the insured does
> not give an informed consent to continued
> representation, counsel must cease to
> represent both. Moreover, in the absence
> of such consent, where there are divergent
> interests of the insured and the insurer
> brought about by the insurer's reservation of
> rights based on possible non-coverage under
> the insurance policy, the insurer must pay
> the reasonable cost for hiring independent
> counsel by the insured. The insurer may not
> compel the insured to surrender control of
> the litigation. (…[citations]). Disregarding the
> common interests of both insured and insurer
> in finding total non-liability in the third party
> action, the remaining interests of the two
> diverge to such an extent as to create an actual,
> ethical conflict of interest warranting payment
> for the insureds' independent counsel.[457]

Cumis allows the agency to object to representation of the
attorney selected by the insurance company because that law
firm's loyalty to the carrier conflicts with loyalty to the agency
due to the existence of substantial non-covered causes of action.
The carrier must pay for separate counsel if the agency does not
waive the conflict.

Cumis also anticipates the insurance company's argument that an agency waived the right to independent counsel by the terms of its contract. *Cumis* said:

> While it has been said a policy provision requiring the insured to permit the insurer to employ the attorney to defend the third party suit amounts to a consent in advance to the conflict of interest (...[citation]), where the insured affirmatively withdraws that consent by hiring independent counsel, no doubt motivated by the insurer's reservation of rights, any such consent may be deemed withdrawn (...[citation]).[458]

When California became a state, it adopted English common law until such time as the State Legislature would adopt a statute covering the same subject. Sometimes, the California Legislature did not get around to changing the common law. This is the case with "sovereign immunity." In merry old England, the king could not be sued because of "sovereign immunity." There are many sensible reasons for this for immunity for chief executives of high profile government, such as the President of the United States. The Presidents would be in court for most of the term of office without sovereign immunity. That's no way to run a country. The reason for the theory is less compelling with local government. The courts and the legislature have evolved exceptions to sovereign immunity for local government. But sovereign immunity remains the rule and liability remains the exception. Public agencies face liability only if a statute creates liability.

Sovereign immunity is the basis of the Tort Claims Act. This Act contains a complicated procedure for filing claims against the government and includes a number of general and specific immunities. A "claim" must be filed with a public agency and acted upon by a public agency before a lawsuit can be filed against a public agency or public employee for money damages. The claim must be written and contain specific information. Claimants who fail to provide the information required on the statutory claim form have filed an insufficient claim. The local agency can reject the claim for insufficiency.

The claim must be filed within a relatively short period of time after the "accrual of the cause of action." An attorney is probably needed to determine when a cause of action accrues. Claims for personal injuries must be filed within six months of accrual. Other claims, such as claims for property damage, must be filed within a year of accrual. Claims can be rejected for lateness. A lawsuit can not be filed if a claim is rejected due to lateness unless the claimant obtains a leave of court to file a late claim. The court will usually permit a claimant to file a late claim if any plausible excuse is offered. But a court cannot allow a claim to be filed more than one year after accrual of the cause of action even if a plausible excuse is offered.[459]

Because of sovereign immunity, agencies cannot be sued unless legislation specifically authorizes the lawsuit.[460] Legislation authorizes many types of lawsuits. The Tort Claims Act contains the most organized list of permitted lawsuits:

- Acts or omissions of employees within the scope of employment.[461]

- Acts or omissions of independent contractors.[462]

- Breach of a mandatory duty imposed by the Constitution, statute, or demand or regulation.[463]

- Damages caused by dangerous condition of public property.[464]

Other important sources of statutory liability include:

- Negligent or wrongful operation of a motor vehicle.[465]

- Interference with rights of disabled.[466]
- Nuisance.[467]
- Common carrier liability.[468]
- School liability.[469]

The Tort Claims Act also contains immunities, including:

- Discretionary acts.[470]
- Public employees or elected officials for acts of others.[471]
- Money stolen from official custody.[472]
- Misrepresentation.[473]
- Malicious prosecution.[474]
- Health and safety inspection of property.[475]
- Adoption and enforcement of laws.[476]
- Failure to legislate.[477]
- Failure to enforce laws.[478]
- Good faith enforcement of invalid laws.[479]
- Authorized entry on private property.[480]
- Licensing activities.[481]
- Gradual earth movement.[482]
- Communications in the proper discharge of official duty, including during official proceedings.[483]

Some of these immunities are nuanced. For example, a public agency enjoys near absolute immunity from liability for misrepresentation but a public employee is not immune to liability for intentional or malicious misrepresentation. Also remember, we are addressing liability for money damages. The immunities frequently do not apply to lawsuits for injunctive relief. For example, refusal to issue a license will not support a claim for damages but can result in a lawsuit to compel the issuance of the license.

When an agency "takes" property for public use without paying for it, the owner cannot reacquire possession but can obtain "just compensation" for the taking. This is called inverse condemnation. Taking claims can take many forms.

When an agency uses public property causing damage to private property, the private owner cannot stop the agency's activities but may be able to obtain compensation for another variety of inverse condemnation. This type of taking claim is a popular way to attack an agency. For example, an agency which constructs a highway causing subsidence on adjoining lands can be held accountable under inverse condemnation.[484] Increased flights to and from a municipally owned airport or water damage caused by storm drainage or water distribution systems have also produced successful taking claims.[485]

Inverse condemnation actions can also be brought in most situations where a property damage action would otherwise lie against the agency. In these types of inverse cases, the lawsuit must be brought within three years of the damage.[486] In an inverse condemnation case, a successful property owner will be able to recover not only the value of the property taken, but also attorney fees and expert fees as well.[487]

Finally, an inverse condemnation case can be brought even when there has been no physical invasion. These cases allege a regulation is "taking" property by restricting its use. These are the most troublesome inverse cases because they go to the heart of government action. The courts created this action. But the courts are only beginning to deal with the subtle problems they have created. A "regulatory taking" claim requires a showing the regulation is unreasonable, the agency failed to reverse the regulation and a substantial part of the property's value has been lost as a result of the regulation. Cases involving a regulatory taking are subtle. In one case, the California Supreme Court allowed an inverse claim against a city that imposed an open space designation on property already assessed for the cost of sewer trunk lines and a sewage treatment facility.[488] The Court allowed the city to reduce damages by reconsidering the assessment and refused to award damages for general diminution in value caused solely by the open space designation. In other words, inverse cases will turn on fine points of law.

Officials may incur personal liability regardless of state immunities when recovery is based on federal law. The most prominent source of federal liability is the Federal Civil Rights Act.[489] Originally, a means to secure racial equality, this statute covers any deprivation of a federal right by agencies or their employees. The Federal Civil Rights Act makes it unlawful to deprive a person of a federal right under color of law.[490] This Act applies whenever a person is deprived of *any* federal rights.[491] Local agencies and their employees can be held liable under this Act for a variety of reasons unrelated to discrimination.[492] Officers may avoid liability on the basis of good faith. However, good faith will not protect the agency.[493] But a "policy decision" is required to hold the agency liable.[494] A city council has been held to answer under the Civil Rights Act for allegedly firing employees who criticized the council members and supported rivals.[495]

The officers and employees of a local agency, including elected officers, should be allowed to perform their work without fear of lawsuit. Even though an agency may be liable for incorrect decisions, individuals are basically free to work without personal liability. This does not mean victims will fail to recover. Instead, the law requires the agency to pay for the defense of officers and employees and pay judgments in many cases.

If an employee's (officers and employees are treated the same) conduct is within the course and scope of employment and not fraudulent, corrupt or malicious, the agency must provide for the official's legal defense. The agency must provide the officer with legal representation, pay attorney fees, and other costs of defense.[496] If the defense conflicts with the defense of the agency, the agency must notify the officer in writing of the conflict and inform the officer of the right to obtain "outside counsel."[497]

The agency must indemnify employees from any judgment based on official acts if:

(1)   a written request is made at least 10 days before trial for the agency to defend;

(2)   the agency has conducted the defense;

(3)   the officer has cooperated in the defense; and

(4)   the officer's actions are within the scope of employment and not fraudulent, corrupt or misconduct.[498]

To emphasize, the duty to defend and the duty to pay judgment are two different duties.

A lawsuit based on conduct outside of the scope of work or amounting to fraud, corruption, or actual malice, does not obligate the agency to defend or to indemnify. When the complaint alleges such conduct, the agency may determine whether the allegations are true. If the agency determines the allegations are not true, the agency may defend. If the court thereafter determines the allegations are true, the officer may be required to pay the judgment even though the agency provided a defense.[499] If the agency determines the allegations are true and refuses to defend, the officer can recover costs of defense and obtain indemnification if the court determines the allegations were not true.[500]

Of course, it is not always easy to determine the truth immediately after charges are filed. Agencies sometimes reserve the right to object later. There is no rule on the subject. But insurance carriers usually provide a defense when the allegations could be untrue and reserve the right to refuse to pay a judgment based on the court's findings. Determining when an employee is acting within the scope of employment can be very difficult. One court found a teacher did not act within the scope of employment when he molested a student.[501] Another court found a police officer was acting within the scope of his employment when he stopped a drunken motorist, followed her home and raped her.[502] In another case dealing specifically with an agency's duty to defend a police officer accused of sexually harassing a female co-worker, the court found the officer was acting outside the scope of his employment and did not deserve defense by the agency.[503]

When the members of the governing board are named as defendants in a lawsuit, the decision to provide defense and indemnity is complicated by conflicts of interest laws. Clearly, providing defense and indemnity is economic gain to the officer. Normally, this would be enough to disqualify the officer from making the decision. The FPPC recognizes elected officials should not needlessly be exposed to litigation without the agency bearing the cost. On the other hand, elected officials cannot be allowed to take advantage of their office. The FPPC has taken a middle ground. The officer may participate in the decision to provide a defense when the agency is potentially mandated to provide defense and indemnity. For example, the official can participate in the determination of whether the lawsuit arises within the course and scope of office. The officer cannot participate when the agency is not required to provide defense and indemnity. For example, the official cannot participate if the lawsuit does not involve activities within the course and scope of office.[504]

CHAPTER 7

ENVIRONMENTAL

The "Green Revolution" is responsible for substantial improvements in air, land and water quality. The improvement comes with a price: government regulations at all levels. The California Environmental Quality Act ("CEQA") is the environmental law affecting virtually every aspect of government operations. The Endangered Species Act ("ESA") is responsible for many important environmental successes but, unlike CEQA, is not an informative Act. CEQA and ESA are the most important but not the only environmental laws affecting California local agencies.

CEQA and its federal counterpart, NEPA, require government to inventory environmental impacts of projects, consider the impacts, and, if possible, mitigate the impacts. CEQA does not require government to take environmentally beneficial actions. Government must merely understand environmental impact before acting. CEQA and NEPA are process laws. CEQA recognizes procedures for environmental review are best developed at the local level, subject to safeguards for statewide uniformity.[505] State law and state guidelines contain minimum standards for the local guidelines. [506]

The "lead agency" prepares the environmental documents for "responsible agencies."[507] If a responsible agency believes the environmental document prepared by a lead agency is not adequate, the responsible agency must file a lawsuit within 30 days after the lead agency files a notice of determination.[508] Unless a challenge is successful, the lead agency's document must be used by the responsible agency to evaluate the project. A responsible agency complies with CEQA by consulting with the lead agency in the preparation of the environmental document and by considering the document prepared by the lead agency before reaching its own conclusions on whether and how to approve the project.[509]

CEQA requires environmental documents for "projects" which public agencies may approve. The lead agency determines whether an activity is a "project." A "project" is an action by a public agency, including a decision to issue a lease, permit, license, certificate or other entitlement of use approved by government for a private party that could significantly impact the environment.[510] The term does *not* include activities over which an agency exercises no discretion, or emergency work to maintain public services.[511] The lead agency must next determine what kind of environmental documents to prepare for the project. Four types of documents are possible:

- A "notice of exemption" can be filed if the project is exempt from further review because it falls within a specified category.

- A "negative declaration" can be prepared if the project has no significant environmental impacts.

- A "mitigated negative declaration" can be prepared if the project is changed to have no environmental impacts.

- An "environmental impact report" must be prepared if the project is expected to have significant environmental impacts.

The lead agency determines the project is exempt by filing a notice of exemption.[512] The State Guidelines identify dozens of "categorical exemptions."[513] The exemptions cover projects not expected to have a significant effect on the environment. For example, rehabilitation of an existing structure is a "class 1" exemption.[514] The filing of the notice of exemption starts a 30-day statute of limitations for court challenge.[515] Exemptions can be highly technical. For example, initiative measures which originate with the voters are exempt because the agency has no discretion to reject the initiatives but agency sponsored ballot measures are not because the agency has discretion whether to propose the measure to the voters.[516] The agency's decision on the exemption will be upheld if there is a "fair argument" the decision is correct.[517]

The lead agency must consult with responsible agencies in the preparation of an "initial study" if a project is not exempt.[518] The initial study describes the project and tentatively determines whether significant environmental impacts are expected.[519] When evaluating potential impacts, the lead agency must consider both the primary and secondary consequences of the project. Primary consequences are immediately related to the project. Secondary consequences are more related to the primary consequences than to the project itself.[520] A project has significant effect on the environment if the project has potential to:

(a) Degrade the quality of the environment; substantially reduce the habitat of a fish or wildlife species; cause a fish or wildlife population to drop below self-sustaining levels; threaten to eliminate a plant or animal community; reduce the number or restrict the range of a rare or endangered plant or animal; or eliminate important examples of the major periods of California history or pre-history;

(b)   Achieve short-term environmental goals to the disadvantage of long-term environmental goals;

(c)   Produce environmental effects individually limited but cumulatively considerable; *or*

(d)   Produce substantial adverse effects on human beings, either directly or indirectly.[521]

The lead agency may prepare a "negative declaration if the initial study reveals the project is not likely to have significant environmental impact."[522] The lead agency must circulate the negative declaration and consider the comments of responsible agencies and the public before approving or disapproving the negative declaration.[523] If a negative declaration is approved, a "notice of determination" is filed and the CEQA process ends.[524]

A mitigated negative declaration can then be used if the project proponent revises the project to eliminate impacts.[525] The mitigated negative declaration is processed the same way as a negative declaration. When significant environmental impacts are *not* eliminated by revisions to the project, an environmental impact report (EIR) must be prepared.[526]

The process for an EIR is considerably more complicated than the process for exemptions or negative declarations. The lead agency must send a "notice of preparation" of the proposed draft EIR to responsible agencies and consult with responsible agencies with respect to the resources affected by the project that are the responsible agency's responsibility.[527] At the conclusion of this round of consultation, the lead agency prepares a draft EIR, files a "notice of completion" of the draft EIR and invites public review.[528] The lead agency reviews the comments on the draft EIR and prepares a final EIR that includes the comments and the response to the comments.[529] The final EIR is then "certified."[530] A subsequent EIR can be required when new information of substantial importance becomes available which was not previously available to the lead agency or when the project is substantially modified.[531]

The EIR provides information about the environmental impact of a project, lists ways the impacts may be minimized and indicates alternatives to the project.[532] The draft EIR includes a description of the project, the environmental setting of the project, the environmental effects of the project, the effects found not to be significant, and a list of organizations and persons consulted.[533] The EIR must evaluate the "cumulative impacts" of the project. Sometimes, cumulative impacts cannot be predicted when the environmental review is required. Reservation of the discussion to a time when the severity of the impact and likelihood of occurrence is better known does not make an EIR inadequate. However, known cumulative impacts must be discussed to the extent feasible. The distinction between an impact which can be discussed later and an impact which must be discussed immediately is difficult and a frequent source of litigation.

After the environmental documents are approved, the agency can make a decision on the underlying project.[534] A "notice of determination" links the environmental documents to the decision on the project by stating how the agency reacted to the anticipated environmental impacts. Agencies must mitigate or avoid significant adverse impacts when feasible.[535] The notice of determination must list the mitigation measures. The project may be approved if economic, social or other conditions make it unfeasible to mitigate an adverse impact. But the agency must find an overriding need. The notice of determination must describe the impacts not feasible to mitigate and the overriding need.[536] A project cannot be approved on the basis of overriding consideration if the agency finds "feasible" alternatives or mitigation measures within its powers would substantially lessen the significant impacts of the project.[537] The notice of determination describes how the mitigation measures are to be monitored and implemented.[538] The filing of this notice starts the running of the statue of limitations.[539] Court decisions have not resolved many questions on the scope of the mitigation requirement.[540]

When considering alternatives and mitigation measures, a responsible agency is more limited than a lead agency. A responsible agency must mitigate or avoid only the environmental impacts within the scope of its statutory authority.[541] When a responsible agency completes its environmental review (using the lead agency's document) and makes its decision, it must likewise file a notice of determination.[542]

Any interested person may file an action to test compliance with CEQA. The action can complain about failure to follow the mandated process or can raise more substantive concerns. The petitioner may allege the agency has wrongfully used a negative declaration instead of an EIR, the EIR does not adequately discuss the significant effects on the environment, or the agency has not properly acted upon the information contained in an otherwise adequate EIR. The time limits for bringing such action vary from 30 days to 180 days, depending on the issues presented.[543] The California Attorney General must be notified when a CEQA action is filed.[544] (No penalty is assigned for failure to notify the Attorney General.) In addition to the short statute of limitations, the petitioner must set the matter for hearing within 90 days of filing or the case will be dismissed.[545] A practice developed of "sandbagging" projects by withholding CEQA comments at the local agency level but raising the objections at the courthouse. The courts may be reluctant to dismiss such cases when the failure to participate earlier is innocent and public interest may be damaged.[546] However, CEQA states the court tests are barred unless objections are raised at the administrative level.[547] After an action is filed, the petitioner must attempt to meet with the agency to resolve the dispute without further litigation.[548]

An action brought on the grounds of noncompliance with CEQA terms questions whether there was a prejudicial abuse of discretion by the agency.[549] Abuse of discretion is established if the agency has not proceeded as required by law or the determination is not supported by substantial evidence.[550] The substantial evidence test is a common test for reviewing public agency decisions in many areas. Traditionally, the substantial evidence test carries a strong presumption in favor of a public agency. However, the substantial evidence test has not been a significant bar in environmental litigation.

Don't get the idea that detailed state guidelines have eliminated uncertainty. The courts have supplied many "missing links" but have sometimes made matters worse. Take the problem of the big development project. "New communities" comprised of thousands of homes must develop over decades, often in reaction to changing market conditions. Agencies are supposed to create an EIR for the "entire" project which discloses environment impacts for the whole project. Courts have tried to develop precedent on how much detail is required. The courts have not succeeded.[551]

The National Environmental Policy Act, "NEPA," was enacted before CEQA.[552] Much of CEQA is borrowed from NEPA. However, NEPA is different in scale. NEPA requires federal administrators to assemble, to consider and if possible to mitigate the adverse environmental impact of *federal* projects, including local projects receiving federal assistance. An environmental impact statement (EIS) must be prepared for the project when a project is expected to have "significant" adverse impacts. NEPA is administered on a national level and the judgment of NEPA's administrators is applied nationally. For a project to be "significant" under NEPA, it must affect a part of the nation. NEPA requires the preparation of an EIS for larger scale projects.

The California and United States Endangered Species Acts are similar in form and function. They can be discussed together, but the State and Federal governments do not necessarily agree on which species are endangered.[553] ESA operates when a decision affects an endangered species or the habitat of an endangered species. ESA does not usually apply in developed urban settings but ESA greatly impacts urban areas because larger public works projects needed to serve communities frequently start in rural areas. Water and highway projects are a prime example.

When ESA applies, the response is severe and mandatory. Government may not undertake a project adversely affecting an endangered species or its habitat.[554] However, a "habitat conservation plan" can be prepared to implement "adequate" steps to minimize the impact and to protect the species.[555] Because of ESA's dramatic impact, most of the notorious landmark cases have involved large public works projects stopped by an obscure endangered species.[556]

This law fulfills an important purpose; when a species becomes extinct it is gone forever. But this law has significant shortcomings.

- First, most species are endangered somewhere and some species are endangered everywhere. For example, the coyote is the common pest to farmers but rare in the cities. It is meaningless to protect a species at the limits of its range. Species are supposed to be endangered at the limits of their range.

- Second, most species have evolved subspecies. Few species are endangered in all evolved forms. The Endangered "Species" Act is sometimes used to protect subspecies. For example, the *Mojave* ground squirrel is protected though no one believes ground squirrels are endangered. Subspecies are always endangered because subspecies represent the cutting edge of the evolutionary process. ESA does not effectively distinguish a healthy species from the endangered subspecies.[557]

- Third, ESA often violates the biological principle it is designed to advance. By attempting to protect "nature's way", ESA intrudes into the evolutionary process. Nature depends on the evolution of healthy plants and animals. Superior species thrive and inferior species become extinct. ESA protects inferior species (usually cute varieties) because our knowledge is feeble. ESA also prevents the extinction of species not threatened by man. ESA is threatening nature's balance. When a predator is protected, the predator runs rampant. The species upon which the predator preys becomes threatened. Cute sea otters threaten the ugly abalone. ESA is founded on the premise interference with nature produces unintended affects. ESA ignores its own impact on nature.

- Finally, ESA does not adequately distinguish between natural and artificial habitats. ESA can require the owner of an artificial habitat to maintain the habitat to support an endangered species. For example, if a spring from sewage ponds supports an endangered species, the Department of Fish and Game will attempt to prevent the owner of the ponds from stopping the leak.

Continuation of life demands attention to conditions making life possible. Every living thing is an environmentalist to some degree. "Toxic dumpers" believe nature will survive despite man's intervention. The "environmental druids" believe nature cannot survive without heavy human intervention. When extremists establish the environmental agenda, decision-makers spend their time on the fringe, dealing with marginally relevant topics. Unfortunately, extremists offer the best theater and are often portrayed as the majority. Extremists win if their agenda is debated; the environment is the loser. The living things affected by this debate, the rest of us, must reject the extremists and recapture the podium to establish the parameters of debate. Industrialists embarrassed by toxic dumpers and environmentalists disgusted by the druids must assert their interests.

Anti-pollution laws are a direct and focused mechanism to protect the environment. While CEQA and NEPA give the appearance of providing environmental protection, other laws do the real work.

A century ago, mankind polluted the environment with simple chemicals. Pollution was controlled with simple processes. A hundred years later, unimaginably complex chemical, biological and radioactive pollutants are discharged into the water environment. Sophisticated technology is needed to detect and to nullify these potent hazards. The shift from relatively simple, easily remedied water pollution to more complex and interrelated forms of pollution is accompanied by an evolution from relatively simple and straightforward pollution laws to complex and interrelated water, air and land pollution laws.

The "Chemical Age" produced everything from computer chips to potato chips. Industrial processes unimaginable prior to World War II are now common. Even when chemicals are handled properly, they often produce dangerous byproducts, which are impossible to keep out of the air, land or water environment. During the decade of the 80's, the Legislature turned its attention from regulating "old fashioned" pollutants such as sewage waste to "high tech" contaminates such as VOC's, PCB's, or the other unpronounceable organic chemicals.[558] As a result, the federal and state Clean Water Acts are now augmented by federal and state laws dealing with hazard or toxic wastes.[559] A definitive synopsis of hazardous waste laws is difficult because new laws are adopted as technology advances and the law runs to catch up.[560] To complicate matters further, each law must be reconciled with one another.[561]

Proposition 65 was a statewide ballot initiative approved by the voters in 1986. This initiative prohibits the use of carcinogens by private industry. Public agencies are exempted from this part of the measure.[562] A governor's task force lists carcinogenic chemicals.[563] Proposition 65 also requires "designated employees" to notify County officials immediately of hazardous spills or face criminal sanctions.[564] This law uses the same definition of the term "designated employee" as used by conflicts of interest laws. Elected officials and much of top management must make these disclosures.

Problems have arisen with respect to the Proposition 65 disclosure requirement. First, every designated employee has a separate disclosure responsibility. This means multiple notices must be given to county officials. A notice by one designated employee not accompanied by notice by designated employees could be embarrassing to the person who fails to give the notice and possible grounds for prosecution. Agencies should establish a process for handling notifications. Most District Attorneys are responsible for enforcing the notice requirements. Most District Attorneys will agree only one notice need be given on behalf of all of the agency's designated employees. If the District Attorney agrees *in writing*, the agency can create a process where a designated employee notifies the general manager of the hazardous condition and the general manager notifies county authorities on behalf of all designated employees. Counties have a similar problem. Both the local health officials and the board of supervisors must be notified to comply with Proposition 65. The board of supervisors and health department must establish a bureaucratic connection and verify notices are received by both. Some counties have handled this problem by stating notices need only be sent to the health department, and the health department is responsible to notify the board of supervisors.

Violation of the notice requirement carries heavy fines and jail terms. But the law provides little guidance in how to judge whether a hazardous condition actually exists. Some designated employees may be professionals trained in the evaluation of hazardous waste. More often, the designated employee is an elected official, manager or other person experienced in entirely different areas. Such a person cannot be expected to assess the threat posed by a chemical spill correctly. Cautious, designated employees will give notice any time a spill could be hazardous. The difference between an oil spill from a leaky automobile in a parking lot and a diesel spill on the freeway from a damaged truck is a matter of degree. Both or neither may be hazardous depending on circumstances. The framers of Proposition 65 can be commended for enthusiasm but not for their common sense. The notice requirement inundates the public with notices of hazards raging from the trivial to the profound. Like the boy who cried wolf, the volume of these warnings produces apathy, not alarm.

The Underground Tank Law affects businesses, public or private, which store chemicals underground for reasons of economy or efficiency.[565] Many water agencies have found it convenient to store chemicals, including fuel, underground for safety. The Underground Tank Law requires the State Department of Health Services to compile a master list of hazardous substances.[566] This list is used to determine which tanks require permits.[567] If a permit is necessary, operation without a permit is in violation of the law.[568] Owners must apply for the permit[569] and pay the required fees.[570] Local agencies may obtain permission to administer the program.[571] Owners must notify the administering agency of any changes made on the tanks or in the storage of new hazardous substances.[572] The application must list information about the owner, about the tank, and about the monitoring program. It must also include a 24-hour phone number to contact the owner in case of emergency.[573] Public agencies must also include the name of the supervisor of the division operating the tank.[574] The administering agency may revoke or modify a permit if:

(1)   there is a violation of the terms of the permit,

(2)   the permit was obtained through misrepresentation, or

(3)   there is a change in condition that justifies a change in the status of the tank.[575]

The administering agency must inspect the tanks every three years.[576] The administering agency may require the permittee to employ special inspectors to inspect the tank and write an inspection report to be filed with the administering agency.[577]

The Act sets the minimum requirements for newly installed tanks.[578] Tanks are required to have primary and secondary containment levels.[579] They must not only be "product-tight" but able to withstand corrosion from released hazardous substances.[580] The containers must have a monitoring system to detect the presence of leaks and equipment to prevent them.[581] Before the containers are used, their integrity must be tested by a licensed inspector.[582] Moreover, tanks (1) may not have unauthorized releases, (2) must be structurally sound, and (3) must be operated by "a person with sufficient training…in preventing corrosion" when equipped with cathodic protection.[583]

Owners must maintain evidence of financial ability to compensate for injuries caused by the material.[584] Operators must monitor the tanks using the method specified on the permit[585] and a report must be kept of the monitoring.[586] If hazardous substances leak from the containers, the operator must report it within 24 hours of detection of the leak.[587] To close down an underground tank, the permittee must present evidence to the administering agency that: hazardous substances have been removed and neutralized; the tank has been sealed; the tank's maintenance will be carried out if the agency desires; and the site has been determined to have no present or past undetected releases.[588]

Penalties for the violation of this Act include civil penalties[589] and injunctive relief.[590] The U. S. Environmental Protection Agency, State Water Resources Control Board, Regional Water Quality Control Board, State and County Departments of Health Services, the local purveyor and, of course, the public have an interest in cleanup of groundwater contamination. Groundwater cleanup can involve wellhead treatment and a comprehensive construction program. The engineers are expert at describing cleanup plans. The formation of a cost recovery program involves several disciplines.

Typically, the biggest technical issue facing a cleanup program is how to recover the cost from the responsible party. There are many cleanup cost recovery programs. The "Comprehensive Environmental Response, Compensation and Liability Act" (CERCLA) is a potential source of funding.[591]

CERCLA was enacted by Congress to: (1) prevent further contamination by hazardous chemicals; (2) identify existing contaminated sites; (3) prepare cleanup plans; (4) provide money to implement the plans; and (5) provide a mechanism for recovering the cost of cleanup from the responsible parties. CERCLA is an important starting point because EPA and the State Board concentrate on CERCLA. CERCLA is also an important starting point because it is a federal law that can preempt other federal or state laws dealing with groundwater cleanup. The extent of CERCLA's reach must be understood before it can be determined whether other laws will survive preemption by CERCLA. Other federal laws dealing with groundwater pollution include: the Resource Conservation and Recovery Act (RCRA),[592] Clean Water Act (CWA),[593] Safe Drinking Water Act (SDWA),[594] Toxic Substances Control Act (TSCA),[595] and Hazardous Materials Transportation Act.[596] Confusion over CERCLA's meaning lead to the passage of legislation known as "Superfund Amendments and Reauthorization Act" (SARA) which removed some of the ambiguities but introduced additional interpretive issues.[597] The federal financial assistance offered under CERCLA is so massive it has introduced a new word to the English language: *Superfund*. Cleanup programs usually include an effort to insure eligibility for the federal superfund.[598] The fund is used by the EPA to cover its investigatory and cleanup costs, as well as to pay for certain damages to natural resources.[599] The fund may be used to reimburse other parties who have incurred response costs. The EPA uses CERCLA's cost recovery provisions to reimburse the fund.

EPA must establish a national contingency plan (NCP) that describes how contaminated sites are to be cleaned. A cleanup program identified in the NCP is eligible for superfund assistance. Local authorities may implement other cleanup strategies. However, if the local cleanup programs are not consistent with the NCP, federal funding will not be available.[600]

The California Department of Health Services (DHS) is the "lead agency" for the purpose of implementing the CERCLA cleanup program. DHS works closely with EPA and the State Water Resources Control Board and the Regional Water Quality Control Board in administering the program as the lead agency. DHS can delegate the lead agency designation to local agencies.

One of the problems with the superfund program is the monies are not disbursed to keep pace with construction. Most experts concede superfund cannot provide enough assistance to completely fund cleanup efforts. Looking to the polluters can mitigate these shortcomings. Cost recovery from polluters is important because:

(1) it sends a message to potential polluters groundwater is off limits;

(2) it forces the polluters to bear a fair share of cleanup cost;

(3) it is a prerequisite to certain types of state and federal financial assistance; and

(4) it is a highly visible way of communicating the importance of cleanup to the public.

These goals are important elements of an overall cleanup program. Litigation can be one of the elements of the overall cleanup program. Litigation can be self-sustaining and may even produce enough revenue to help implement the cleanup program. Litigation alone usually cannot clean up a basin.

CERCLA allows the government to recover cleanup costs from the responsible parties. CERCLA is an attractive tool because liability under CERCLA is strict: if groundwater has been polluted, the polluter must pay the cleanup costs whether or not the polluter acted reasonably or negligently when the pollution occurred. CERCLA is also a powerful tool because it creates joint and several liability. The government does not have to identify all of the polluters or apportion the damages among several responsible parties.

CERCLA has some limitations.[601] Cleanup costs can be recovered under CERCLA but other damages cannot.[602] Although recovery of cleanup costs should be significant, not all damages suffered by a basin or water purveyors in a basin are directly associated with cleanup costs. For example, if a producer takes a well out of service because of pollution, the producer has been damaged yet it may be difficult to demonstrate putting the well back into production constitutes a cost of cleanup.[603]

Responsible parties are jointly and severally liable for the cost of cleanup under CERCLA. One party can be made to bear the entire cost. The responsible parties can argue among themselves how to apportion costs but this does not affect the recovery of damages. Responsible parties include not only the owner and former owners and operator of the contaminated site, but also anyone who has transported, or arranged for the transportation of, the hazardous materials to the site and anyone who has generated the waste. The owners and operators of the property generating the pollution will undoubtedly seek a contribution from transporters and anyone who could have arguably arranged for the movement of the pollutant to the site. As a result, cleanup lawsuits are large multi-party suits.[604]

The "Carpenter-Presley-Tanner Hazardous Substance Account Act" (HSA) is another potential source of clean-up money. HSA was enacted by the State to provide response authority for hazardous substance releases, to compensate persons for losses resulting from releases of hazardous substances, and to provide matching funding for CERCLA grants. HSA is patterned after CERCLA.[605] In many ways, the uncertainties of CERCLA carry over to HSA. In some cases, HSA improved on CERCLA by removing uncertainties.

The DHS adopts regulations for the selection and ranking of sites for removal and remedial action under HSA. Removal consists of physical cleanup to mitigate the damage. Remedial action can consist of a permanent remedy, monitoring, assessment and site operations and maintenance. Funds appropriated to DHS must be expended in accordance with the priority ranking. "Priority One" is a site that possesses a known or probable immediate threat to public health. "Priority Two" is a site that poses a substantial but less immediate threat to public health and safety in the environment. "Priority Three" presents only a limited and defined threat to human health or the environment. DHS remedial plans must be consistent with the National Contingency Plans prepared under CERCLA. A potentially responsible party named in the final plan may seek judicial review of the plan.

HSA creates two funds: the Hazardous Substance Account and Hazardous Substance Cleanup Fund. Monies in the Hazardous Substance Account may be expended to fulfill the state's obligations under CERCLA to pay for removal and remedial action performed by the State and for a variety of other purposes. Cleanup costs incurred by a local agency with the approval of the DHS director can be funded under this part. The Hazardous Substance Cleanup Fund may be used for cleanup of sites included within a final remedial action plan. Cleanup from the fund expenditure cannot be made unless DHS is unsuccessful in obtaining cleanup by the potentially responsible parties. The California Attorney General is authorized to commence lawsuits to recover cleanup costs from potentially responsible parties. Strict liability will be imposed and a penalty of up to three times the cleanup cost can be awarded.

Traditional tort law is sometimes inadequate to deal with pollution because of difficulties in proving a connection between a hazardous waste condition and a contaminated site or between a contaminated site and plaintiff's damages. The new statutes also have shortcomings. It would be a mistake to overlook the possibility of recovery under traditional tort law for damages accruing from the disposal of hazardous wastes.

Several "old fashioned" court remedies can be brought to bear to obtain pollution cleanup. "Negligence" is a tort theory familiar to most. Briefly, a person is liable under a negligence theory for damages caused by unreasonable i.e. negligent, conduct. There are well-established doctrines under this theory important in the hazardous waste context. Under the doctrine of res ipsa loquitur (the "thing speaks for itself"), the defendant's negligence can be inferred in the absence of direct proof if the incident is the kind of event ordinarily not occurring in the absence of negligence. Under the "negligence per se" doctrine, violation of a statute will prove negligence without other direct evidence. Finally, "joint tortfeasor" liability may exist where it can be shown one of two actors is responsible for the damage but the identity of the responsible party cannot be established by the plaintiff. Negligence remains the most common basis for suit to recover damages. Negligence will be pleaded in virtually all hazardous waste tort cases. A "trespass" action may be brought if the hazardous waste invades the plaintiff's property. For example, if the plaintiff is a groundwater producer, a trespass suit could be brought against an up gradient polluter. Trespass is an intentional tort, and the defendant is responsible for damages whether or not the actions were reasonable. A "nuisance" action lies somewhere between negligence and trespass. In a nuisance case, the plaintiff is not required to prove the defendant's conduct was unreasonable. But the plaintiff is required to show the defendant exercised some degree of control over the offending wastes. Finally, an action can be brought to recover damages to a "public trust" asset (water).[606] A tort action can be brought to recover property damage, personal injuries or even wrongful death. Regardless of the type of damages sought, the plaintiffs will experience difficulty in proving causation in most cases.

When the Legislature fails and traditional legal concepts are inadequate, the courts are compelled to craft new remedies. In

Potter v. Firestone Tire and Rubber Co., property owners adjacent to an abandoned dumpsite sued the Firestone Tire and Rubber Co. for emotional distress resulting from the fear of contracting cancer as a result of drinking water contaminated by the chemicals.[607] The plaintiffs showed Firestone's waste disposal practice contaminated private wells located on the plaintiff's property. The first causation issue was surmounted. However, the plaintiffs were unable to show they contracted cancer as a result of the contamination. Indeed, although "cancer causing" chemicals are often described, proving a particular chemical causes a particular cancer is almost impossible.[608] The *Potter* case avoids this second causation issue by allowing the plaintiffs to recover for the "emotional distress" caused by the reasonable "fear" of contracting cancer. In other words, the plaintiffs were not required to show a causal link between the contamination and cancer. They were allowed to show a causal link between contamination and reasonable fear. This is a much more relaxed burden of proof. While it is true plaintiffs will not be able to recover as much for "fear" as for actually contracting cancer, it is also true juries will be inclined to award as much as possible when the actions of the polluters are egregious. The *Potter* case is an example of how an ingenious court can craft a remedy in a difficult area. Other water quality issues can be confronted in this manner.

Many environmental laws have been adopted on the state and national level. Some of these laws have been on the books for generations. Others are the products of recent scientific discovery. Most will not have the kind of widespread impact of the laws mentioned above. Federal laws on natural resource protection include:

Water
River and Harbor Act of 1968, 33 U.S.C. Section 59c
Wild and Scenic Rivers Act of 1968, 16 U.S.C. Section 1271

Federal Water Pollution Control Act (Clean Water Act),
33 U.S.C. Section 1251
Rivers and Harbors Act of 1899, 33 U.S.C. Section 403
Safe Drinking Water Act, 42 U.S.C. Section 300f

Land

Organic Act of 189/, 16 U.S.C. Section 471 *et seq.*
Multiple Use - Sustained Yield Act of 1960, 16 U.S.C. Section 528 *et seq.*
Forest and Rangeland Renewable Resources Planning Act of 1974, 16 U.S.C. Section 1600 *et seq.*
Mineral Leasing Act of 1920, 30 U.S.C. Section 181 *et seq.*
Taylor Grazing Act of 1984, 43 U.S.C. Section 315 *et seq.*
Classification and Multiple Use Act (of 1964), 43 U.S.C. Section 1411 *et seq.*
Federal Land Policy and Management Act (of 1976), 43 U.S.C. Section 1701 *et seq.*
National Park Service Act of 1916, 16 U.S.C. Section 1 *et seq.*
Cooperative Forestry Assistance Act, 16 U.S.C. Sections 2101–2111
Public Rangelands Improvement Act, 43 U.S.C. Sections 1901–1908
General Mining Law of 1872, 30 U.S.C. Section 21 *et seq.*
Reservoir Salvage Act of 1960 and the Archaeological and Historical Preservation Act of 1974, 16 U.S.C. Sections 469-469c
Surface Mining Control and Reclamation Act of 1977, 30 U.S.C. Section 1201 *et seq.*

Ocean

Outer Continental Shelf Lands Act, 43 U.S.C. Sections 1331-1343

Marine Sanctuaries Act, 16 U.S.C. Sections 1431-1434

Wilderness Act of 1964, 16 U.S.C. Section 1131 *et seq.*

Endangered American Wilderness Act of 1978, 16 U.S.C. Section 1132

National Park Service Organic Act (of 1916), 16 U.S.C. Section 1 *et seq.*

Antiquities Act of 1906, 16 U.S.C. Section 431

Archaeological Resources Protection Act, 16 U.S.C. Section 470a, *et seq.*

Historic Sites Act of 1935, 16 U.S.C. Section 461 *et seq.*

Federal Coastal Zone Management Act, 16 U.S.C. Section 1451 *et seq.*

Fish and Wildlife

Endangered Species Act of 1973, 16 U.S.C. Section 1531 *et seq.*

Migratory Bird Conservation Act, 16 U.S.C. Section 715 *et seq.*

Migratory Bird Hunting and Conservation Stamp Act of 1983, 16 U.S.C. Section 718 *et seq.*

Migratory Bird Treaty Act, 16 U.S.C. Section 703

Bald Eagle Protections Act, 16 U.S.C. Sections 668-668(d)

Wild Free-Roaming Horses and Burros Act, 18 U.S.C. Section 1331 *et seq.*

Fishery Conservation and Management Act, 16 U.S.C. Section 1801

Fish and Wildlife Coordination Act of 1958, 16 U.S.C. Sections 661-666(b)

Anatropous Fish Conservation Act of 1965, 16 U.S.C. Sections 757a–757f

Lacey Act of 1900, 16 U.S.C. Section 6673; 18 U.S.C. Sections 42-44

Pittman-Robertson Program, 16 U.S.C. Sections 669-669(i)

Dingell-Johnson, 16 U.S.C. Sections 777-777k

Land and Water Conservation Fund Act of 1964, 16 U.S.C. Sections 4601-4601-11

Hazardous and Toxic Wastes

Resource Conservation and Recovery Act of 1976, 42 U.S.C. Section 6901 *et seq.*

Comprehensive Environmental Response, Compensation and Liability Act of 1980, 42 U.S.C. Section 9601 *et seq.*

Federal Insecticide, Fungicide and Rodenticide Act, 7 U.S.C. Section 135 *et seq.*

Toxic Substances Control Act, 15 U.S.C. Section 2600 *et seq.*

Hazardous Materials Transportation Act, 49 U.S.C. Section 1801

Federal Mine Safety Act, 30 U.S.C. Section 901

Ports and Waterways Safety Act, 33 U.S.C. Section 1221

Dangerous Cargo Act, 49 U.S.C. Section 170

Federal Hazardous Substances Act, 15 U.S.C. Section 2051

Poison Prevention Packaging Act, 15 U.S.C. Section 1471

Lead-Based Paint Poisoning Prevention Act, 42 U.S.C. Section 4801

Food Drug and Cosmetic Act, 21 U.S.C. Section 342

Air

Noise Control Act of 1972, 42 U.S.C. Section 4901 *et seq.*

Clean Air Act of 1970, 42 U.S.C. Section 7401 *et seq.*

Environmental laws have a way of evolving. Waste discharge laws were once limited to water collected with wastes. Federal waste discharge laws were once limited to waters of the United States. Over time, federal waste discharge laws have evolved to cover virtually all water, regardless of source. Since water touches nearly everything, this development means waste discharge laws affect nearly every development.

A navigable stream which cannot be degraded by pollution has become any streambed which cannot be altered without permission of the federal government or its surrogates in state government. This is not a good thing for the environment. The federal-state bureaucracy is understandably very large. No large bureaucracy acts quickly or efficiently. Streambed alteration permits are too time-consuming and too costly to obtain. Instead of seeking permits, those who propose to alter a streambed, wait for the inevitable catastrophe when emergency conditions make the permit more or less automatic. Streambeds are degraded while work is delayed and when the failure occurs, remedial work following an emergency is more costly and frequently less thoughtful.

Storm water runoff has long been recognized as a source of pollution. Implementation of storm water runoff regulations was delayed for decades because of the magnitude of handling every street drain in the United States. The final regulations were even more ambitious: <u>every</u> building project must provide for on-site collection of storm water and treatment before disposal to a waterway.

Local governments mostly dictate to others how to meet storm water containment policies by the review of subdivisions or building permits. However, local government is also on the receiving end. Every public works project, including maintenance, must be implemented in such a way as to avoid runoff during construction. Every project must be designed to avoid runoff. Compliance is completed because the federal program also has the large federal-state bureaucracy.

PART 3

CUSTOMERS AND TAXPAYERS

Public agency customers come in two sizes. Residents obtain property related service such as water, sewer, energy or fire protection. Nonresidents "consume" park and recreation services, street and sidewalk services, and police services. Cities and counties can provide all public services. A few special districts can provide all public services. Many districts provide some public services. This part is about consumer rights, but is focused on water and sanitation.

CHAPTER 8
WATER

Every community needs an efficient and constant water supply. Water purveyors can acquire water by purchase or from the source. Purveyors must comply with laws when acquiring water and to ensure quality of service.

In California, economic activity has a way of cropping up distant from water supplies. Water-rich areas contribute water to the overall benefit of the state.[611] Water purveyors can <u>purchase</u> water. Most water sold in California is purchased from a half-dozen major water projects.

Large water projects are an integral part of water service for most Californians. The Hetch Hetchy project annually transports approximately 316,000 acre-feet of Tuolumne River water to the city of San Francisco and Alameda, San Mateo and Santa Clara counties. The Central Valley Project ("CVP") serves much of California's central valley agriculture with approximately 6,000,000 AF annually through 500 miles of canals. The State Water Project ("State Project") serves much of California with approximately 23,000,000 AF/Y annually through a 444-mile aqueduct. The Los Angeles Aqueduct serves approximately 350,000 acre-feet per year to the city of Los Angeles through a 240-mile canal. The Colorado River Aqueduct delivers approximately 1,000,000 AF of water annually to Southern California through a 240-mile aqueduct. The All-American and Coachella Canals serve approximately 3,600,000 AF annually to Southeast California through 160 miles of canals. Together, these projects account for approximately 34,000,000 AF of water annually![612] These major projects were constructed with local, regional, state and federal monies. The use of public funds created public obligations.

The largest federally funded water project in California is the CVP. This project was authorized as an irrigation project under the state Central Valley Project Act.[613] The federal government stepped in to finance the project after the state was unable to proceed.[614] The reclamation laws governing the payment for these facilities require the Secretary of Interior to enter repayment contracts with water purveyors. These contracts reflect the populist policies that brought the federal government in the water business in the West. The most controversial Reclamation Act requirement is a 160 acre limitation on the size of beneficiary farms. [615]

The most prominent project is the State Water Project. This project was authorized under the Burns-Porter Act to meet domestic and agriculture needs. [616] The project was financed through the issuance of bonds secured by payments from water purveyors under contracts administered by the Department of Water Resources. The State Project could not proceed without legislation protecting the "areas of origin" of the water for the project.[617]

Water projects provide the opportunity for water marketing and conjunctive use project. Water Marketing takes many forms. In simple terms, water marketing allows water to be freely sold when and where the marketplace dictates. Water marketing is based on the belief that the marketplace is the most efficient way to allocate water supply. Some types of water marketing are historical, well-tested, water management techniques. For example, neighboring water purveyors have always "exchanged" or "wheeled" water for one another. An exchange is like a bank account. A purveyor with surplus will deliver the surplus to a neighbor with a deficit. When the receiving purveyor has a surplus, the water is returned. Wheeling occurs when a purveyor is allowed to transport water through another purveyor's system. Wheeling takes advantage of surplus conveyance capacity. These traditional methods have increased the available supply for years. Usually these methods are employed on a small scale by neighboring purveyors without any adverse impact. These methods are the model for the more ambitious statewide, inter-watershed transfers and banking programs.

Water marketing is also being promoted under a rubric: water transfer.[618] Currently, the law gives local and regional purveyors primary jurisdiction to determine when and how surplus water may be "transferred."[619] The Department of Water Resources established a bureau to examine the concept and to promote water marketing. No one is required to engage in water marketing.[620] But, another law – called the Katz bill – furthers water marketing in mandatory terms.[621] Under this law, a water purveyor must allow others access to unused pipeline or aqueduct capacity upon the payment of fair market value to the owner of the water transport facility. The use of surplus capacity cannot interfere with the owner's use.

The popularity of marketplace economics overshadows some basic policy issues. A free-market efficiently allocates financial resources. But, some resources should not be allocated on a fiscal basis. Few would argue water cannot be denied the poor simply because a wealthier person can afford to purchase it on the open market. Water marketing ultimately promotes this result.[622]

Any summary of water law oversimplifies a complex subject. In California, there are nine basic water rights: the right to: (1) purchase water from someone else; (2) exercise riparian rights to surface water; (3) exercise an overlying right to groundwater; (4) exercise appropriative right to surface water; (5) exercise an appropriative right to groundwater; (6) exercise a prescriptive right to groundwater; (7) exercise a public trust right to surface water; (8) exercise a pueblo right to surface water; and (9) exercise a federal right. Water purveyors use a combination of these rights. Water rights can be lost as a result of a variety of environmental laws. "New" water can be created by recycling.

Californians fortunate to own land touching a river or stream can exercise the rights of a <u>riparian</u> owner. As with most important legal doctrines, the basic principles of riparian law are easily stated but difficult to apply. Originally, a property owner had the right to the use the "natural flow" of a river on property contiguous to the river if the use could be accomplished without injury to other riparians.[623] Water could be wasted if other riparians were not harmed. Non-riparian users could be deprived of supply by the riparian's waste. In 1928, California joined a majority of jurisdictions in holding the riparian's usage must be "reasonable and beneficial."[624] Riparians are now entitled to the reasonable use of the waters of a stream on riparian lands for beneficial uses.[625]

The question of reasonableness is pivotal. Because California shares the riparian rights doctrine with other states, nationwide precedent is somewhat applicable. A useful summary of this precedent is contained in the *Restatement of the Law of Torts*, which describes reasonable use as follows:

The determination of the reasonableness of a use of water depends upon a consideration of the interests of the riparian proprietor making the use, of any riparian proprietor harmed by it and of society as a whole. Factors that affect the determination include the following:

(a)　The purpose of the use,

(b)　the suitability of the use to the water course or lake,

(c)　the economic value of the use,

(d)　the social value of the use,

(e)　the extent and amount of the harm it causes,

(f)　the practicability of avoiding the harm by adjusting the use or method of use of one proprietor or the other,

(g)　the practicability of adjusting the quantity of water used by each proprietor,

(h)　the protection of existing values of water uses, land, investments and enterprises, and

(i)　the justice of requiring the user causing harm to bear the loss.[626]

Land adjacent to a natural watercourse is riparian land.[627] Riparian lands are continually being diminished as land is "severed" from the stream by the subdivision process. The smallest tract of land adjacent to the stream under one title in the chain of title is riparian.[628]

Riparian rights cannot be lost by non-use.[629] Riparian rights are "prior" and "paramount" to appropriative rights. Prior downstream appropriators can lose rights when a later upstream riparian use commences.[630] Unexercised riparian rights have same priority as exercised riparian rights.[631]

The State Water Resources Control Board ("State Board") administers many water rights. The State Board attempted to reduce the uncertainty of unexercised riparian rights by "adjudicating" riparian stream systems. Under the adjudicating process, riparian claimants must come forward so the amount of present and future entitlement can be quantified. This process has limitations. The courts have explained the limited power of the State Board:

> The Board is authorized to decide that an unexercised riparian claim loses its priority with respect to all rights currently being exercised. Moreover, to the extent that an unexercised riparian right also may create uncertainty with respect to permits of appropriation that the Board may grant after the statutory adjudication procedure is final, and may thereby continue to conflict with the public interest in reasonable and beneficial use of state waters, the public interest in reasonable and beneficial use of state waters, the Board also may determine that the future riparian rights shall have a lower priority than any uses of water it authorizes before the riparian in fact attempts to exercise his right. In other words, while we interpret the Water Code as not authorizing the Board to extinguish altogether a future riparian right, the Board may make determinations as to the scope, nature and priority of the right that it deems reasonably necessary to the promotion of the state's

interest in fostering the most reasonable and beneficial use of its scarce water resources.[632]

Groundwater law evolved parallel to surface water law. A person adjacent to a surface stream is called a riparian. A person owning property over the basin, is an overlying owner. Just as a riparian may use a reasonable proportion of the surface flow on riparian lands, an <u>overlying owner</u> may use groundwater for reasonable, beneficial purposes on overlying lands.[633] Each overlying owner has an equal and "correlative right" to the use of groundwater.[634] In times of shortage each overlying user must proportionately reduce the amount of water produced from the basin. Overlying rights are not lost by non-use. An overlying owner can assert rights against a prior appropriator.[635] Riparian and overlying rights are analogous in many important aspects. However, riparian and overlying rights are not identical.[636]

Under the <u>appropriative rights</u> doctrine, water flowing in a natural channel surplus to riparian needs may be appropriated for reasonable, beneficial use on non-riparian lands. Only "surplus" water can be appropriated. Appropriative rights are always "junior" to riparians.[637] As among appropriators, the earliest appropriator has prior rights.[638]

Prior to 1914, appropriative rights were acquired by use. These appropriative rights are still called "pre-1914 rights". After 1914, an appropriative right cannot be acquired except in compliance with the statutory scheme.[639] The State Board issues the appropriation permits.[640] A person desiring to appropriate water must apply for a permit.[641] If the State Board finds unappropriated water is available and the proposed use is reasonable and beneficial, the State Board will grant an appropriation permit with conditions necessary to "best develop, conserve and utilize in the public interest the water sought to be appropriated."[642] When the permittee has complied with the permit conditions, a license is issued confirming the rights to the appropriator.[643]

Appropriative rights can be lost.[644] This can occur when water is not used for reasonable, beneficial purposes[645] or when an appropriator changes the point of division, place or purpose of use.[646] A statutory procedure is available to determine whether nonuse has occurred or whether the point of diversion, place of use, or purpose of use can be changed.[647]

In theory, the appropriation process is simple, first come, first served.[648] However, the State Board may consider competing interests in reviewing appropriation applications.[649] A difficult question arises when a "higher" use attempts to defeat a "lower" but prior use. There is a strong policy favoring "higher" uses regardless of when asserted:

> [T]he people of the State have a paramount interest in the use of all the water of the State and the State shall determine what water can be converted to public use or controlled for public protection.[650]

Domestic use is "the highest use of water" and irrigation is the next highest use to the detriment of prior rights.[651] This priority must be considered by the State Board when acting on application to appropriate water.[652] Moreover, an application by a municipality to appropriate water for domestic purposes is deemed first-in-right regardless of whether it is filed first.[653] The State Board must reserve potential municipal uses for future appropriation.[654]

The State Board's power to insist water be used for beneficial purposes is a basis for conditions. The State Board cannot grant a permit for "in-stream" uses, such as fisheries and recreation, because a permit cannot be granted without a diversion.[655] However, the State Board must consider the in-stream uses when granting permits to others.[656] Court decisions point to enlarging the power to adopt conditions affecting existing appropriations permits.[657]

Overlying owners enjoy correlative rights to groundwater analogous to riparian rights. A similar analogy exists for appropriative rights in groundwater.[658] If surplus groundwater exists after the rights of overlying owners are satisfied, the surplus may be appropriated for reasonable and beneficial use off the overlying lands.[659] This right is extremely important because a water purveyor is usually not an overlying owner. The purveyor is usually an appropriator.[660]

The statutory procedure for obtaining appropriations permits does not apply to groundwater. The State Board may file a court action to protect the quality of a ground-waterbasin.[661] The State Board can issue permits to store water underground.[662] The State Board may require certain reports to be filed concerning groundwater production in specified areas of Southern California.[663] The state has no general jurisdiction over groundwater management; the appropriation system does not apply to groundwater.[664] Groundwater rights, particularly rights to surplus water, are protected only by the courts.[665]

Property may be "acquired" by adverse possession or prescription. Prescription occurs when a person occupies or uses the property of another for five years in an open, notorious and hostile manner. Water is property. Water rights may be acquired by adverse possession or prescription.

The primary issue in resolving a prescription dispute is whether a surplus exists. A surplus exists when less water is extracted from the basin than naturally replenished.[666] When more water is extracted than replenished and the basin is damaged, an "overdraft" exists.

In 1948, the Court concluded the gradual deepening of wells throughout the Raymond Basin in Pasadena put each water producer on notice that water was being taken by someone and the existence of an overdraft demonstrated such taking was hostile because surplus was not available for appropriation.[667] The Court found each party had "mutually prescribed" a quantity of water the party had produced from the basin continuously for five years preceding the filing of the complaint.[668] As a result of this decision, pumpers maximized their production from basins threatened with overdraft. This "race to the pump house" protected pumper's rights but had the unfortunate side-effect of exacerbating the overdraft.

The Court reexamined the doctrine in light of this problem.[669] Although the Court did not expressly overrule the mutual prescription doctrine, in at least three respects, it made it extremely difficult to apply the doctrine in the future:

- First, the Court found the commonly understood definition of overdraft did not take into account that the natural yield of the basin could be increased if producers temporarily "mined" a basin. Under such circumstances, additional pumping would not be "hostile" because the overdraft would be illusory. The additional temporary storage capacity would allow the capture of flood waters.

- Next, overdraft was too difficult for a pumper to determine by mere deepening of wells. Actual notice had to be given to each overlying owner. As a practical matter, few producers are motivated to determine the existence of an overdraft and then warn all other producers.

- Finally, prescription cannot run against a public agency.

Prescriptive rights are not evidenced by a deed or other legal document. To establish a prescriptive right "of record," a court action must "quiet title" or "adjudicate" water rights.[670] Typically, the quiet title action is accompanied by an offer to solve the physical problems of overdraft. In fact, the possibility of a physical solution is usually the predominant motive for suit, with the establishment of water rights secondary.

In 1983, the California Supreme Court worked legal magic to create the <u>public trust doctrine</u>.[671] To understand the scope and breadth of the public trust doctrine, it is necessary to examine how the doctrine arose. In 1942, the city of Los Angeles obtained an appropriation permit to divert waters from streams tributary to the Mono Lake for urban consumption. Over the years, the Owens River Aqueduct was improved and expanded. Mono Lake was lowered as a result of these diversions to the potential damage of a brine shrimp population and sea gull rookery. The National Audubon Society sued the city to reduce the diversions and protect the ecological uses of Mono Lake.[672] The city defended itself by citing the long held licenses and by arguing the Audubon Society could not upset vested rights. The Audubon Society argued the licenses were always subject to the state's rights as trustee of water resources to preserve and protect public trust uses. In other words, the Audubon Society argued the 40-year-old permits were subject to the state's continuing right to preserve and protect commerce, navigation, recreation and ecological uses.

At the time of the decision, the public trust doctrine was well established only with respect to tidelands. The doctrine originated when the U.S. Supreme Court revoked a grant to the Illinois Central Railroad giving the railroad control of the entire Chicago waterfront.[673] The public trust doctrine was modified in California to enable the state to protect commerce and navigation along the Pacific Coast.[674] California cases applied the doctrine to other types of navigable waters.[675] Another California case, expanded public trust uses to include fishing, navigation and ecological protection.[676] On the eve of the *National Audubon* case, the doctrine was routinely invoked to prevent adjoining landowners from interfering with the water in a navigable stream or lake. But the doctrine was not used to prevent the diversion of water from a stream or lake for use for beneficial purposes.

The Supreme Court made the quantum leap and applied the public trust doctrine in water rights context by relying upon ancient laws, including the Institutes of Justinian to find the laws under which Los Angeles obtained its appropriation license were always subject to the state's prior and paramount right and obligation to protect public trusts uses.

The case is clearly poor legal scholarship. First, a similar argument was rejected by the California Supreme Court close to 100 years earlier.[677] Second, the courts cannot overturn the Constitution and statutes in favor of common law, let alone Justinian law.[678] For example, many ancient laws approved slavery. If ancient laws can overturn statutes or the Constitution, slavery can be permitted in California. Finally, the court did not have to "reach" to the doctrine to provide relief. The California Constitution with its requirement that water be put to reasonable beneficial use, provided a basis for finding the Mono Basin diversions should be reviewed and modified.[679]

Despite its dubious ancestry, the public trust doctrine is now part of the California water rights landscape. Like other court-made laws, those affected by the decision must now raise and resolve unanswered questions that should have been addressed by the Legislature as a part of a statutory scheme. But because this doctrine is based on something even above the Constitution, legislation may be theoretically impossible.

A few California cities enjoy a <u>pueblo right</u> that is prior and paramount to other rights except federal rights. There is no rational basis for this right. This right is simply a creature of the judiciary, invoked for expedience.

The federal government also affects water supply by asserting ownership claims to water on federal lands. The United States Supreme Court confirmed the federal government's right to assert a <u>reserved right</u> to sufficient water to operate and manage Indian properties.[680] Indian tribes enjoy an important special category of federal rights. Under the law, tribes are separate nations existing within the United States as a result of treaties. Of course, native Americans are also American citizens. Each tribe's treaty elaborates the rights adhering to native Americans which are different than other Americans.

The nature and extent of this specie of federal right is set forth in each tribe's treaty. In general, treaties will "reserve" sufficient water for the tribe to enjoy independence. Non-Indian reserved rights are also established.[681]

To assert a supreme federal right, Congress must express intent to exert its jurisdiction. In some cases, Congress specifically reserves water rights when establishing a federal preserve or federal project. However, in the absence of specific language (which is usual) "intent can be inferred if previously unappropriated waters are necessary to accomplish the purposes for which the federal reservation [project] was created."[682] Sometimes, a legal "implication" is the court's way of saying that people act with common sense. However, legal implications are also used to rationalize a result otherwise barred by the law. Because the reserved rights doctrine depends ultimately on one's political philosophy, the doctrine has an uneven development depending upon whether proponents of state's rights or proponents of federal rights have held sway in Washington, D.C. Through the years, the Supreme Court has also embellished its original handiwork.[683]

Under the United States Constitution, lawsuits between states must be heard by the United States Supreme Court. Disputes between States over the rights in boundary waters are heard by the United States Supreme Court. The Supreme Court has established its own water rights law, the so-called "equitable apportionment doctrine" to deal with these disputes.[684] Under this doctrine, each state is entitled to receive its "equitable" share of interstate waters. If each state recognizes the same water rights doctrine, e.g. appropriative rights, the concept of first-in-time, first-in-right will be considered by the court as it bears upon the equitable rights of each state.[685] The court will not be bound by each state's laws.[686]

Interstate equitable apportionment lawsuits lost favor perhaps because of the tremendous cost in bringing a United States Supreme Court action or perhaps because of the risk involved with a doctrine as nebulous as equitable apportionment.

States then attempted to resolve their interstate water disputes by agreement, called "interstate compacts." The agreement between the upper Colorado River states and lower Colorado River states is such an agreement.[687] To be effective, interstate compacts require congressional approval.[688]

The United States Supreme Court must hear lawsuits between the states. Congress must approve interstate compacts. Given this heavy federal involvement in resolving interstate issues, it was inevitable that Congress would legislate solutions to interstate disputes without Supreme Court action or an interstate compact. This occurred when the lower Colorado River water users failed to resolve their differences after years of dispute. The Supreme Court upheld the authority of Congress to legislate a physical solution to interstate water disputes.[689]

Water wars are legendary in the Wild West. Government has tried to devise ways for water disputes to be resolved quickly and cheaply. Historically, the courts are where civilized water warriors engage in battle. Landmark water decisions are among the earliest reported California cases. Three basic types of judicial relief exist today. First, a water user who interferes with the rights of another can be subjected to a nuisance action similar to nuisance actions in other areas of the law. Second, a water user who is running out of water can demand a watershed adjudication to declare the respective rights of all users. Third, a water user can demand an equitable apportionment of water flowing interstate.

One of the best examples of grass-roots lawmaking is the formulation of physical solutions for water management issues. A physical solution is an agreed method of maximizing the available water resources by management practices. A physical solution is typically court-imposed but seldom the result of truly adversary proceedings. Usually, the parties will negotiate a physical solution to water problems with the aid of hydrogeologists and water lawyers. The Court is then asked to set the agreement in a judgment. Regardless of how the physical solution is presented, the Court has the ultimate responsibility under the Constitution to determine whether the resource is being put to reasonable, beneficial use.[690]

The quantification of a right owned by each party is usually part of a basin management program. The program typically involves prorating the cost of basin management on the basis of each party's share of the basin. In effect, each water producer owns a *pro rata* portion of the basin. As long as no producer extracts more than its share, the basin is in (theoretical) equilibrium. But, pumpers seldom extract precisely the same amount of water from a basin from year to year and the same amount of yield is seldom available. Physical solutions may allow excess production but require the producer to purchase unused rights or supplemental water to replace over-pumping. Many Southern California physical solutions have operated successfully for generations on this basis.[691]

There are fifteen adjudicated basins managed by Watermasters.[692] About the only pattern is the basins are in Southern California.[693] The organization of each Watermaster reflects the powers exercised by the Watermaster. For example, when the Watermaster simply accounts for production, the Department of Water Resources ("DWR") is often the Watermaster.

Central Basin: This basin is located in southeastern Los Angeles County.[694] Production is about 180,000 AF/Y. The Watermaster accounts for production. The Watermaster is DWR.[695]

Chino Basin: This basin is located in Western San Bernardino County. Production is about 140,000 AF/Y. The Watermaster consists of persons appointed by various interest groups.

Cucamonga: This basin is located in the North-Central part of Upper Santa Ana Valley Basin, San Bernardino County. Production is about 41,865 AF/Y.

Cummings: This basin is located in the Cummings Valley Floor in Tehachapi. The Watermaster is the Tehachapi-Cummings Water District. Production was about 1,940 AF/Y in 1987. The Watermaster accounts for data useful to the monitoring of groundwater production by the parties, and the keeping of records, reporting on the annual production.

Main San Gabriel Basin: This basin is located in eastern Los Angeles County.[696] Production is about 260,000 AF/Y. The Watermaster accounts for production, determines safe yield, levies assessments, and makes a variety of substantive decisions affecting basin operations. The Watermaster is a nine-member board, nominated annually by the producers and wholesale water agencies.[697]

Mojave River: This basin is around the City of Barstow in San Bernardino County. Production is about 160,000 AF/Y. The Watermaster accounts for production and manages the basin. The Watermaster is the Mojave Water Agency.

Puente Basin: This basin is located in the San Gabriel Valley Basin, excluding Raymond Basin, and the Main San Gabriel Basin. The Watermaster accounts for production; poor water quality has led to no production. The Watermaster consists of a three-member board: one consultant representing the Walnut Valley Water District and Rowland Water District, one consultant for the City of Industry and Industry Urban Development Agency, and a third neutral party.

Raymond Basin: This basin is located in the Pasadena/La Cañada/Flintridge area of Los Angeles County. Production is about 30,000 AF/Y. The Watermaster accounts for production, regulates storage, and performs monitoring. The Watermaster is selected annually by the Raymond Basin Management Board.

San Bernardino Basin Area: This basin is located in the northeast part of Upper Santa Ana Basin, San Bernardino and Riverside counties. Production is about 201,408 AF/Y. The Watermaster monitors compliance with 1969 Judgment. The Watermaster consists of one representative each from Western Municipal Water District and San Bernardino Valley Municipal Water District.

Santa Margarita River Watershed: This basin consists of the entire Santa Margarita River Watershed, including three groundwater basins — Santa Margarita Valley, Temecula Valley and Cahuilla Valley, San Diego and Riverside. The Watermaster accounts for production, but no groundwater is extracted. The Watermaster is a U.S. District court appointee.

Santa Paula Basin: This basin consists of the sub-basin of Santa Clara River, Ventura County. Production is about 20,578 AF/Y. The Watermaster is the keeper of the records; the technical advisory committee performs same functions as a Watermaster would. The Watermaster consists of a three-person technical advisory committee from the United Water Conservation District, City of Ventura, and Santa Paula Basin Pumpers Association.

Six Basins: These basins are located in the Pomona-Claremont Area of Los Angeles County. Production is about 20,000 AF/Y. The Watermaster accounts for the overseeing of the extraction of the basins, determines safe yield, and enters into storage and receiving agreements. The basins are administered by Three Valleys Municipal Water District. The Watermaster consists of a multi-member board consisting of Southern California Water Company, City of La Verne, City of Pomona, City of Claremont, Pomona College, Pomona Valley Protection Association, San Antonio Water Company, and Three Valleys Municipal Water District.

Tehachapi: This basin is also located in the Tehachapi area. The Watermaster is the Tehachapi-Cummings Water District. Production is about 2,938 AF/Y. (5,500 AF/Y - safe yield.) The Watermaster accounts for data useful to the monitoring of groundwater production by the parties, keeps records, and files annual groundwater production reports. Watermaster is to interpret and enforce requirements of installing measuring devices.

Upper Los Angeles River Area: This basin is located in the San Fernando Valley Basin (entire watershed). Production is about 75,000 AF/Y. The Watermaster is a Superior Court appointee.

Warren Valley: This basin consists of 51 square miles in the Yucca Valley area, San Bernardino County. Production is about 2,500 AF/Y. The Watermaster accounts for the monitoring and regulating of water related items in the basin. The purpose is to cure the overdraft of the Warren Valley. The Watermaster is the Hi-Desert Water District.

West Coast Basin: This basin is located in southwestern Los Angeles County.[698] Production is about 50,000 AF/Y. The Watermaster accounts for production. The Watermaster is DWR.[699]

In the San Gabriel Valley, groundwater adjudication resulted in an aggressive physical solution. In this case, groundwater rights were adjudicated on the basis of mutual prescription. The Main San Gabriel Basin judgment allocates shares of the basin's yield based on each producer's prescriptive rights and requires pumpers producing more than their share to purchase supplemental water. The judgment allows the free exchange of water rights. Over-producers also can obtain water by leasing or buying rights from under-producers. The Main San Gabriel Basin Watermaster annually determines yield based upon current basin water levels. A pumper may produce in excess of prescriptive rights without having to purchase supplemental water if the safe yield is high enough. Conversely, a pumper can produce less than allocated rights and still be required to purchase water if the yield is low.

The acquisition of water rights has been curtailed by the State and Federal governments' Wild River statutes. These Acts preserve rivers in a native state. In many cases, projects are unable to satisfy contractual commitments.

Traditionally, water conservation meant preventing water from "wasting" to the ocean by the construction of dams. Conservation now refers to measures to reduce consumption. These two approaches to conservation are fundamentally different. The first approach attacks the problem of shortage by collecting more water; the second approach reduces consumption. Supporters of each type denigrate the other. Dam builders debate the effectiveness of efforts to reduce consumption; those promoting reductions criticize the inefficiency of new dams. This conflict comes to a head in preservation of wild and scenic rivers.

Under the federal Wild and Scenic Rivers Law, the Secretary of Interior designates rivers to be preserved in a natural state because of unique attributes.[700] The Secretary acts on the basis of state recommendations. California also enacted a Wild and Scenic Rivers Law.[701] Under this law, the Secretary of Resources designates rivers to be preserved in a natural state for recreational purposes.[702] The following rivers in California have been designated: Smith, Trinity, Klamath, Van Duzen, Eel, Feather, American and Tuolumne.[703]

Water rights can also be lost by unwise use. The Constitution requires riparians and appropriators to use water only for reasonable, beneficial purposes.[704] The State Board may require appropriators and purveyors to eliminate wasteful practices. [705] The consumer can be similarly restrained by their purveyors.

In addition to general authority, [706] the Principal Acts of various agencies usually provide express authority to require conservation.[707] The law upholds "reasonable" regulations. What is reasonable will vary. The severity of regulation must be compared to the need for conservation. The reasonable use test is both elegant and frustrating. It is elegant because it allows the law to take into consideration the expectations of the community. It is frustrating because policy makers can not know in advance how proposals will fare in a judicial setting.[708]

The reasonableness of a water conservation measure will vary over time and from place-to-place. A couple of decades ago, it may have been unreasonable for an agency to require showerhead flow restricters. Such a requirement is now universally accepted even in the absence of drought. A requirement for drought-tolerant plants may be reasonable in the southern part of the State. Such a requirement might not be reasonable in parts of the water-rich north. When there is uncertainty, Water Code Section 375 can be invoked. This Section states:

> Notwithstanding any other provision of the law to the contrary, any public entity which supplies water at retail for the benefit of the inhabitants therein may, by ordinance or resolution adopted by a majority of the members of the governing body thereof after holding a public hearing upon notice thereof and making appropriate findings of necessity therefor, adopt and enforce a water conservation program to reduce the quantity of water used by the inhabitants therein for the purpose of conserving the water supplies of such public entity. Such ordinance or resolution may, for other than agricultural uses, specifically require the installation of water-saving devices which are designed to reduce water consumption. For the purposes of this section, 'public entity' means a city, county, district, agency, or any other political subdivision of the state.[709]

By the middle of 1991, water agencies throughout the state shared a concern on the need for water conservation. This resulted in agreement concerning "best management practices" for water conservation. The list of practices was circulated throughout the state among the various water agencies in the form of a memorandum of understanding. Beginning in August 1991, agencies signaled their approval of the best management practices by the execution of a "memorandum of understanding" (MOU) which provided strong political and weak legal implementation of water conservation. The MOU is interesting for a number of reasons. First, by listing what constitutes "normal" water conservation practices, it provides ready support for arguments confronting a water agency over what might constitute "reasonable" conservation measures. Second, the MOU was developed outside of traditional channels.

The memorandum is not a statute adopted by the Legislature, a rule adopted by the executive branch or a decision of the judiciary. The MOU is like a contract among water purveyors, environmental groups and other interested parties.

One problem of water conservation is all purveyors do not treat the scarcity of supply with similar concern. This is understandable because even during severe drought some areas have adequate supplies. An agency's lack of conservation can be because the agency does not find it in its best interest to conserve water. For example, leaders of a large city might not call for conservation because the lack of water reflects poor planning and stresses the voters. Agricultural interests have little incentive to promote conservation if conservation increases the cost of water and makes water available for the competition. Most people willingly engage in water conservation (and pay income taxes) if they believe the program is uniformly and fairly applied. Enthusiasm for water conservation is extremely difficult to maintain if the public believes that someone is taking advantage of the system. The majority of purveyors promote water conservation (at least during a drought).

Local water purveyors can not deal effectively with the profligate neighbor. An agency with broad responsibilities can judge local conservation in the context of larger policy issues. The seminal question: What level of government should be responsible for water conservation standards?[710]

California and the federal government have adopted complementary drinking water laws.

The federal Safe Drinking Water Law mandates drinking water standards for water purveyors.[711] The federal act also provides financial assistance to purveyors to meet the requirements. The federal act delegates responsibilities for administration to the various states.[712]

California accepted the invitation of the federal government to develop drinking water standards with the adoption of the California Safe Drinking Water Act.[713] This law directs the Department of Health Services to establish safe levels for various constituents in the drinking water supply.[714] A water purveyor is generally prohibited from distributing water exceeding the drinking water standards and must notify customers when standards are exceeded. Constituent levels may be exceeded occasionally at a low level without the notification provisions of the Act coming into play.

Water purveyors must distribute a variety of reports to water customers. Every public water system must annually prepare a "Consumer Confidence Report" and mail or deliver a copy of the report to each customer (other than an occupant of a recreational vehicle park). The report must contain the following:

1. The source of water provided by the system.

2. A "brief and plainly worded definition" of "maximum contaminant level," "primary drinking water standard" and "public health goal."

3. If a regulated contaminant is detected during the past year, the report shall also state:

   a. The level of the contaminant and corresponding public health goal and primary drinking water standard;

   b. Description of violations of primary drinking water standards occurring as a result of the presence of the contaminant and a "brief and plainly worded statement" of health concerns.

   c. Public water system's [sic] address and phone number for further information.

4. Information on levels of unregulated contaminants, if any, for which monitoring is required pursuant to state or federal law or regulation.

5. Variances or exemptions from primary drinking water standards granted to the system and the basis therefor.[715]

Aside from the dubious benefit of sending a report to every customer, whether they want it or not, the most problematical requirement of this provision is providing information on "unregulated contaminants." Purveyors are expected to provide information on constituents being studied and for which there is no scientific evidence of health threat. Additionally, purveyors can expect the health department to promote language in the notices which frighten customers, and purveyors will be interested in providing notices which reassure customers.

In addition to the annual consumer confidence report, each water system having more than 10,000 service connections must provide plain language reports commencing July 1, 1998, and every three years thereafter if contaminants are detected exceeding public health goals. This report must: (1) identify the contaminant which exceeds public health goal; (2) disclose the numerical public health risk associated with the maximum contaminant level to identify the category of risk to public health; (4) describe technology to remove the contaminant; (5) estimate the cost per customer of using technology described above to reduce the concentration of the contaminant; and (6) describe what action has been taken to reduce the contaminant.[716] The purveyor must also hold a public hearing to accept and respond to public comment on the report.

Once again, purveyors are asked to inform their customers about the constituents not yet found to actually pose a danger. In fact, this provision reaffirms the Department of Health Services shall not require the water system to take action to reduce or eliminate excedence of public health goals.

Health and Safety Code states the *minimum* requirements for these reports. Nothing prevents the purveyor from adding information to provide perspective. For example, the report could begin with a disclaimer:

> "The state and federal laws require water
> purveyors to give notices to customers when

a constituent is found in the water supply threatening the public health. Ironically, purveyors are also required to give notice if certain constituents appear in the water supply even though scientists are unable to say there is a real public health risk. The following report shows no known public health risk has been detected in your water supply. The report also discloses the existence of some constituents which scientists have not concluded pose a public health risk, but we are asked to address as a 'public health goal.' You can judge for yourself whether it is worth the effort to remove these 'suspected' constituents because the report also explains it will cost you about $_____ a month to accomplish this goal."

The Department of Health Services is responsible for issuing permits to supply water for domestic purposes. The Department can impose conditions as "necessary to assure a reliable and adequate supply of water at all times that is pure, wholesome, potable and does not endanger the health of consumers."[717] The Department is competent to judge these matters. However, the Department is also authorized to refuse to issue permits to a "public water system" not in existence on January 1, 1998, unless the "water supplier possesses adequate financial, managerial, and technical capability to assure the delivery of pure, wholesome, and potable drinking water." Furthermore, a permit will not be issued to an unincorporated association existing after December 31, 1990.

The Department of Health Services will not issue a public water system permit for the use of a reservoir as a source of supply if the reservoir is augmented with recycled water, unless the department performs engineering studies and evaluates the treatment technology and finds there is no significant threat to the public health and conducts a public hearing before the first use. What is interesting about this provision is, in a backhand way, it says recycled water may be placed in a potable water reservoir.

One interesting but overlooked sidelight to the pursuit for pure water is that communities are not permitted to tolerate *substandard* water. The federal government, the state and counties dictate the minimum standards to be met by purveyors. However, there was a time when a community could decide it could not afford modern water pumps, storage and distribution facilities. Many small rural water systems operated with apparent success for decades. Areas that could not afford water system improvements must now spend considerable amounts for system upgrades, testing, and compliance with new operating standards. In many cases, the character of the community changes as a result.

Under the Safe Drinking Water Act amendments of 1986, the EPA may establish "wellhead protection" for aquifers that are a sole source of an area's water supply and could create a significant hazard to public health if contaminated. Once an area is designated, no federal assistance may be provided for a project in an area where the aquifer is contaminated. The 1986 amendments restrict underground injection of hazardous wastes, establish a sole source aquifer demonstration program and encourage state programs to develop wellhead protection programs.

Rate setting is a major consumer issue associated with publicly financed projects. The Principal Acts of public agencies prohibit discrimination in the establishment of water rates. This does not mean rates must be the same. Reasonable classifications are possible. The reasonableness of a classification is determined on a case-by-case basis. The courts established some guidelines worth reviewing. A fee cannot exceed the reasonable cost of service without being a disguised tax. This is the first principle for water rates. However, the purveyor still has discretion to arrange rates to promote equity and water policy. For example, many agencies charge more for services to higher elevations. Agencies can create block rates to encourage conservation by making the purchase of large quantities more expensive.[718] Service to property outside the agencies can be at a different rate than service to property within the agency.[719] But the out-of-agency rates must still bear a relationship to the agency's costs.[720]

Many Principal Acts allow a separate rate classification for service to other public agencies.[721] Tax-exempt agencies can be required to pay a higher rate to compensate for the lack of tax revenue.[722]

Type of use, i.e., domestic or commercial agricultural, and certainty of supply, i.e., interruptible or uninterruptible, are other common classifications having passed the test of time and should survive judicial challenge as long as the facts continue to show that the cost of providing service will vary from class-to-class. Even though the courts will usually defer to the agency on the propriety of a class, not all classifications have survived judicial scrutiny. For example, a separate class for rental housing has been rejected.[723]

Courts have also upheld long-term water supply contracts. In effect, such contracts create a separate class of service. Five-year and longer negotiated water rates have been upheld.[724] These cases are usually decided without reference to the problem of discriminatory rates on the basis of necessity.

Every few years, horror stories report on the unfortunate consequences of termination of water service. The axiom, hard cases make bad law, is also apparent in this area. The United States Supreme Court introduced customer protections in this area.[725] The Court found the due process clause of the United States Constitution required utilities to give reasonable notice of anticipated termination of service and opportunity to contest the facts or make arrangements for payment. Subsequently, the California Legislature addressed the issue by enacting laws with specific notice and hearing requirements.[726] District purveyors must give single family residential customers at least 13 days prior written notice of termination.[727] Termination must be preceded by a "reasonable attempt" to contact an adult residing at the premises at least 24 hours prior to cut-off. If personal notice cannot be accomplished, a notice must be posted on the property 48 hours before the cut-off.[728] The notice must give the customer the opportunity to contest the facts upon which termination is based.[729] Further, poor or infirm customers must be given the opportunity to make installment payments to pay the delinquencies on conditions subsequent bills are paid in due course.[730]

Purveyors must live with the public policy pronouncements of the state legislature. This usually means special interest groups or pet programs get special attention. There are special rules when water is served through a master meter to a multi-residential structure, mobile home park or farm labor camp or through individual meters for such uses when the owner, manager or farm labor employer is the customer of record. The purveyor must make "every good faith effort to inform the actual users" when the account is delinquent.[731] The purveyor must give the actual users at least 10 days prior notice of intent to terminate and give the actual users the opportunity to become a customer without having to pay the delinquent amount.[732] A requirement for individual service can be satisfied if the actual users comply with the terms and conditions of service and one of the actual users accepts responsibility for the tenants or the units can be separately terminated.[733]

When the tenant is a customer, service may be terminated to the delinquent tenant but the agency may not refuse service to a subsequent tenant. If the District terminates service to a landowner-customer, the actual water users must be notified and given the opportunity to become the customer.[734] An agency cannot terminate service on Saturday, Sunday, a legal holiday or at any time during which the business offices of the agency are not open to the public.[735]

While an agency may demand a service deposit from a customer who has been terminated for non-payment, including a chronically delinquent customer, an agency cannot demand service deposits from all applicants or from a class of applicants, such as renters.[736] The agency must establish lack of credit worthiness on an individual basis. Residence and proof of prompt payment of rent will satisfy deposit requirements.[737]

Low cost housing has been a favored state policy for years. Beginning in July 2006, purveyors were required to grant priority for service allocations to developments which included affordable / low-cost housing.[738] Applications for service cannot be denied for developments containing affordable / low-cost housing unless the agency makes a finding that capacity is not sufficient to serve the project.[739]

A public agency purveyor cannot serve water for municipal and industrial purposes outside its boundaries without the permission of the Local Agency Formation Commission ("LAFCO").[740] However, LAFCO's permission is not needed if: there is an agreement with the agency where service is to be provided; the water is non-potable or untreated; service is incidental to agricultural service, or the service is for conservation purposes.

Water Code Section 350, *et seq.*, allows a public water purveyor to declare a water shortage emergency. The emergency may be localized, such as the sudden loss of production facilities, or widespread, such as a statewide drought. Under these provisions, the agency conducts a public hearing to give customers the opportunity to comment on whether supplies are inadequate and on the proposed regulations. Like all regulations, water shortage emergency regulations must be reasonable and nondiscriminatory. The basis of a water shortage emergency regulation is that the water supply is inadequate to satisfy the regular needs of water customers and requirements for human habitation.[741] The penalties for violating a water shortage emergency regulation can be harsh, imprisonment or termination of water service.

Under Section 350, the agency must recognize the priority enjoyed by human habitation, including sanitation and fire protection. Commercial and industrial uses, agricultural and irrigation uses, and stock watering must be curtailed sooner or to a greater extent than domestic uses when the water shortage emergency statute is invoked.[742] This sometimes conflicts with community standards. Most communities seem willing to allow business to share the burden of cutbacks. Orchards and stock watering usually enjoy favor. For this reason, water shortage emergency regulations typically allow a certain amount of commercial, industrial, agricultural uses to occur even while domestic uses are curtailed.

On the face of it, it is not possible to rationalize approval of new service connections when a water shortage emergency threatens existing customers. On the other hand, harsh economic consequences befall work in progress when such regulations are adopted. Further, emergencies and even droughts don't last forever. Commitment to serve after the emergency ends doesn't violate rights of existing customers. Regulations can allow service to be extended to persons with work in progress or to allow the processing of applications for service to persons who have not even begun constructing on the condition service will not actually commence until the water shortage ends.

The question sometimes arises whether water service can be denied to protect the environment. It is unquestioned the design and timing of the installation of water distribution systems routinely affects the manner and rate of growth. Additionally, shortages in supply, production, storage or transmission capacity limit the development of property. There is no question a water district can legally influence development patterns. The purveyor may refuse service to new customers when there is a shortage of supply. The more difficult question is whether a purveyor may refuse to acquire additional supply to meet anticipated demand.

> The decision of various communities to manage growth has been prompted by a

variety of interrelated factors many laudable and some suspect. ...However one evaluates these factors, the growth management movement of recent years has had the effect of making land use planning and control law a more popular and controversial topic at the grass roots level than ever before. ...There is little if any doubt that exclusionary motives including even racial and economic discrimination lurk behind some of the proposals but at the very least the controversies that envelop nearly all growth control proposals have brought much needed public interest and attention to the land use planning and control process. In fact, it seems quite possible that growth management provides the primary theme and coherence for land use regulation and environmental protection for the remainder of the twentieth century.[743]

Many cases can be cited for the proposition the purveyor may refuse to extend service to new customers when supplies are inadequate.[754] These cases are interesting but not profound.[755] Only a few cases address the question of whether the District has a duty to augment supply to serve anticipated demands. A water district can refuse applications for new service during a water shortage emergency, but politically, the power to "cut off one's water" by the simple expedient of imposing another moratorium is a potent weapon in effecting a no-growth policy within a community. Since District has neither the power nor the authority to initiate or implement such a policy, the imposition of any restriction on the use of its water supply for that purpose would be invalid:

...[W]e do foresee a continuing obligation on the part of the District to exert every reasonable effort to augment its available water supply in order to meet increasing demands.[744]

The Legislature enacted several statutes confirming the inadequacy of California's housing stock and mandating that local agencies address the housing problem rather than make excuses for failing to do so.[745] Each year the legislation makes it more difficult for *cities* to declare building moratoria on the basis of the inadequacy of infrastructure.[746]

There is no legislative or judicial authority for the proposition water agencies may manage growth by refusing to augment supply when necessary to meet anticipated demands.[747] Advocates of growth control by utility shortage often admit there is no legal authority to support such a practice but argue the law is developing in that direction. There is nothing to support this view.

In the mid-seventies, Southern California was in the middle of one of its periodic boom cycles. In desperation, many voters tried to limit the rate of growth by restricting access to utility services, particularly water and sewer service. By the end of the seventies, the bust cycle had begun. This made utility service moratoria academic. Most communities have used this breathing spell to formulate programs of phased growth.[748] Most areas no longer use utility service as a mechanism for growth control.

The shift away from utility based growth control is beneficial to the advocates of managed growth. Land planning agencies, particularly cities, have an array of land use management tools, broad jurisdictional powers and access to the necessary data to make intelligent, long-term, land use planning decisions which will command enduring support by the community. A community which relies on water shortage to control growth will inevitably run out of water.[749] Serious and responsible growth management advocates are wary of using a water supply shortage as a basis for growth control because of the inevitable adverse reaction when no-growth policies produce water rationing.

Serious and responsible growth management advocates are also reluctant to allow utility services shortages to displace the established land planning process because it allows land planners to escape responsibility for the consequences of their actions. If poor land planning decisions are being made by the agencies responsible for land planning, the elected and appointed officials can be held accountable by democratic processes. If the majority of the population is unwilling to reverse unwise land planning decisions at the ballot box, this implies that the majority expects that utility service will be provided in due course by the agencies responsible for such service.[750] When supervisors, council members or water district directors cross jurisdictional lines, they are ignoring the will of the voters who elected the governing board of the other agencies and they are brushing aside the compact with their own electors.

Cities and counties are responsible for determining how land may be used. Land use regulators have always had the responsibility to consider water supply. In recent years, legislation has been adopted to remind cities and counties of their responsibility and to mandate water purveyors to cooperate in the effort. These statutes mandate what was once good business practice: land planning agencies must confer with water suppliers about the availability of water for new developments.

CHAPTER 9
SANITATION SERVICE

The precursor of human habitation is water. The inevitable byproduct of human society is wastewater (sewage). Except to rural areas, sanitation service has become the "utility" only slightly less important than water service. The two have much in common. Many agencies with the power to provide water service can provide sanitation service. Sewage disposal is heavily influenced by laws designed to keep water pure. Water laws increasingly promote reduction in wastewater.

The federal government's involvement in water pollution control is longstanding. It dates from 1899 with the Rivers and Harbors Act. This early law attempted to regulate water pollution by setting quality standards for the receiving waters such that a pollutant could be discharged into a water system if the overall quality of the water system was not degraded below specific levels. [751] The Rivers and Harbors Act worked well for years probably because receiving waters had an unused capacity to assimilate pollutants. As pollutants became more numerous, complex and toxic, the receiving water approach became inadequate.

In 1968, Congress began to heavily regulate the quality of the materials discharged into navigable waterways with the adoption of the Federal Water Pollution Control Act (now called the Clean Water Act).[752] Under the federal Clean Water Act, no person may discharge a "pollutant" or "contaminant" from a "point source" without first obtaining a discharge permit from the Environmental Protection Agency or a state agency approved by the EPA. Under this law, "effluent limitations" are established for various types of biological, chemical and radioactive wastes. These limitations are incorporated in the National Pollution Discharge Elimination System (NPDES) permits that are a prerequisite to the discharge to navigable waters.[753] The Federal Clean Water Act allows states to administer the program if the EPA certified minimum standards were achieved in the state program. California accepted the invitation. The State Water Resources Control Board assumed this responsibility and delegated the authority for the issuance of permits to the nine Regional Water Quality Control Boards. The Regional Board considers requests for federal permits to discharge to the "waters of the United States" and for state permits to discharge to waters not affected by the federal act.

Only navigable waterways are regulated by the federal government. The test of navigability under the federal Clean Water Act is easily met.[754] The term "navigable waterway" even includes "wetlands" and land tributary to wetlands.[755] However, "navigable" does not include all water Congress could regulate under the Commerce clause. The water must actually be navigable.[756] Additionally, the terms "pollutant" and "contaminant" are broadly defined so that virtually any foreign substance can be regulated.[757] Despite the foregoing, the federal Clean Water Act fails to regulate water pollution completely in at least three areas. First, "non-point" source pollution is only lightly regulated.[758] Second, the Act fails to address groundwater pollution other than to control the injection of waste into wells for disposal purposes.[759] Finally, non-navigable waters are not regulated.

The Porter-Cologne Water Quality Control Act was adopted long before it became fashionable to be concerned about water pollution. Porter-Cologne regulates discharge of waste into waters of the state. In many ways, the Porter-Cologne Water Quality Control Act, has a more profound effect on the quality of waters in the State than the federal Act. The State Clean Water Act also requires a permit before any pollutant may be discharged.[760] However, the State Act defines "pollutant" even more broadly than the federal act. Further, the State Act applies to all waters within the state, including non-navigable waters. The breadth and scope of the State Act has continued to expand. For example, the owners of a recreational lake have been found to violate the state Act by releasing sediment from the lake.[761] The Court upheld an injunction against further releases and mandated clean-up.

Enforcement of both the State and Federal Acts is left up to Regional Water Quality Control Board.[762] The regional board may seek court injunctions, levy civil fines and seek criminal sanctions against violators.[763] If the regional board fails to enforce the Clean Water Acts by demanding a permit as a condition to a discharge or by imposing inappropriate permit conditions, an aggrieved party may appeal the decision to the State Board or the EPA regional administrator (in the case of the federal act).[764] If the State Board fails to produce satisfactory results, an aggrieved person may resort to the courts.[765] In reviewing the administrative decision of the State Board, the Court makes an independent evaluation of the evidence before it, which includes the records of the state and regional boards and any evidence it finds relevant.[766] Only the EPA or the state can actually enforce an NPDES permit. However, a nuisance action can be brought against a polluter, separate and apart from the state or federal Clean Water Acts under general common law principles.[767] But there is no federal common law with respect to water pollution.[768] Thus, a federal water pollution nuisance action is impossible.

"Progress" in the expansion of community sanitation systems has been remarkable and, in many respects, helpful to the cause of public health. Top down regulation from federal and state governments has a mania for uniformity which can produce unnecessary projects. Not everything new is good; not everything old is bad. On-site septic disposal of human waste avoids environmental cost in many cases. (Huge amounts of electrical energy and large tracts of otherwise productive land are consumed by community sanitation systems.) Environmental opportunities are presented by septic systems. (Properly maintained septic systems recharge basins, making water available for reuse without government intervention.) Then again, not everything new is bad, nor is everything old good. The point is public policy is not well-served by edicts-from-on-high. Sanitation policy currently lacks the fundamental flexibility needed to address real problems with real answers.

Many purveyors undertake reuse programs to conserve potable water. Recycling is a convenient way to generate modest revenue while disposing of treated effluent. A water agency can be forced into a water reuse program by the State Board, and a purveyor can force its customers to use recycled water if the circumstances are right.[769] The State Board must consider reuse potential when reviewing appropriations permits:

> The use of potable domestic water for the irrigation of greenbelt areas, including, but not limited to, cemeteries, golf courses, parks, and highway landscaped areas, is a waste or an unreasonable use of such water within the meaning of Section 2 of Article X of the California Constitution when reclaimed water which the state board, after notice and a hearing, finds meets the following conditions is available:
>
> (a) The source of reclaimed water is of adequate quality for such use and is available for such use.
>
> (b) Such reclaimed water may be furnished to such greenbelt areas at a reasonable cost for facilities

for such delivery. In determining reasonable cost, the state board shall consider all relevant factors, including, but not limited to, the present and projected costs of supplying potable domestic water to affected greenbelt areas and the present and projected costs of supplying reclaimed water to such areas, and shall find that the cost of supplying such reclaimed water is comparable to, or less than, the cost of supplying such potable domestic water.

(c) After concurrence with the State Department of Health Services, the use of reclaimed water from the proposed source will not be detrimental to public health.

(d) Such use of reclaimed water will not adversely affect downstream water rights, will not degrade water quality, and is determined not to be injurious to plant life. The state board may require a public agency or person subject to this article to furnish such information as may be relevant to making the finding required by this section.[770]

This legislative finding on the importance of water reuse is repeated elsewhere. The Water Code also provides:

A person or public agency...shall not use water from any source of quality suitable for potable domestic use of the irrigation of greenbelt areas when suitable reclaimed water is available as provided in Section 13550. ...[771]

The State Board can mandate local agencies to undertake reuse programs and local agencies can require its customers to use reclaimed water in lieu of potable water if the reclaimed water is not more expensive than potable water.[772]

In the early 1990's, a series of statutes encouraged reuse for a variety of specific uses, including: [773]

(1)   residential landscaping;[774]

(2)   floor trap priming, cooling towers and air-conditioning devices;[775] and

(3)   toilet and urinal flushing in structures.[776]

In these situations, "any public agency" may require the use of recycled water if the water satisfies Water Code Section 13550 (as determined by the State Board); use does not diminish existing water rights and the irrigation system meets Health Department requirements.[777] These laws are curious in that any agency can mandate reuse but the State Board must make findings. An interesting issue arises if a water purveyor wishes to exercise its independent power to prohibit waste and mandate conservation.

The growing popularity of water reuse is starting to generate disputes over the ownership of untreated effluent from wastewater treatment plants distributed as recycled water. Such disputes may arise when a purveyor not ready to use the effluent attempts to block another purveyor about to embark on a reuse program.[778]

CHAPTER 10

INTERGOVERNMENTAL RELATIONS

In the hierarchy of American government, the federal government is supreme by virtue of the United States Constitution. The same Constitution guarantees a role for state government. At the state level, the California Constitution similarly says state government preempts local agencies but guarantees a role for local government. The state has adopted a few statutes dealing with the relationships among local agencies. Because the hierarchy of government is mainly based on constitutional law, most details of have been worked out by the courts.

The U.S. Constitution is the supreme law of the land; this establishes the prime position of the federal government. Some of the most important events in U.S. history occurred because of the need to define federal supremacy.[779] Under the supremacy clause, if Congress enacts a program *it has authority to enact*, the federal executive branch may implement the program and other levels of government cannot interfere.[780] (The italicized portions of the preceding sentence has been overlooked during the last decade.)

Under one line of cases, the Court determines whether Congress has shown an intent to *occupy the field*.[781] With this approach, other levels of government are completely barred from acting in the area. With another line of cases, the Court conducts a *conflict analysis*.[782] Under this approach, the Court bars state or local action only to the extent it directly conflicts with a federal enactment. The Court seems to choose between these two theories on the basis of whether it wishes to overturn the local enactments. Legal scholars have much to argue about.

Seldom does the law create a rule without exceptions. Historically, the supremacy clause included a major exception because the U.S. Constitution reserves jurisdiction to the states over matters of state concern.[783] The Court once held the terms and conditions of public employment were protected from federal interference.[784] More recently, the Court adopted a different test: if a matter was part of a congressional program, the supremacy clause applies. The court now holds federal wage and hour laws apply to public employees.[785]

California allocates jurisdiction between state and local government in a manner similar to the U.S. supremacy clause. Under the California "preemption" doctrine, local government cannot enact laws that conflict with a state law when the state legislature intends to occupy the area.[786] Like the state's rights provision of the U.S. Constitution, the State is theoretically powerless to act in fields that are "municipal affairs." Like "states rights," "municipal affairs" have been consistently eroded over the years. The court has stated:

> Because the various sections of article XI fail to define municipal affairs, it becomes necessary for the courts to decide, under the facts of each case, whether the subject matter under discussion is of municipal or statewide concern.[787]

> No exact definition of the term 'municipal affairs' can be formulated, and the courts have made no attempt to do so, but instead have indicated that judicial interpretation is necessary to give it meaning in each controverted case. The comprehensive nature of the power is, however, conceded in all the decisions...[788]

The California Supreme Court acknowledged how subjective the preemption doctrine has become:

> Justice Richardson acknowledged this Court's ineluctable duty under the "municipal affairs" clause to allocate political supremacy between the Legislature and charter cities "without the benefit of guidance from history, constitutional tradition, or sharply delineated principles." The approach to that demanding task historically taken in our cases has been one of ad hoc intuition informed by pragmatic common sense rather than a rigid fidelity to some theoretical model. In an area of constitutional law so deeply marked from the beginning by conceptual uncertainty and inherent factual ambiguity, we should not expect doctrinal tidiness: "Constitutions," as Justice Holmes said, "are intended to preserve practical and substantial rights not to maintain theories."[789]

The allocation of jurisdiction among counties, cities and special districts is not part of the Constitution or a comprehensive statutory scheme. The jurisdiction of counties and cities is geographically separated. Interagency issues are more likely to arise between cities and counties and special districts because districts overlap counties and cities. There are a variety of laws directly and indirectly dealing with the relationship among *equal* levels of government. Cooperation is more common than dispute. The conflict typically occurs in two areas: cities and counties adopt planning, zoning and building laws impacting special district projects and cities (and counties) sometimes regulate how special districts provide service.

Under the California Planning Law, districts must present projects to the planning agency for review for compliance with the general plan.[790] Districts are encouraged to submit 5-year capital improvement plans for this purpose.[791] Districts must also request the planning commission to determine whether proposed property acquisition and disposition will be in compliance with the general plan.[792] Failure to comply carries no penalty.[793]

Occasionally, cities or counties will attempt to dictate how a special district will provide service. The preemption doctrine resolves such a conflict by tracing each agency's power back to their respective sources in state law. In a leading case, the Court examined a county regulation dictating the design of pipelines in a new subdivision.[794] The Court found the state law delegated authority to the water district and preempted the county's subdivision controls. This principle has been codified. The "building" and "planning" ordinances of a city or county do not apply to water production, transmission or storage facilities of a public agency purveyor.[795] Further, city and counties cannot charge public agency purveyors' fees for official services.[796] The city or county may require a permit to specify the time, place and manner of placement, and may demand a deposit to ensure street restoration. An inspection fee cannot be charged.[797]

Local agencies often resolve institutional deficiencies by creating partnerships called joint powers authorities.[798] Some problems are too large for a single agency to handle and some too small for the next larger governmental unit. Rather than eliminate the existing agencies, better suited to address other issues, the agencies can form a joint powers authority to specifically deal with the common problem. An authority is created by contract between two or more public agencies to solve common problems. The authority only uses the powers common to both. The Authority's mission is defined by the mutual agreement of the agencies.

The Knox-Cortese Local Government Reorganization Act establishes a framework for dealing with formations, annexations, detachments, mergers, and dissolutions under the auspices of Local Agency Formation Commissions, known as "LAFCO."[799] The LAFCO process is designed to avoid interagency conflict by acting carefully when entities are formed or boundaries revised.

In the case of water purveyors, anti-paralleling laws are designed to prevent wasteful competition for customers.[800] Under the service duplication law, a public water agency which extends pipelines into an area served by a public utility must pay the utility for the value of facilities rendered functionally obsolete.[801]

The separation of powers doctrine is important to how each government operates but not to how government agencies interact. The separation of powers doctrine is not mentioned expressly by the United States or California Constitution. The documents separate power among branches of government. More often than not, separation of powers crises arise on the federal level.

> [I]t remains a basic principle of our constitutional scheme that one branch of the government may not intrude upon the central prerogatives of another. …
>
> Even when a branch does not arrogate power to itself, moreover, the Separation of

> Powers Doctrine requires that a branch not impair another in the performance of its constitutional duties. ...

> Another strand of our separation of powers jurisprudence, has developed to prevent Congress from forsaking its duties.[802]

The doctrine applies with equal force to state or even local relationships.

It is fair to say the judiciary was the least important branch of the federal government at our nation's founding. The Separation of Powers Doctrine seems to relegate the judiciary to a very small role. That changed with the landmark decision in *Marbury v. Madison*.[803] The United States Supreme Court decided it had the power to review certain legislation despite the Separation of Powers Doctrine. The facts of this case are interesting. President Adams signed but did not deliver general appointments during the end of his administration. During the transition from the administration of President Jefferson, he instructed Secretary of State Madison to withhold the commission. Marbury sought a Supreme Court writ to compel Madison to honor the appointment under the Judiciary Act of 1789. Chief Justice Marshall found the Act of 1789 to be unconstitutional. This means two things: the Constitution prevails over legislation, and the court has the power to decide when a conflict exists.

Judicial power has been exercised wisely or unwisely since. Legislative enactments (at the federal, state or local level) must be implemented by the executive without interference by the judiciary. However, someone has to decide whether the Legislature has exceeded its constitutional authority or violates the Separation of Powers Doctrine. Someone has to interpret vague legislation. That someone is the Court. The court's powers with respect to legislation are passive. The Court cannot write laws. The power to interpret laws is not misused to interpret the law out of existence, most of the time the Court is not second-guessing the Legislature. Only when a legislative decision is unconstitutional or violates the Separation of Powers Doctrine can the Court overturn the decision.

The Court's deference to the Legislature becomes complicated in practice. Often the complications arise because it is difficult to define what constitutes a legislative act. For example, when the board of directors of a water district adopts a rate structure to discourage water consumption, the board is acting in a legislative capacity. When the rates are subsequently challenged, the Court must limit its review to whether the rates have *any* rational connection to water conservation. The Court will be tempted to decide whether the rates are actually effective in promoting water conservation. Under the Separation of Powers Doctrine, the Court may determine if there is a rational connection to the legislative purpose but may not determine whether the purpose is actually being accomplished.

Most of the executive branch's work involves the implementation of laws and policies adopted by the legislative branch. The legislative and judicial branches are usually wise enough to avoid being drawn into questioning whether the executive branch is efficiently and effectively implementing legislative decisions. However, the current debate over the structure of government will inevitably produce some clash in this area.

Sometimes the executive branch fails to implement programs adopted by the Legislature. Given the lack of judicial precedent in this area, however, it appears this problem arises infrequently. Surprisingly, the converse is not true. The Courts have overturned statutes delegating legislative authority to the executive branch. In effect, the Court is saying to the Legislature it cannot avoid making difficult legislative decisions by delegating issues to the executive branch.

ENDNOTES

1   Only one per diem can be earned per day regardless of the number of meetings or events attended by a director.

2   Public Utilities Code Section 22407.

3   Water Code Section 20201.

4   Water Code Section 20202.

5   Directors of a private corporation are not considered employees for federal income tax purposes. *Steffons v. Commissioner* (1084) TC Memo 1984-592; Special ruling March 8, 1945, 454 CCH 6202.

6   Government Code Section 53232.2(d).

7   Government Code Section 53232.2(c).

8   See 75 Ops. Cal.Atty.Gen 20 (1992) (district cannot pay expenses of spouse at conference).

9   Retired directors elected before 1998 can obtain group medical insurance after twelve years of office holding. Directors elected after 1998 are not permitted to continue to be enrolled in the agency's group health plan after they cease holding office. Government Code Section 53208.

10 83 Ops.Cal.Atty.Gen. 124 (2000). But see, 89 Ops.Cal.Atty.Gen. 107 (2006) (general law city can redirect premiums to deferred compensation plan).

11 *Department of Alcoholic Beverage Control v. Alcoholic Beverage Control Appeals Board* (2006) 40 Cal.4th 1, 50 Cal.Rptr.3d 585.

12 Government Code Section 87406.3.

13 See e.g., Water Code Section 71274 (municipal water district)

14 See e.g., Public Utilities Code Section 22410 (airport district).

15 Many agencies are able to criminally enforce ordinances only for limited purposes. See e.g., Water Code §71600 (municipal water district enforcement of sanitation regulations).

16 For example, an irrigation district cannot act by ordinance.

17 Government Code Section 36931, *et seq.*

18 Some ordinances have a longer waiting period. For example, a director's compensation ordinance under the Uniform Act for Director's Compensation has a 60-day waiting period.

19 Elections Code §9340, *et seq.*

20 Elections Code §9142.

21 Elections Code §9141.

22 Elections Code §9144.

23 The initiative process is largely unregulated. But this important, and often abused process, is beginning to come under closer scrutiny. In 1998, a statute banned foreign government contributions to promote initiatives (or referendum or recall.).

24 Elections Code §9200, *et seq.*

25 *City of Burbank v. Burbank-Glendale-Pasadena Airport Authority* (2003) 113 Cal.App.4th 469, 6 Cal.Rptr.3d 367 (local initiative cannot restrict airport operations because of conflict with State Aeronautics Act).

26 *DeVita v. County of Napa* (1995) 9 Cal.4th 763; 38 Cal.Rptr.2d 699.

27 Govt. Code §50075, *et seq.*

28 Elections Code §9205.

29 Elections Code §9206.

30 Elections Code §9208.

31 Elections Code §9214.

32 *Id.*

33 *Id.*

34 Elections Code §9211.

35 Elections Code §9214(b).

36 Elections Code §9217.

37 Robert's Rules of Order, Revised (1970), p. xlii. Further references in this section are to Robert's Rules unless otherwise indicated.

38 The rules concerning secondary motions are responsible for most of the trepidation and confusion surrounding parliamentary law.

39 Elections Code Section 13307.

40 Government Code Section 85703. Some agencies have used this authority to limit the *amount* of campaign contributions. Real campaign reform is possible by prohibiting campaign contributions by vendors, consultants, and those planning to do business with the agency.

41 Government Code Section 1770.

42 *Ibid.*

43 Government Code Section 53227.

44 California Constitution, Article XX, Section 3.

45 Government Code Section 1780(a).

46 *Ibid.*

47 Government Code Section 1780(c).

48 *Ibid.*

49 Government Code Section 1780(a).

50 Government Code Section 1780(b).

51 Government Code Section 1780(c)(1).

52 Elections Code Section 11000, *et seq.*

53 An officer who is serving the first or last six months of a term or who has had a recall election favorably decided in the prior six months may not be recalled. Elections Code Section 11007.

54 Recall proponents who argue the process is fundamental to a democracy forget the person being recalled was elected, and the recall process is instituted on the initiative of a relatively small group, often a special interest group.

55 The county election official may be the county clerk or registrar of voters. The county clerk fulfills the function of the county election official in the case of a city recall petition.

56 Government Code Section 3060.

57 *People v. Ward* (1890) 85 Cal. 585, 24 P. 785.

58 *Steiner v. Superior Court* (1996) 50 Cal.App.4th 1771, 58 Cal.Rptr.2d 668.

59 Government Code Section 54956.

60 With small agencies, the CEO is directly responsible for personnel matters. In larger organizations, a human resources director will

report to the CEO on personnel matters. In either event, the CEO must administer the personnel program. These skills are difficult to master.

61 The severance cannot exceed eighteen months. Government Code Section 53260.

62 Some agencies attempt to list what may constitute cause and inevitably, the list will be incomplete. "Cause" is a longstanding concept in personnel practice and despite its apparent ambiguity, has a meaning that is known by most practitioners.

63 California Constitution, Article XX Section 3.

64 *Bagley v. Washington Township Hospital District* (1966) 65 Cal.2d 499; 55 Cal.Rptr. 401.

65 *Garcetti v. Ceballos* (2006) 547 US 410, 126 S.Ct. 1951, 164 L.Ed.2d 689.

66 *Lubey v. San Francisco* (1979) 98 Cal.App.3d 340, 159 Cal.Rptr. 440. A name clearing hearing is just that, not an opportunity to recover the job. Needless to say, the name clearing can generate a controversy and make publicly elected officials uncomfortable.

67 Large organizations can afford to engage permanent, full-time counsel, treasurer, secretary and auditor. Most local agencies engage part-time counsel, appoint a member of the governing body as treasurer and secretary, and engage part-time independent auditors. Counsel and auditors are usually selected during a consultant hiring process.

68 This will allow the board to evaluate cost of services but the board cannot expect the lawyer to work more time than estimated and the lawyer cannot expect the agency to pay for more time than estimated, so the fees may have to be adjusted in the long-term.

69 Agencies can pay lawyers any amount and under any terms. The State Bar encourages lawyers to have a written professional services agreement which discusses consumer rights, including the right to arbitrate fee disputes. The lawyer must disclose the nature and extent of malpractice insurance coverage. Potential conflicts of interest must be disclosed. A written agreement is a convenient instrument to memorialize the disclosures.

70 Government Code Section 4529.10.

71 Civil Code Section 2782.8.

72 California Constitution Article XX, Section 3.

73 Govt. Code §50085.

74 Govt. Code §50084.

75 Govt. Code §12940.

76 Govt. Code §12945.2.

77 Govt. Code §12940.

78 42 U.S.C.A. §12132.

79 As discussed elsewhere in this work, these laws also mandate physical access to public facilities and services.

80 *Sterling v. Fair Employment and Housing Commission* (1981) 121 Cal. App.3d 791, 175 Cal.Rptr. 548.

81 Govt. Code §12926.1(a).)

82 Govt. Code §12926.1(b).

83 Govt. Code §12961(c).

84 See also, www.ed.gov/about/offices/list/osers/nidrr/index.html

85 Govt. Code §12926(h), 12945(c)(1).

86 Govt. Code §12945.2.

87 Govt. Code §12941.(a).

88 *Id.*

89 Govt. Code §12941(b).

90 (1979) 24 Cal.3d 458, 156 Cal.Rptr. 14.

91 *Soroka v. Dayton Hudson Corp.* (1991) 235 Cal.App.3d 654, 1 Cal. Rptr.2d 77.

92 Chapter 915, Stats. 1992, Section 1.

93 Labor Code §1102.1(b)(1), (2).

94 Govt. Code §12949; see also *Schwenk v. Hartford*, 204 F.3d 1187, 1202 (9th Cir. 2000).

95 Military and Veterans Code §394.

96 Military and Veterans Code §395.1.

97 Govt. Code §50083.

98 *Graham v. Kirkwood Public Utilities District* (1994) 21 Cal.App.4th 1631, 26 Cal.Rptr. 793. See also, 56 Ops. Cal. Atty. Gen 57 (agency may impose residency requirements related to ability of employee to perform service for which she is hired.)

99 Proposition 209.

100 Govt. Code §50085.5(a).

101 *Wygant v. Jackson Board of Education* (1986) 476 U.S. 267, 90 L.Ed.2d 260.

102 476 U.S. at 277, 90 L.Ed.2d at 271.

103 *United States v. Paradise* (1987) 480 U.S. 149, 94 L.Ed.2d 203.

104 480 U.S. at 171, 94 L.Ed.2d at 223.

105 *Johnson v. Transportation Agency* (1987) 480 U.S. 616, 94 L.Ed.2d 615.

106 The U. S. Supreme Court's more recent decision in *Adarand Constructors, Inc. v. Pena* (1995) 519 U.S. 200, 132 L.Ed.2d 158, can be squared with this decision because *Adarand* only says race cannot be the *sole* factor in awarding contracts.

107 Cal. Const. Article I, Section 31 (Prop. 209).

108 See e.g., *Domar Electric Co. v. City of Los Angeles* (1996); 9 Cal.4th 161, 36 Cal.Rptr.2d 521; but see *Monterey Mechanical Company v. Wilson* (9th Cir. 1997) 125 F.3d 702.

109 *Nelson v. Thornberg* (E.D.Pa.1983) 567 F.Supp. 369. But see, *Carter v. Bennett* (1988) 840 F.Supp. 63.

110 *County of Fresno v. Fair Employment and Housing Commission* (1991) 226 Cal.App.3d 1541, 277 Cal.Rptr. 557. But see, *Vickers v. Veterans Administration* (1982) 549 F.Supp. 85 (no accommodation required for nonsmokers).

111 *Ackerman v. Western Electric Co., Inc.* (9th Cir. 1988) 860 F.2d 1514.

112 *Arneson v. Heckler* (8th Cir. 1989) 879 F.2d 393.

113 *Fields v. Lyng* (D.Md. 1988) 705 F.Supp.1134.

114 *Ackerman v. Western Electric Co., Inc., supra.*

115 *Arneson v. Heckler, supra.*

116 *Arneson v. Heckler, supra* (back pay and reinstatement); *Nelson v. Thornburgh, supra* (injunction to provide accommodation).

117 Military and Veterans Code §395.1.

118 Military and Veterans Code §395.1(b).

119 Labor Code §6404.5.

120 Labor Code Section 6404.5(c).

121 Labor Code Section 6404.5(c)(14).

122 Labor Code Section 6404.5(d)(13).

123 41 U.S.C.A. Section 701-707; 3 CFR 224.

124 *Collins v. Longview Fibre Co.* (9th Cir. 1995) 63 F.3d 828; see also Govt. Code §8350, *et seq.* (state agency work plan).

125 49 U.S.C.A. 31306, Omnibus Transportation Employee Testing Acat of 1991 (PL 102-143); See also 49 CFR 382, 101.

126 *Loder v. City of Glendale* (1997) 14 Cal.4th 846, 59 Cal.Rptr.2d 696.

127 *AFL-CIO v. California Unemployment Insurance Appeals Board* (1994) 23 Cal.App.4th 1306.

128 IBEW, *Local 1245 v. U.S. NRC* (9th Cir. 1992) 966 F.2d 521, 525, fn.9; *Taylor v. O'Grady* (7th Cir. 1989) 888 F.2d 1189, 1196.

129 IBEW, *Local 1245 v. U.S. NRC, supra*, at 526.

130 See *Semore v. Pool, supra*, 217 Cal.App.3d at 1097; *Gerdom v. Continental Airlines, Inc.* (9th Cir. 1982) 692 F.2d 602, 609; *Diaz v. Pan Am World Airways, Inc.* (5th Cir. 1971) 442 F.2d 385, 389 (hiring discrimination).

131 *Skinner v. Railway Labor Executives' Association* (1989) 489 U.S.602, 103 L.Ed.2d 639.

132 *Skinner v. Railway Labor Executives' Associaiton, supra, Treasury Employees v. Von Raab* (1989) 489 U.S. 656.

133 *Skinner v. Railway Labor Executives' Association, supra*, at 624.

134 *Treasury Employees v. Von Raab, supra*.

135 *Acton v. VCR Nonik Schook District* (9th Cir. 1995) 66 F.3d 217.

136 Cal. Const. Article I, Section 1.

137 *Wilkenson v. Times Mirror Corporation* (1989) 215 Cal.App.3d 1034, 264 Cal.Rptr. 194.

138 *Hill v. National Collegiate Athletic Association* (1994) 7 Cal.4th 1, 26 Cal.Rptr.2d 834.

139 Govt. Code §24001.

140 *Wilbur v. Office of City Clerk* (1956) 143 Cal.App.2d 636, 644.

141 *Spreckels v. Graham* (1924) 194 Cal.516. Peace officers are "officers." Govt. Code §1031. See also Penal Code §§830, *et seq*.

142 Govt. Code Section 3504.5 empowers local agencies to adopt rules and regulations governing employer-employee relations after consultation with employee groups. This process typically results in the adoption of an employer-employee relations ordinance or resolution which contains the procedures which the various parties will follow.

143 Govt. Code §3541.3(a).

144 Govt. Code §§3544 to 3544.9.

145 Govt. Code §3504 (local agency employees); Govt. Code §3529 (educational employees).

146 Govt. Code §3505 (local agency employees); Govt. Code §3543.3 (educational employees), cf. Govt. Code §3530 (state employees).

147 Govt. Code §3505.1 (local agency employees).

148 The law dealing with school employees establishes the independent Public Employment Relations Board (PERB) to act as an independent commission to settle employee relations issues.

149 Since the fact-finder will end up taking a "side," it is unusual and unwise to allow a mediator or conciliator to act as a fact finder because the mediator's neutral and confidential status will be jeopardized.

150 Govt. Code §3509.

151 *McCoy v. Superior Court* (2001) 87 Cal.App.4th 354, 104 CR 2d 504.

152 See e.g. *San Diego Teacher's Assn. v. Superior Court of San Diego County* (1979) 24 Cal.3d 1, 154 Cal.Rptr. 893, 593 P.2d 838 (strikes illegal unless authorized by statute); *Baker v. Wadsworth* (1970) 6 Cal.App.3d 253, 85 Cal.Rptr. 880 (strike may be grounds for dismissal of employee). But see, *IBEW v. Gridley* (1983) 34 Cal.3d 191, 193 Cal.Rptr. 518 (strike not grounds for decertifying union or for dismissing employee unless duration indicates abandonment of position.)

153 (1985) 38 Cal.3d 564, 214 Cal.Rptr. 424.

154 Govt. Code §1157.4.

155 *Renken v. Compton City School District* (1962) 207 Cal.App.2d 106, 24 Cal.Rptr. 347.

156 Govt. Code §1157.4.

157 Govt. Code §3502.5(b).

158 *Ford Motor Co. v. Huffman* (1953) 345 U.S. 330, 97 L.Ed. 1048.

159 Public agencies are not required to participate in the California State Disability Income Act (SDI). Most public agencies participate since the program is funded only by employee contributions.

160 29 U.S.C. Section 203.

161 Time-off by the next pay period will be considered reasonable. A longer delay must be justified in a case-for-case basis.

162 Labor Code §510.

163 Govt. Code §12945.2(c)(2).

164 Govt. Code §12945.2(a).

165 Govt. Code §12945.2(c)(3).

166 Govt. Code §12945.2(e), (h).

167 Govt. Code §12945.2(a).

168 Govt. Code §12945.2(r).

169 Govt. Code §12945.2(s).

170 Unemployment Insurance Code §605.

171 Govt. Code §53200 *et seq.*

172 Govt. Code §§53201, 53205, 53205.1; See also 76 Ops. Cal. Atty. Gen. 91 (dependant coverage for retired employees does not require "specific declaration of policy").

173 Govt. Code §53216.

174 Govt. Code §53200.

175 Labor Code §233(a).

176 *Ibid.*

177 *Ibid.*

178 *City of Long Beach v. Allen* (1956) 143 Cal.App.2d 35, 38, 300 P.2d 356.

179 *Kern v. City of Long Beach* (1947) 29 Cal.2d 848, 851, 179 P.2d 799.

180 *DiGiacinto v. Ameriko-Omspr Corporation* (1997) 59 Cal.App.4th 629, 69 Cal.Rptr.2d 300.

181 *Williams v. County of Los Angeles* (1978) 22 Cal.App.3d 731, 150 Cal. Rptr. 475, 586 P.2d 956 ("reoccurring" employer); *IBEW v. Gridley, supra,* (any non-civil service employee who has a right not to be discharged without cause.)

182 See *Williams v. City of Los Angeles* (1982) 130 Cal.App.3d 682, 181 Cal.Rptr. 868 (no *Skelly* for part-time employees); *Murden v. Sacramento* (1984) 160 Cal.App.3d 302, 206 Cal.Rptr. 699 (temporary, part-time not entitled to *Skelly* but entitled to *Lubey* rights); *Schultz v. Regents of the University of California* (1984) 160 Cal.App.3d 768, 206 Cal.Rptr. 910 (no *Skelly* rights for reclassification of positions); *Turturici v. Redwood City* (1987) 190 Cal.App.3d 1447, 236 Cal.Rptr. 53 (personnel evaluation does not constitute punitive action within meaning of Peace Officers Bill of Rights); *Siegert v. Gilley* (1990) 500 U.S. 226, 114 L.Ed.2d 277 (negative letter does not deprive liberty interest); see also *Phillips*

v. California State Personnel Board (1986) 184 Cal.App.3d 651, 229 Cal.Rptr. 502 (collective bargaining agreement may supplement discharge procedures but the procedures must still comply with due process requirements.)

183 *Lubey v. San Francisco* (1979) 98 Cal.App.3d 340, 159 Cal.Rptr. 440; *Gaydowski v. County of Los Angeles* (1984) 158 Cal.App.3d 406, 204 Cal.Rptr. 643); *Phillips v. Credit Service Commission of the County of San Diego* (1987) 192 Cal.App.3d 996, 237 Cal.Rptr. 751 (no back pay for *Lubey* violation, public disclosure necessary for damages); *Heger v. City of Costa Mesa* (1991) 231 Cal.App.3d 42, 282 Cal.Rptr. 341 (reserve officer entitled to hearing).

184 *Bagley v. Washington Township Hospital District* (1966) 65 Cal.2d 499, 55 Cal.Rptr. 401, 421 P.2d 409.

185 Government Code Section 12940. The California Attorney General concluded it is unlawful for a public agency to discriminate against homosexuals in employment. (66 Ops. Cal. Atty. Gen. 486.)

186 Even volunteers can receive protection. See *Hyland v. Wonder* (9th Cir. 1992) 97 F.2d 1129.

187 Government Code Sections 53298, 53296(c).

188 Government Code Section 532998.5.

189 2 Cal. Code of Regs. Section 7287.6.

190 Government Code Section 12940(h)(1).

191 *Ellison v. Brady* (9th Cir. 1991) 924 F.2d 872.

192 Government Code Section 12950 (minimum requirements to ensure harassment free workplace).

193 *Janken v. Hughes Electronics* (1996) 46 Cal.App.4th 55, 53 Cal. Rptr.2d 741.

194 A temporary employee cannot force an accommodation which results in permanent status. *Jenkins v. County of Riverside* (2006) 138 Cal.App.4th 593, 41 Cal.Rptr.3d 686; *Raine v. City of Burbank* (2006) 135 Cal.App.4th 1215, 37 Cal.Rptr.3d 899.

195 *Sutton v. United Air Lines* (1999) 527 US 471.

196 *Murphy v. United Parcel Service, Inc.* (1999) 527 US 516.

197 *Wellington v. Lyon County School* (9th Cir. 1999) 187 F.3d 1150.

198 *Gelfo v. Lockheed Martin Corp.* (2006) 140 Cal.App.4th 34, 43 Cal. Rptr.3d 874.

199 Government Code Section 12945(a).

200 Government Code Section 12945(b).

201 Government Code Section 12956(c).

202 *Bagley v. Washington Township Hosp. Dist.* (1969) 65 Cal.2d 499, 55 Cal.Rptr. 401; *Hyland v. Wonder* (9ᵗʰ Cir. 1992) 972 F.2d 1129 (volunteer workers).

203 Here's another area where public employees have special privileges because their employer is a government body.

204 *Waters v. Churchill* (1994) 511 US 661, 128 L.Ed.2d 686.

205 *Jordan v. Workers' Comp. Appeals Bd., et al.* (1985) 175 Cal.App.3d 162, 220 Cal.Rptr. 554.

206 *Jackson v. County of Los Angeles* (1997) 60 Cal.App.4ᵗʰ 171, 70 Cal. Rptr.2d 96.

207 Government Code Section 1091.5.

208 Government Code Section 1091. Section 1091.5(a)(9) is the same as Section 1091(b)(13). The first does not require disclosure and abstention; the second does.

209 Government Code Section 1092.

210 *Carson Redevelopment Agency v. Padilla* (2006) 140 Cal.App.4ᵗʰ 1323, 44 Cal.Rptr.3d 881.

211 Government Code Section 1097.

212 Government Code Section 87100.

213 Government Code Sections 91000(b), 91002. An official is not guilty of aiding and abetting violations merely by participating in a decision where another official has a conflict. Letter to Janet Lealy (March 1, 1995) FPPC File No. A-95-038.

214 "Income" does not include campaign contributions or salary, benefits or expense reimbursement paid by a public entity or per diem paid by a 501(c)(3) charitable corporation. Government Code Section 82030. As a result, officials can participate in non-contractual decisions involving these matters. See also Letter to Phillip Romney (March 23, 2003) FPPC File No. A-99-292 (decision to indemnify and defend lawsuit).

215 Government Code Section 87103.

216 The Political Reform Act authorizes the FPPC to adopt rules and regulations implementing the Act. FPPC has issued numerous

advice letters, opinions, rules and regulations interpreting the non-contractual conflicts of interest laws. The rules, regulations, letters and opinions of the FPPC are the interpretive base for this body of law.

217 2 Cal. Code of Regs., Section 18700 *et seq.*

218 The regulations contain multiple negatives and many provisions are unintelligible.

219 2 Cal. Code of Regs., Section 18708(a).

220 2 Cal. Code of Regs., Section 18708(c).

221 2 Cal. Code of Regs., Section 18708(b).

222 Letter to James Heisinger, Jr. (November 6, 1995) FPPC File No. A-95-333.

223 2 Cal. Code of Regs., Section 18703.

224 2 Cal. Code of Regs., Section 18703(b).

225 2 Cal. Code of Regs., Section 18703.1.

226 2 Cal. Code of Regs., Section 18703.5(a). A good faith effort to identify multiple sales must be used in making this calculation.

227 Letter to Wallace Peck (May 5, 1992) FPPC File No. 1-92-215; See also A-84-108 (disqualification of director-renter); Letter to DeVoe (March 12, 1993) FPPC File No. 1-93-094 (director-developer); Letter to Weinkle (April 17, 1992) FPPC File No. 1-91-484 (director-developer).

228 2 Cal. Code of Regs., Section 18703(b).

229 2 Cal. Code of Regs., Section 18702(b).

230 2 Cal. Code of Regs., Section 18702.1(a)(1).

231 2 Cal. Code of Regs., Section 18702.1(a)(2). Councilman attorney may participate in decision regarding workers' compensation matters affecting his law firm unless the decision will have a material financial effect on the councilman. Letter to Robert S. Bower (January 1995) FPPC File No. 1-94-406.

232 2 Cal. Code of Regs., Section 18702.1(a)(3).

233 2 Cal. Code of Regs., Section 19702(a)(4). Office holders may not participate in decisions pertaining to defense of litigation seeking punitive damages because personal interests are affected. Letter to David Olivas (April 4, 1995) FPPC File No. A-95-068.

234 2 Cal. Code of Regs., Section 18702.1(b).

235 *Id.*

236 *Id.*

237 2 Cal. Code of Regs., Section 18702.2(a).

238 2 Cal. Code of Regs., Section 18702.2(b).

239 2 Cal. Code of Regs., Section 18702.2(c).

240 2 Cal. Code of Regs., Section 18702.2(g).

241 2 Cal. Code of Regs., Section 18702.3(a)(1).

242 2 Cal. Code of Regs., Section 18702.3(a)(2).

243 2 Cal. Code of Regs., Section 18702.3(a).

244 2 Cal. Code of Regs., Section 18702.3(b).

245 2 Cal. Code of Regs., Section 18702.4(a).

246 2 Cal. Code of Regs., Section 18702.4(b).

247 2 Cal. Code of Regs., Section 18702.4(c).

248 2 Cal. Code of Regs., Section 18702.4(d).

249 2 Cal. Code of Regs., Section 18702.4(e).

250 2 Cal. Code of Regs., Section 18702.5(a).

251 2 Cal. Code of Regs., Section 18702.5(b).

252 2 Cal. Code of Regs., Section 18702.5(c).

253 2 Cal. Code of Regs., Section 18702.5(d).

254 2 Cal. Code of Regs., Section 18702.5(e).

255 2 Cal. Code of Regs., Section 18702.5(f).

256 2 Cal. Code of Regs., Section 18702.5(c).

257 2 Cal. Code of Regs., Section 18704.3(e).

258 2 Cal. Code of Regs., Section 18704.3(c).

259 2 Cal. Code of Regs., Section 18704. The FPPC investigators occasionally press claims based on violation of Section 1090 (contracts). The FPPC lacks jurisdiction in this area.

260 Letter to Glenn A. Miller (February 21, 1991) FPPC File No. 1-91-066 and letter to Joe Pandit (May 6, 1992) FPPC File

No. A-92-172.

261 Letter to Minna Williams (March 19, 1992) FPPC File No. 1-92-140.

262 Government Code Section 53227.

263 Letter to Fred Galante (December 23, 1997) FPPC No. A-97-585; Letter to Phillip Romney (March 23, 2000) FPPC File No. A-99-292.

264 *City of Vernon v. Central Basin Municipal Water District* (1999) 69 Cal.App.4th 508, 81 Cal.Rptr.2d 650. Only about two dozen utilities were served by the District.

265 Letter to Anthony Condotti (July 9, 1999) FPPC File No.

A-99-154; See also Letter to Michael Woods (April 19, 1999) FPPC File No. A-99-089 (water conservation measures).

266 Letter to Bill Daniels (January 28, 1999) FPPC File No. I-98-306.

267 Government Code Section 1098.

268 See e.g., 37 Ops.Cal.Atty.Gen 21. But see, 75 Ops.Cal.Atty.Gen. 10 (No. 91-906). (*Quo warranto* not filed for water district director and council member because only four months remains on term of office.)

269 See e.g. 30 Ops. Cal. Atty. Gen. 184 (councilman and transit district director); 33 Ops. Cal. Atty. Gen. 49 (council member and director of District Agriculture Assoc.); 37 Ops. Cal. Atty. Gen. 21 (council member and county water district director); 91 Ops. Cal. Atty. Gen. 98 (council member and sanitation district director); 48 Ops. Cal. Atty. Gen. 141 (council member and school district trustee); 58 Ops. Cal. Atty. Gen. 241 (district attorney and school district trustee); 58 Ops. Cal. Atty. Gen. 323 (county planning commission and water district director); 63 Ops. Cal. Atty. Gen. 610 (county planning commission and city planning commission); 63 Ops. Cal. Atty. Gen. 916 (county supervisor and regional air quality board); 64 Ops. Cal. Atty. Gen. 137 (county supervisors and public utility district director); 64 Ops. Cal. Atty. Gen. 288 (county planning commissioner and county water district director); 64 Ops. Cal. Atty. Gen. 795 (county supervisor outside activities); 65 Ops. Cal. Atty. Gen. 606 (council member and school district board member); 66 Ops. Cal. Atty. Gen. 176 (county fire chief and member of board of supervisors); 66 Ops. Cal. Atty. Gen. 293 (county planning commissioner and city planning commissioner); 66 Ops. Cal. Atty. Gen. 383 (school district trustee and "full-time city attorney); 67 Ops. Cal. Atty. Gen. 347 (city attorney and airport authority board); 67 Ops. Cal. Atty. Gen. 409 (county water district general manager and board of supervisors); 68 Ops. Cal. Atty. Gen. 7 (deputy sheriff

and member of board of supervisors); 68 Ops. Cal. Atty. Gen. 240 (county committee on school organizations and school district trustees); 69 Ops. Cal. Atty. Gen. (Suppl) 1 (community services district director and hospital district administrator or superintendent of schools or fire captain); 73 Ops. Cal. Atty. Gen. 268 (county water district and school district); 92 Ops. Cal. Atty. Gen. 4 (city council and local water districts); 80 Ops. Cal. Atty Gen. 242 (municipal water district director and city treasurer); 84 Ops. Cal. Atty. Gen. 91 (No. 01-502), (City Planning Commissioner and School District Trustee); (86 Ops.Cal.Atty.Gen. 205 (No. 03-901), (irrigation district director and county supervisor).

270 The failure to investigate cannot justify making a false accusation.

271 To terminate an employee, the agency must show a nexus between the unethical conduct and job performance.

272 Government Code Section 89501; 2 Cal. Code of Regs. Section 18930, *et seq.*

273 2 Cal. Code of Regs. Section 18930.

274 Government Code Section 89501. The gift of a dinner for an office holder and spouse does not require the reporting of the value of the gift to the spouse. Letter to Robert Coffman (February 27, 1995) FPPC File No. A-95-046.

275 Government Code Sections 87207 and 87460, *et seq.*

276 Government Code Sections 91000-91019; 2 Cal. Code of Regs. Section 18901. The regulations are not limited to a mailing. Hand delivery of over 200 documents to an organization can violate the law. Letter to Bill Lockyer (July 5, 1989) FPPC File No. A-89-342.

277 2 Cal. Code of Regs. 18901(a)(1), (a)(3), (a)(4). Letter to Michelle Curtis, dated March 18, 1994 (No. A-94-053), says a Chamber of Commerce directory is a mass mailing if any of the costs of directory are paid with City funds. The regulations cover many types of documents. See e.g., Letter to Theodora Giattina (August 5, 1996) FPPC File No. A-96-206 (annual reports); Letter to Arnoldo Beltran (October 31, 1997) FPPC File No. A-97-509 (Newsletters); Letter to Frances Moore (August 24, 1999) FPPC

File No. A-99-234 (Newsletters; Letter to Don Gartner (August 27, 1999) FPPC File No. A-99-224 (Newsletters). But see, Letter to Andrew Peterson (February 23, 1999) FPPC File No. A-99-013 (Websites not covered).

278 Government Code Section 89501(a)(2)(B).

279 Id. At (b)(2) through (b)(10). Letter to Richard Mayer (May 8, 1995) FPPC No. A-95-147 (reply to inquiries).

280 Letter to Jane Moore (July 30, 1998) FPPC File No. A-98-171.

281 A mailing list does not lose its unsolicited character if the list includes a purge notice similar to the following: "The law does not permit this office to use public funds to keep you updated on items of interest unless you specifically request it to do so."

282 2 Cal. Code of Regs. Section 18901(b)(1).

283 Letter to Al Vollbrecht (April 21, 1997 FPPC No. A-97-155 (Chamber of Commerce); Letter to Frances Moore (August 24, 1999) FPPC File No. A-99-234 (Chamber of Commerce).

284 2 Cal. Code of Regs. Section 18438.2.

285 Government Code Section 85705. Letter to Gail Vasquez-Connolly (May 1, 1997) FPPC No. A-97-181 (planning commissioner cannot serve as treasurer of council member's campaign).

286 Government Code Section 3205.

287 Government Code Section 3205.5.

288 Government Code Section 54953.

289 Government Code Section 54951.

290 Government Code Section 54951.7.

291 Government Code Section 54952.

292 Government Code Section 54952.3. But see, *Farron v. City of San Francisco* (1989) 216 Cal.App.3d 1071, 265 Cal.Rptr. 317.

293 Government Code Section 54952.5.

294 Government Code Section 54952.

295 Government Code Section 54952.2(a).

296 79 Ops. Cal. Atty. Gen. 69.

297 81 Ops. Cal. Atty. Gen. 156 (No. 97-1207.

298 Government Code Section 54952.6.

299 Government Code Section 54952.2(c).

300 Government Code Section 54954.

301 *Id.*

302 Government Code Section 54956,

303 A waiver of notice may be filed by a member with the clerk or secretary of the legislative body prior to the time of the meeting. (*Id.*)

304 Government Code Section 54956.5.

305 Government Code Section 54955.

306 Government Code Section 54954.1.

307 Government Code Section 54954.2(a).

308 Government Code Section 54954.2(b).

309 Government Code Section 54954.2(b)(1).

310 Government Code Section 54954.2(b)(2).

311 Government Code Section 54954.2(b)(3).

312 Government Code Section 54954.2(b).

313 Government Code Section 54956.

314 Government Code Section 54954.3.

315 The public comment section of the meeting is also an opportunity for members of the legislative body or staff to submit brief comments for items not on the agenda.

316 This requirement can be satisfied by allowing comment during committee meetings.

317 Government Code Section 54954(b).

318 Government Code Section 54954.2.

319 Government Code Section 54953(b).

320 Government Code Section 54956.7-54957.8.

321 Government Code Section 54957.1.

322 The appointment or dismissal of non-elective positions of city manager, city attorney, department head, chief administrative officer, general manager, chief engineer, legal counsel, district secretary, auditor, assessor or treasurer may be considered in closed session, but elected officials or other persons appointed by the legislative body are not covered.

323 Government Code Section 54957.6. But see *San Diego Union v. City of San Diego* (1083) 146 Cal.App.3d 947, 196 Cal.Rptr. 45 (salary deliberations must be public when union negotiations not involved).

324 Government Code Section 54957.

325 Government Code Section 54957.9.

326 *Id.*

327 *Id.*

328 Government Code Section 54956.8. See *Sacramento Newspaper Guild, Local 92 v. Sacramento County* (1967) 255 Cal.App.2d 51, 62 Cal.Rptr. 819.

329 Government Code Section 54956.9.

330 Government Code Section 54956.8.

331 Government Code Section 54956.7.

332 Government Code Section 54956.94.

333 Government Code Section 54957.

334 Government Code Section 54957.7. The litigation must be identified before the closed session unless disclosure would prejudice the agency.

335 Government Code Section 54954.5.

336 *Id.*

337 *Trancas Property Owners Association v. City of Malibu* (2006) 138 Cal.App.4th 172, 41 Cal.Rptr.3d 200.

338 89 Ops.Cal.Atty.Gen. 110 (2006).

339 Government Code Section 54957.1(a).

340 Government Code Section 108.

341 *Hamilton v. Town of Los Gatos* (1989) 213 Cal.App.3d 1050, 261 Cal. Rptr. 888.

342 Government Code Section 54957.2.

343 Government Code Section 54954.3(a).

344 Void.

345 Government Code Section 54954.3(b).

346 Government Code Section 54953.3.

347 Government Code Section 54953.5. See also Government Code Section 6091 (radio and television broadcasts are permitted).

348 Government Code Section 6091.

349 Government Code Section 54956.6.

350 Government Code Section 54961.

351 Government Code Section 549575. Writings otherwise exempt from public disclosure under the Public Records Act are exempt from this requirement.

352 *Kindt v. Santa Monica Rent Control Board* (9th Cir. 1995) 67 F.3d 266.

353 76 Ops. Cal. Atty. Gen. 281 No. 93-308, December 15, 1993.

354 Government Code Section 54959.

355 Government Code Section 54960.1(a).

356 Government Code Section 54960.1(b).

357 Government Code Section 54960.1(c).

358 The Act may be violated if a director on the losing side privately asks a director on the prevailing side of a vote to reconsider the vote because the contact could represent a new majority.

359 79 Ops. Cal. Atty. Gen. 69.

360 62 Ops. Cal. Atty. Gen. 150.

361 Government Code Section 6250, *et seq.*

362 Government Code Section 6254.

363 *Los Angeles Unified School District v. Superior Court* (2007) 151 Cal. App.4th 759, 60 Cal.Rptr.3d 445 (2007 DAR 8181).

364 Government Code Section 60200.

365 Government Code Section 60201. Under this section, the board of directors may authorize the destruction of a two-year-old map of the property upon which the district's offices are constructed because such a map is not required by state statute. On the other hand, the board could not authorize the destruction of an inundation map for a reservoir owned by a water district or an airport layout map of an airport owned by an airport district because such maps are required by state statute.

366 Government Code Section 60202. routine video monitoring tapes can be destroyed after one year.

367 Government Code Section 34090.6.

368 Government Code Section 60203.

369 *Ibid.*

370 Only one provision in the Municipal Water District Law of 1911 even mentions public records. Water Code Section 71596 provides: "A district may disseminate information concerning the rights, properties, and activities of the district. Such powers shall not be construed as an exception to the California Public Records Act."

371 Government Code Section 34090.

372 Government Code Section 34090.5.

373 The reserve will decrease when revenues are less than expenditures and will increase when revenues exceed expenditures.

374 Local government has little opportunity to levy excise or income taxes. These taxes are beyond the scope of this work.

375 Legislature is fond of tinkering with the apportionment of *ad valorem* taxes.

376 See e.g., *AB Cellular LA, LLC v. City of Los Angeles* (2007) 150 Cal. App.4th 747, 59 Cal.Rptr.3d 295 (voters must approve tax on use of cell phones).

377 *Collier v. City and County of San Francisco* (2007) 151 Cal.App.4th 1326, 60 Cal.Rptr.3d 698.

378 *Richmond v. Shasta Community Services District* (2004) 32 Cal.4th 409, 9 Cal.Rptr.3d 121.

379 *Bighorn-Desert View Water Agency v. Verjil* (2006) 39 Cal.4th 205, 46 Cal.Rptr.3d 73. See also, *Pajaro Valley Water Management Agency v. Amrhein* (2007) 150 Cal.App.4th 1364, 59 Cal.Rptr.3d 484 (groundwater augmentation charge is property-related and subject to Proposition 218).

380 California Constitution Article XIII D, Section 6(a)(2); Government Code section 53700. Proposition 218 apparently overturned another longstanding rule. Before Proposition 218, the initiative process could not be used to set rates. The Court has held a local initiative can set property related fees as long as the initiative does not require voter approval of future fee increases.

381 The obvious is frequently missing in the Legislature and the court's analysis.

382 Article XIII B Section 6 ("state mandated costs").

383 See e.g., *County of Los Angeles v. California* (1987) 43 Cal.3d 46, 233 Cal.Rptr. 38 (no reimbursement for services uniquely associated with government).

384 *County of Los Angeles v. Commission on State Mandates* (2007) 150 Cal.App.4th 898, 58 Cal.Rptr 3d 762.

385 Presumably, the voters don't mean for government to emulate businesses such as IBM, which disintegrated because its size prevented it from adapting to changes in the market place.

386 Government Code Section 53646.

387 Government Code Section 53600.3.

388 Government Code Section 53600.5.

389 Government Code Section 53646(a)(2).

390 Government Code Section 53646(b)(1).

391 *Ibid.*

392 Government Code Section 53646(g).

393 Government Code Section 53601(a)-(d).

394 Government Code Section 53601(e).

395 Government Code Section 53601(f), (g), (h), (i). How this provision squares with California Constitution Article XVI, Section 17, which prohibits public agencies from lending their credit to private firms is a discussion for another time.

396 Government Code Section 53821.5.

397 Government Code Section 53601. The fund must be registered under the Securities Act of 1940. No commissions can be paid. The fund must have achieved the highest rating of one of the two nationally recognized services, or the fund must be managed by a person registered with the SEC with five years' experience in handling a security of type in the mutual fund with assets of $500,000 or more. Revenue and Taxation Code Section 23701(m).

398 Government Code Section 16429, *et seq*.

399 Government Code Section 53601.

400 Government Code Section 53646(b).

401 Government Code Section 53631, 53635.

402 Government Code Section 53638.

403 Government Code Section 53653.

404 Government Code Section 50569.

405 Government Code Section 50572, only if transferred to housing corporation.

406 Government Code Section 54222. State lands must be offered to local agencies for similar purposes. Government Code Section 11011.1.

407 Government Code Section 54221(b).

408 Government Code Section 54222(a), Health and Safety Code Section 50079. The offer must be sent first-class mail and include the location and a description of the property. Priority must be given to development of such housing in deciding to lease or sell the surplus property.

409 Government Code Section 54222(b).

410 Government Code Section 54222(c).

411 Government Code Section 54222(d).

412 Government Code Section 54222(e).

413 Government Code Section 54222(f).

414 Government Code Section 54223.

415 Government Code Section 54221(e).

416 Government Code Section 1090.

417 40 U.S.C. 276a, *et seq.*

418 18 U.S.C. 874.

419 48 CFR 52.22-26.

420 48 CFR 52.219-8.

421 48 CFR 52.222-55.

422 48 CFR 52.222-36

423 42 U.S.C. 1352.

424 48 CFR 52.223-1, 223-2.

425 24 CFR 85.20(b), (c).

426 Earlier, we discussed the need for the preparation of environmental documents before an agency acquires real property. The environmental document must be completed before the adoption of the resolution of necessity. The property owners can object to the resolution of necessity on the basis of a lack of environmental review if environmental documents are not prepared.

427 Most agency attorneys are probably capable of filing eminent domain cases. However, eminent domain specialists are often hired by agencies.

428 The property owner is required to repay the agency for the amount of the agency's earlier payment, plus the difference between the current value and the amount paid earlier.

429 See *Miller v. McKinnon* (1942) 20 Cal.2d 83, 124 P.2d 34.

430 See *Reams v. Cooley* (1015) 171 Cal. 150, 152 P. 293.

431 *Perry v. Los Angeles* (1909) 157 Cal. 146, 106 P. 410.

432 Public Contracts Code Section 5110. See also, e.g., *Martin v. Corning* (1972) 25 Cal.App.3d 165, 101 Cal.Rptr. 678.

433 Government Code Section 1092.

434 Civil Code Section 3251.

435 A violation of CEQA procedures can also directly impact a public works contract. *COAC, Inc. v. Kennedy Engineers* (1977) 67 Cal.App.3d 916, 136 Cal.Rptr. 890 (the contractor recovers damages from the consultant who prepared documents violating CEQA).

436 Public Contracts Code Section 20101.

437 Labor Code Section 1770.

438 Labor Code Section 1773.1.

439 Labor Code Section 1777.5.

440 Labor Code Section 1861. The contractor is usually also required to provide certificates of automobile, comprehensive general liability, property damage and other types of "insurance," but state law only requires that the agency demand a worker's compensation certificate.

441 Public Contracts Code Section 7104. This provision is not particularly startling because courts usually allow relief for delays caused by *force majeure*. What is unique about this provision is it contains a specific definition of what constitutes an act of God.

442 Government Code Section 4215.

443 Labor Code Section 6705.

444 Public Contracts Code Section 7103.

445 Government Code Section 7550.

446 Public Contracts Code Section 4104.

447 Public Contracts Code Section 20104, *et seq.*

448 Public Contracts Code Section 7104.

449 Public Contracts Code Section 7106.

450 Government Code Section 4201.

451 As will be explained, this problem also arises with respect to joint powers insurance authorities, even though they are not "insurance" companies because the problem is a matter of professional legal ethics, not insurance law.

452 Although *Cumis* involved an insurance carrier, the defendant's status as an insurance company was unimportant to the decision. The court repeatedly refers to the "insurer" and the "insured," but it is clear from context this is just a convenient way to refer to parties.

453 *San Diego Navy Federal Credit Union v. Cumis Ins. Society, Inc.* (1984) 162 Cal.App.3d 358, at page 364.

454 *Id.* At pages 373-374.

455 *Id.* At pages 365-366.

456 *Id.* At pages 373-374.

457 *Id.* At page 375.

458 *Id.* At page 375, footnote 4. This is inconsistent with the Rules of Professional Conduct which state a client's waiver of conflict must be knowledgeable.

459 The Tort Claims Act says claims are not required in limited circumstances. For example, the Act does not require a public agency to file a claim. However, the Act permits agencies to adopt a local regulation covering any subject not covered by the Act. Local agencies should adopt regulations requiring claims to be filed whenever the Act does not require a claim.

460 Government Code Section 815(a). Government employees can be liable under common law theories. Government Code Section 820(a).

461 Government Code Section 815.1(a).

462 Government Code Section 815.4.

463 Government Code Section 815.6.

464 Government Code Section 835, 830(a).

465 Vehicle Code Section 17001.

466 Civil Code Section 54.3.

467 Civil Code Section 3479-3503.

468 Civil Code Section 2100.

469 Education Code 44807.

470 Government Code Section 820.2.

471 Government Code Section 820.8.

472 Government Code Section 822.

473 Government Code Section 818.8 (absolute immunity for agency); Government Code Section 822.2 (qualified immunity for public employee).

474 Government Code Section 821.6.

475 Government Code Section 830(c).

476 Government Code Section 818.2.

477 *Ibid.*

478 *Ibid.*

479 Government Code Section 820.6.

480 Government Code Section 821.8.

481 Government Code Section 818.4, 821.2.

482 Government Code Section 865-867.

483 Civil Code Section 47.

484 *Albers v. City of Los Angeles* (1965) 62 Cal.2d 250, 42 Cal.Rptr. 89; see also *Yee v. Sausalito* (1983) 141 Cal.App.3d 917, 190 Cal.Rptr. 595 (inverse liability for flood damage).

485 *Aaron v. City of Los Angeles* (1974) 40 Cal.App.3d 471, 115 Cal.Rptr. 162; *Baker v. Burbank Airport Authority* (1985) 39 Cal.3d 862, 218 Cal.Rptr. 293 (airplane noise is a continuing nuisance, inverse will lie even if agency lacks power of eminent domain);

Bunch v. Coachella Valley Water District (1989) 214 Cal.App.3d 203, 262 Cal.Rptr. 513; *Yue v. City of Auburn* (1992) 3 Cal.App.4th 751, 4 Cal. Rptr.2d 653 (flood and surface waters distinguished).

486 Civil Procedure Code Section 338.

487 *Holtz v. San Francisco Bay Area Rapid Transit District* (1976) 17 Cal.3d 648, 658, 131 Cal.Rptr. 646, 552 P.2d 430.

488 *Furrey v. City of Sacramento* (1979) 24 Cal.3d 862, 157 Cal.Rptr.684.

489 42 U.S.C.A. Section 1983.

490 California courts have concurrent jurisdiction to hear such claims provided federal rules are followed. *Bach v. County of Butte* (1983) 147 Cal.App.3d 554, 195 Cal.Rptr. 268.

491 *Gilliland v. County of Los Angeles* (1981) 126 Cal.App.3d 610, 179 Cal. Rptr. 73.

492 *Owen v. City of Independence* (1980) 445 U.S. 622, 63 L.Ed.2d 673.

493 *Novich v. City of Los Angeles* (1983) 148 Cal.App.3d 325, 195 Cal. Rptr. 747.

494 *Monell v. New York City Dept. of Soc. Serv.* (1978) 436 U.S. 658; *Bach v. County of Butte, supra; Federer v. Sacramento* (1983) 141 Cal. App.3d 184, 190 Cal.Rptr. 187 (no civil rights liability for agency without policy decision).

495 *Gilbrook v. City of Westminster* (9th Cir. 1999) 177 F.3d 839. But see, *Biggs v. Best, Best & Krieger* (9th Cir. 1999) 189 F.3d (council may threaten to fire city attorney because city attorney fills a policy and confidential position).

496 Government Code Section 825. See also Government Code Section 820.9 (no vicarious liability for governing board members.)

497 Government Code Section 995.

498 Government Code Section 995.2.

499 Government Code Section 996.

500 Government Code Sections 996.4, 825.

501 *Lisa M. v. Henry Mayo Newhall Memorial Hospital* (1995) 12 Cal.4th 291, 58 Cal.Rptr.2d 510; see also Labor Code Sections 1025, 2802.

502 *Mary M. v. City of Los Angeles* (1991) 54 Cal.3d 202, 285 Cal.Rptr. 99.

503 *Farmers Insurance Group v. County of Santa Clara* (1995) 11 Cal.4th 992, 47 Cal.Rptr.2d 478.

504 Letter to Pilot (FPPC No. A-97-265.).

505 CEQA requires the preparation of state guidelines for its implementation. In turn, local agencies are required to adopt "local guidelines" implementing CEQA and the state guidelines. Public Resources Code Section 21083. These guidelines are often referred to as the "State Guidelines" and are contained in 14 Cal. Code of Regs., Section 15000, *et seq.*

506 Public Resources Code Section 21082.

507 14 Cal. Code of Regs. Section 15064. A lead agency is usually, but not always, the first agency to be confronted with the project. In the case of a subdivision development, the city or county would normally be the lead agency. A water agency is normally a responsible agency and *not* a lead agency with respect to a subdivision project.

508 14 Cal. Code of Regs. Section 15096(e).

509 14 Cal. Code of Regs. Section 15096(1), (b).

510 Public Resources Code Section 21065.

511 Public Resources Code Section 21080. But see *Friends of Westwood, Inc. v. City of Los Angeles* (1987) 191 Cal.App.3d 259, 235 Cal.Rptr. 788 (building permits not automatically exempt); compare *Adams Point Preservation Society v. City of Oakland* (1987) 192 Cal.App.3d 203, 237 Cal.Rptr. 273 (demolition permit is ministerial).

512 Public Resources Code Section 21084. Exemptions are narrowly interpreted. *McQueen v. Mid-Peninsula Regional Open Space District* (1988) 202 Cal.App.3d 1136, 249 Cal.Rptr. 439.

513 14 Cal. Code of Regs. Section 15300, *et seq.*

514 14 Cal. Code of Regs. Section 15301.

515 14 Cal. Code of Regs. Section 15062(d).

516 *Friends of Sierra Madre v. City of Sierra Madre* (2001) 25 Cal.4th 165, 105 Cal.Rptr.2d 214.

517 *Banker's Hill, et al. v. City of San Diego* (2006) 139 Cal.App.4th 249, 42 Cal.Rptr.3d 537.

518 14 Cal. Code of Regs. Section 15063(g).

519 14 Cal. Code of Regs. Section 15063(c).

520 14 Cal. Code of Regs. Section 15064(d).

521 14 Cal. Code of Regs. Section 15065.

522 14 Cal. Code of Regs. Section 15070(a). A party attacking the negative declaration must show a "fair argument" exists that the project might have significant adverse environmental impacts. *Newberry Springs Water Association v. San Bernardino* (1984) 150 Cal.App.3d 740, 198 Cal.Rptr. 100.

523 14 Cal. Code of Regs. Section 15074, 15096(d).

524 14 Cal. Code of Regs. Section 15075.

525 14 Cal. Code of Regs. Section 15070(b).

526 14 Cal. Code of Regs. Section 15064; compare *Newberry Springs Water Ass'n v. San Bernardino, supra,* at 105 (existence of public controversy indicates that EIR should be prepared but does not mandate preparation of EIR), with *No Oil, Inc. v. City of Los Angeles* (1974) 13 Cal.3d 68, 118 Cal.Rptr. 34 (EIR necessary if serious public controversy).

527 14 Cal. Code of Regs. Section 15082.

528 14 Cal. Code of Regs. Section 15085(c), (d). The outside consultants, hired by the project proponent, can be used to prepare the environmental documents provided the agency exercises independent judgment in reviewing the applicant's work. *Friends of La Vina v. County of Los Angeles* (1991) 232 Cal.App.3d 1446, 284 Cal.Rptr. 171. The agency should select the consultant (or offer the applicant the opportunity to select from an approved list of consultants) and require the applicant to reimburse the agency for payments made by the agency to the consultant.

529 14 Cal. Code of Regs. Section 15088. The public must have adequate time to review and to respond to environmental documents. 14 Cal. Code of Regs. Section 15087(c), 15203. Public participation is to be encouraged. 14 Cal. Code of Regs. Section 15083, 15201. In cases of statewide, regional or area-wide significance, environmental documents must also be submitted to the State Clearinghouse. 14 Cal. Code of Regs. Section 15087(d), *et seq.* A minimum of 45 days' notice must be given to the State Clearinghouse for EIRs; 30 days for negative declarations. The minimum notice of EIRs without State Clearinghouse involvement is 30 days, and for negative declarations, it is 21 days. Public Resources Code Section 21091.

530 14 Cal. Code of Regs. Section 15090.

531 14 Cal. Code of Regs. Section 15162. See also *Santa Teresa Citizens Action Group v. City of San Jose* (2003) 74 Cal.App.4th 689, 7 Cal. Rptr.3d 868.

532 Public Resources Code Section 20161.

533 14 Cal. Code of Regs. Section 15141, 15142, 15143, 15143.5, 15144.

534 14 Cal. Code of Regs. Section 15090(b), 15092.

535 Public Resources Code Section 21002.1; *Citizens for Quality Growth v. City of Mount Shasta* (1988) 198 Cal.App.3d 433, 243 Cal.Rptr. 727 (findings and mitigation measures inadequate).

536 14 Cal. Code of Regs. Section 15091(a)(3), 15092(b)(2)(B).

537 14 Cal. Code of Regs. Section 15092(b)(2)(A).

538 14 Cal. Code of Regs. Section 15094(a)(6), 15126(c).

539 14 Cal. Code of Regs. Section 15094(d).

540 See e.g., *Concerned Citizens of Calaveras County v. Calaveras County Board of Supervisors* (1985) 166 Cal.App.3d 90, 212 Cal. Rptr. 273 (Cannot identify adverse impacts which accompany a general plan and merely state that other agencies will mitigate); *Laurel Heights Improvement Ass'n of San Francisco v. Regents of the University of California* (1988) 47 Cal.3d 376, 253 Cal.Rptr. 426, 764 P.2d 728 (discussion of mitigation was based on substantial evidence); *Long Beach Savings & Loan Ass'n v. Long Beach Redevelopment Agency* (1986) 188 Cal.App.3d 249, 232 Cal.Rptr. 772 (no duty to mitigate); *No Oil, Inc. v City of Los Angeles, supra* (findings and mitigation deemed adequate).

541 14 Cal. Code of Regs. Section 15096(g)(1).

542 14 Cal. Code of Regs. Section 15096(i).

543 Public Resources Code Section 21167.

544 *Id.*

545 *San Francisco for Reasonable Growth v. City and County of San Francisco* (1987) 189 Cal.App.3d 498, 234 Cal.Rptr. 527 (mandatory dismissal if no hearing in 90 days).

546 *Environmental Law Fund v. Town of Corte Madera* (1975) 49 Cal. App.3d 105, 122 Cal.Rptr. 282 (failure to complain will not prevent court relief.)

547 Public Resources Code Section 21177; See also *Kane v. Redevelopment Agency of Hidden Hills* (1986) 179 Cal.App.3d 899, 224 Cal.Rptr. 922; *Coalition for Student Action v. City of Fullerton* (1985) 153 Cal.App.3d 1194, 200 Cal.Rptr. 855 (failure to protest negative declaration bars later court action); *Gorsuch v. Sonora* (1985) 173 Cal.App.3d 111, 218 Cal.Rptr. 871 (Failure to exhaust bars suit).

548 Public Resources Code Section 21167.8.

549 Public Resources Code Section 21168.5.

550 See *Newberry Springs Water Ass'n v. San Bernardino, supra* (court to determine if there is substantial evidence to support agency's decisions there is no "fair argument" the project may have significant environmental impact); *Heninger v. Board of Supervisors of Santa Clara County* (1986) 179 Cal.App.3d 218, 224 Cal.Rptr. 509 (substantial evidence to support negative declaration).

551 *Concerned McCloud Citizens v. McCloud Community Services District* (2007) 147 Cal.App.4th 181, 54 Cal.Rptr. 3d 1 (future agreement can resolve contingencies); *Western Placer Citizens for Agricultural and Rural Environment v. County of Placer* (2006) 144 Cal.App.4th 890, 50 Cal.Rptr.3d 799 (EIR need not identify guaranteed source of water); *Landwatch Monterey County v. County of Monterey* (2007) 147 Cal.App.4th1001, 55 Cal.Rptr.3d 34 (EIR not required for project using overdrafted basins because impact is mitigated); *Woodward Park Homeowners Assoc. v. City of Fresno* (2007) 150 Cal. App.4th 683, 58 Cal.Rptr.3d 102 ("baseline" must be established in EIR); and *Vineyard Area Citizens for Responsible Growth v. City of Rancho Cordova* (2007) 40 Cal.App.4th 412, 53 Cal.Rptr.3d 821 (long-term water supply must be explained clearly).

552 42 U.S.C. Section 4321, *et seq.*

553 Fish and Game Code Section 2050; 16 U.S.C. Section 1531, *et seq.*; Federal and State Endangered Species Acts are virtually identical, except with respect to listed species and listed habitats.

554 Fish and Game Code Section 2052; 16 U.S.C. Section 1538(a)(2)(B). See also *Cabinet Mountains Wilderness v. Peterson* (1981 Dist. Col.) 510 F.Supp. 1186, 685 F.2d 678.

555 The state and federal regulatory agencies responsible for the administration of ESA often use this feature to negotiate mitigation measures.

556 See, e.g., *Tennessee Valley Authority v. Hill* (1978) 437 U.S. 153, 998 S.Ct. 2279, 57 L.Ed.2d 117 (snail darter blocks major hydroelectric project).

557 "Threatened" species are also protected by ESA. The law provides more administrative flexibility when a species is threatened, rather than endangered.

558 The challenge is to protect society from unwanted side affects without inhibiting progress, The law must lag slightly behind technological advance. If prohibition precedes technology, the law will prohibit something that should be permitted. If the prohibition is too late, the law will permit something that should be prohibited.

559 The technical differences between a hazardous waste and a toxic waste are unimportant to this discussion. All dangerous wastes will be called hazardous wastes.

560 One can hope that some day a hazardous waste law will be generic enough to deal with all future technological advances. However, it is probably no more realistic to hope for a single comprehensive legal solution to technological problems than it is to hope for a unified field theory to describe the physical nature of the universe once and for all. For an interesting discussion of law and science, see, "The Curvature of Constitutional Space: What Lawyers Can Learn From Modern Physics," Tribe, 103 Harvard Law Review 1.

561 Hazardous waste laws deal with water quality, air quality and land pollution. As a result, air pollution, solid waste disposal, and other health-oriented laws are often implicated when dealing with a hazardous waste issue.

562 Legislation is often introduced to eliminate the public agency exemption.

563 Health and Safety Code Section 25249.8. The "list" must contain, at a minimum, known human and animal carcinogens and reproductive toxins identified in the applicable Labor Code Section. See *AFL-CIO v. Deukmejian* (1989) 212 Cal.App.3d 425, 260 Cal.Rptr. 479.

564 Health and Safety Code Section 25180.7.

565 Health and Safety Code Section 25280, *et seq.*

566 Health and Safety Code Section 25282.

567 *Id.*

568 Health and Safety Code Section 25284(a). When a tank is transferred, the agency must transfer the permit. Health and Safety Code Section 25284(b). The transfer form must be submitted within 30 days of the transfer of the tank.

569 Health and Safety Code Section 25286.

570 Health and Safety Code Section 25287. Permits may be waived for tanks under 5,000 gallons.

571 Health and Safety Code Section 25283

572 Health and Safety Code Section 25286

573   Health and Safety Code Section 25286(c)(7).

574   Health and Safety Code Section 25286(c)(8).

575   Health and Safety Code Section 25285.1.

576   Health and Safety Code Section 25288(a).

577   Health and Safety Code Section 25288(b).

578   Health and Safety Code Section 25291.

579   Health and Safety Code Section 25291(a).

580   Health and Safety Code Section 25291(a)(1) and (2).

581   Health and Safety Code Section 25291(b) and (c).

582   Health and Safety Code Section 25291(h). See Health and Safety Code Section 25284.4, for the licensing requirements for integrity testers and the penalties for unlicensed practice.

583   Health and Safety Code Section 25292.

584   Health and Safety Code Section 25292.2. If there is both an operator and an owner, either may maintain the records.

585   Health and Safety Code Section 25293.

586   *Id.*

587   Health and Safety Code Section 25295.

588   Health and Safety Code Section 25298.

589   Health and Safety Code Section 25299 ($500 to $5,000 per tank per day of violation).

590   Health and Safety Code Section 25299.01.

591   42 U.S.C. Section 9601, *et seq.*

592   42 U.S.C. Section 6901, *et seq.*

593   33 U.S.C. Section 1254, *et seq.*

594   42 U.S.C. Section 300 f, *et seq.*

595   15 U.S.C. Section 2601, *et seq.*

596   49 U.S.C. Appx. Sections 1801-1812.

597   For example, leaking underground tanks are now specifically handled by SARA amendments 42 U.S.C. Section 9601, *et seq.*

598   The state superfund program pales by comparison to the federal program, the Carpenter-Presley-Tanner Hazardous Substance Act. Health and Safety Code Section 25300, *et seq.* The Department of Health Services is authorized to carry out "all hazardous waste management responsibilities or authorized" by CERCLA. Health and Safety Code Section 25259.7.

599 No claim shall be paid for natural resource damages until the claimant has exhausted administrative and judicial remedies to recover from responsible parties. CERCLA Section 1119b)(2).

600 If the NCP is compromised by a rival cleanup strategy, the EPA can charge the persons who implement the rival plan with violation of the NCP and seek to recover cleanup costs from that person.

601 The *government* is authorized to bring a CERCLA action. In the first instance, this means that EPA may bring suit. EPA is expected to delegate responsibility for litigation to a *lead agency* which then becomes the EPA's enforcement arm.

602 Future cleanup costs consistent with the NCP can also be recovered.

603 A producer which installs wellhead treatment can argue it has incurred cleanup costs.

604 This also means a CERCLA lawsuit against a landfill operator will produce cross-complaints against cities and the county on the grounds those jurisdictions arranged for trash to be hauled to the landfill by issuance of rubbish collection franchises.

605 The Hazardous Waste Resource and Research Coordination Program was enacted by the State to implement the Federal Resource Conservation and Recovery Act (RCRA).

606 *Selma Pressure Treating Co. v. Osmose Wood Preserving Co.* (1990) 221 Cal.App.3d 1601, 271 Cal.Rptr. 596.

607 *Potter v. Firestone Tire and Rubber Co.* (1991) 6 Cal.4th 965, 25 Cal. Rptr.2d 550.

608 The best example of this difficulty is shown in the case of cigarette smoking. It is probably universally accepted that cigarette smoking causes lung cancer. Yet, lung cancer victims are often unable to recover damages from cigarette manufacturers because of inability to prove causation between smoking and cancer in a particular case.

609 The benefits from a major water project is not one-sided. By exporting water, water-abundant areas can avoid urbanization.

610 Rogers & Nichols, Water Development, contains a complete description of these projects.

611 Water Code Section 11100 *et seq.*

612 49 Stat. 1028, 1038, Ch 831.

613 The "Hammer Clause" increases the limit to 960 acres per family provided the family farmer agrees to pay higher water rates designed to recoup all operation and maintenance costs. (Reclamation Act of 1902: 32 Stat. 388-90.)

614 Water Code Section 12930 *et seq.*

615 Water Code Section 10505.

616 Water Code Section 109 (policy on water transfers). See also, e.g. , Water Code Sections 11011, et seq., The Water Rights Protection and Expedited Short Term Water Transfer Act of 1999.

617 Water Code Section 380 *et seq.*

618 Water Code Section 470-483.

619 Water Code Section 1810-1814.

620 If a Court finds that the right to water is "fundamental," wealth-based discrimination would be unconstitutional. See e.g. *Serrano v. Priest* (1971) 5 Cal.3d 584, 96 Cal.Rptr. 601.

621 *Lux v. Haggin* (1886) 69 Cal. 255, 10 P. 674.

622 California Constitution, Article X, Section 2.

623 *Peabody v. City of Vallejo* (1935) 2 Cal.2d 351, 40 P.2d 486.

624 4 Restatement of Torts (2d ed.) Section 850A.

625 4 Restatement of Torts (2d ed.) Section 843.

626 *Boehmer v. Big Rock Irrigation District* (1897) 117 Cal. 19, 48 P. 908; *Anaheim Union Water Co. v. Fuller* (1907) 150 Cal. 327, 88 P. 978. But see *Strong v. Baldwin* (1908) 154 Cal. 150, 97 P. 178 (conveyance of riparian rights), *Rancho Santa Margarita v. Vail* (1938) 11 Cal.2d 501, 81 P.2d 533 (tenants in common).

627 *Anaheim Union Water Co. v. Fuller* (1907) 150 Cal. 327, 88 P. 978.

628 See also *Pabst v. Finmand* (1922) 190 Cal. 124, 211 P. 11 (riparian rights not affected by downstream prescription).

629 *In re Waters of Soquel Creek Stream System* (1978) 79 Cal.App.3d 682, 145 Cal.Rptr. 146.

630 *In re Waters of Long Valley Creek Stream System* (1979) 25 Cal.3d 339, 158 Cal.Rptr. 350; *Deetz v. Carter* (1965) 232 Cal.App.2d 851, 43 Cal.Rptr. 321; *California ex rel. California Water Resources Control Board v. Forni* (1976) 54 Cal.App.3d 743, 126 Cal.Rptr. 851; and *Niles*

Sand and Gravel Company, Inc. v. Alameda County Water District (1974) 37 Cal.App.3d 924, 112 Cal.Rptr. 846 (groundwater).

631 *Katz v. Walkinshaw* (1903) 141 Cal. 116, 70 P. 663.

632 *Hudson v. Dailey* (1909) 156 Cal. 617, 105 P. 748.

633 *Burr v. Maclay Rancho Water Co.* (1908) 154 Cal. 428, 98 P. 260; *Wright v. Goleta Water District* (1985) 174 Cal.App.3d 74, 219 Cal. Rptr. 740.

634 *Wright v. Goleta Water Dist.* (1985) 174 Cal.App.3d 74, 219 Cal. Rptr. 740.

635 *Lux v. Haggin*, supra.

636 *San Bernardino v. Riverside* (1921) 186 Cal. 7, 198 P. 784.

637 *People v. Shirokow* (1980) 26 Cal.3d 301, 162 Cal.Rptr. 30; But see Water Code Section 1006 (rights vested in municipality prior to 1914 not affected by legislative scheme). Pre-1914 rights are currently treated as a vested property right. This status is probably not deserved because government regulations may affect vested property rights without requiring the payment of compensation under a wide variety of circumstances. See *Keystone Bituminous Coal Association v. DeBenedictus* (1987) 480 U.S. 470, 94 L.Ed.2d 472, 107 S.Ct. 1232.

638 Water Code Section 1250.

639 Water Code Section 1252.

640 Water Code Sections 1253, 1375.

641 Water Code Section 1610.

642 Water Code Sections 1240, 1241.

643 *Los Angeles v. Aitken* (1935) 10 Cal.App.2d 460, 52 P.2d 585; Water Code Section 1627; But see, Water Code Section 1011 (no reduction of right because of water conservation).

644 Water Code Section 1675, *et seq.*

645 Water Code Section 1700 et seq. See also *Environmental Defense Fund v. East Bay Municipal Utility District* (1980) 26 Cal.3d 183, 161 Cal.Rptr. 466 (courts have concurrent jurisdiction to determine issues of beneficial use and waste).

646 Water Code Section 1450.

647 Water Code Section 1330.

648 Water Code Section 104.

649 Water Code Section 106. See also Water Code Section 106.5 (high priority for municipal uses); cf. *Deetz v. Carter* (1965) 232 Cal. App.2d 851, 43 Cal.Rptr. 321 (domestic uses have priority among riparians).

650 Water Code Section 1254. See also Water Code Section 1257 (relative benefit).

651 Water Code Sections 1203, 1460.

652 If a municipality wishes to acquire existing water rights, it must pay "just compensation" for the physical water but no value is assigned to the former users' water rights because the municipality has "prior rights." Water Code Sections 1462, 1463.

653 *Fullerton v. California Water Resources Control Board* (1979) 90 Cal.App.3d 590, 153 Cal.Rptr. 518; *California Trout, Inc. v. California Water Resources Control Board* (1979) 90 Cal.App.3d 816, 153 Cal. Rptr. 672.

654 Water Code Sections 1243, 1257.5; But see *Bank of America v. California Water Resources Control Board* (1974) 42 Cal.App.3d 198, 116 Cal.Rptr. 770.

655 In *California Trout, Inc. v. State Water Resources Control Board and City of Los Angeles* (1989) 207 Cal.App.3d 585, 255 Cal.Rptr. 184, the Court held that a statute which directs licenses in portions of Mono and Inyo Counties issued after September 9, 1953 to insure water for in-stream (fisheries) use, applies to permits or licenses for dams constructed prior to September 9, 1953. The Court found that its interpretation did not divest the city of any rights and does not exceed the legislature's power to allocate water uses.

656 *San Bernardino v. Riverside* (1921) 186 Cal. 7, 198 P. 784 (overlying city's use is appropriative).

657 *Moreno Mutual Irrigation Co. v. Beaumont Irrigation District* (1949) 94 Cal.App.2d 766, 211 P.2d 928. The appropriation doctrine has no application when all users are overlying users. In such a case, all rights are equal and correlative and must be reduced proportionately in times of shortage. *Tehachapi-Cummings County Water District v. Armstrong* (1975) 49 Cal.App.3d 992, 122 Cal.Rptr. 918. See also *Pasadena v. Alhambra* (1949) 33 Cal.2d 908, 207 P.2d 17.

658 *Wright v. Goleta Water District* (1985) 174 Cal.App.3d 74, 219 Cal. Rptr. 740.

659 Water Code Section 2100.

660 Water Code Section 1242.

661 Water Code Section 4999, *et seq.*

662 *Orange County Water District v. Riverside* (1959) 173 Cal.App.2d 137, 343 P.2d 450.

663 See also *Andres v. Charleston Stone Product Co.* (1978) 436 U.S. 604, 56 L.Ed. 570 (no federal groundwater law).

664 *City of Los Angeles v. City of San Fernando* (1975) 14 Cal.3d 199, 123 Cal.Rptr. 1.

665 *Pasadena v. Alhambra* (1949) 33 Cal.2d 908, 207 P.2d 17.

666 For example, a pumper who extracted five acre-feet, four acre-feet, three acre-feet, two acre-feet, one acre-foot would earn a one-acre foot prescriptive right because the maximum amount produced continuously for five years was only one
acre-foot.

667 *City of Los Angeles v. City of San Fernando* (1975) 14 Cal. 3d 199, 123 Cal.Rptr. 1.

668 *San Fernando* may have sounded the death knell to the mutual prescription doctrine. *San Fernando* has not ended the practice of "adjudicating" groundwater basins.

669 *National Audubon Society v. Superior Court of Alpine County*, (1983) 33 Cal.3d 419, 189 Cal.Rptr. 346.

670 The Audubon Society did not rely entirely upon the courts. A massive national publicity program was undertaken by the society. Major articles appeared in national magazines such as Sports Illustrated and the National Geographic Society Journal.

671 *Illinois Central Railroad Co. v. Illinois* (1892) 146 U.S. 287, 36 L.Ed 1018. Commentators have suggested the court's decision may have been reaction to undue influence of the railroad on the Illinois Legislature. If so, the court's reasoning in the Illinois Central case may just be another example that proves the maxim hard cases make bad law.

672 *City of Berkeley v. Superior Court of Alameda County* (1980) 26 Cal.3d 515, 162 Cal.Rptr. 327.

673 *California v. Superior Court of Placer County (Fogerty)* (1981) 29 Cal.3d 240, 172 Cal.Rptr. 713 (Lake Tahoe); *Golden Feather Community Assn. v. Thermalito Irrigation District* (1988) 199 Cal.App.3d 402, 244 Cal.Rptr. 830 (artificial impoundment; case decertified).

674 *Marks v. Whitney* (1971) 6 Cal.3d 251, 98 Cal.Rptr. 790.

675 *Lux v. Haggin, supra.* The court did not even mention the prior decision.

676 Civil Code Section 22.2 states the common law shall prevail only in the absence of a statute. This means ancient laws such as relied upon in *National Audubon* have no standing. However, the way the decision is written, relying on ancient laws and "fundamental rights," casts grave doubt on whether or not the legislature can do any more than tinker with the peripheral issues involved in the doctrine.

677 The California Attorney General argued the reasonable use test should have been applied.

678 *Winters v. United States* (1908) 207 U.S. 564, 52 L.Ed. 340.

679 *Federal Power Commission v. Oregon* (1955) 349 U.S. 435, 99 L.Ed. 1215; See also Trelease, Federal Reserved Rights Since FERC, 54 Denver L.J. 473 (1977). Although the terminology is different, the federal reserve rights doctrine and the state public trust doctrine are essentially the same. In both cases, government asserts "public" rights to defeat pre-existing "private" rights.

680 *Cappaert v. United States* (1976) 426 U.S. 128, 48 L.Ed.2d 523. Since the right is "reserved" from earliest of times, the reserved right is prior and paramount to subsequent private water uses. Federal reserved rights are largely unasserted at this time, this means that future claims of reserved rights could disrupt carefully devised water appropriation decisions.

681 See e.g. *United States v. New Mexico* (1978) 438 U.S. 696, 57 L.Ed.2d 1052 (no reservation for "aesthetic, environmental, recreational and Ôfish' purposes" under the Multiple-Use Sustained Yield Act of 1960).

682 *Kansas v. Colorado* (1907) 106 U.S. 46, 51 L.Ed 956.

683 *Wyoming v. Colorado* (1922) 259 U.S. 419, 66 L.Ed 999.

684 *Nebraska v. Wyoming* (1945) 325 U.S. 589, 89 L.Ed 1815.

685 *Hinderlider v. La Plata River & Cherry Creek Ditch Co.* (1938) 304 U.S. 92, 82 L.Ed 1202.

686 U.S. Const. Article I, Section 10.

687 *Arizona v. California* (1963) 373 U.S. 546, 10 L.Ed.2d 572.

688 Cal. Const. Article X, Section 2; *Tulare Irrigation District v. Lindsay-Strathmore Irrigation District* (1935) 3 Cal.2d 489, 45

P.2d 972.

689 *Pasadena v. Alhambra, supra,* imposed a successful physical solution on the Raymond Basin in the 1950s. There is a general perception judicial actions are unnecessarily time consuming and expensive. Water rights are complicated by nature. It remains to be seen whether alternatives are less time consuming or expensive. Several statutes attempt to short circuit the court system by establishing a method for negotiating "physical solutions" to water problems. These statutes work in concert with court decrees. For example, the Groundwater Replenishment Act allows a groundwater replenishment district to levy assessments to recover the cost of importing water to make up overproduction. More recent legislation is supposed to work without court intervention. The Groundwater Management Act creates a mechanism for water producers to jointly administer a groundwater basin. Unfortunately (or fortunately depending on point of view), this Act depends on the voluntary cooperation of the parties.

690 There are adjudicated basins operating without a Watermaster. There are also stream systems managed by a Watermaster. Adjudicated basins without Watermaster supervision and stream systems with Watermaster supervision are outside the scope of this analysis.

691 The two basins in the Tehachapi area are at the northern edge of this group.

692 The basin is roughly west of Orange County, south of Whittier Narrows, east of the Harbor Freeway, and north of the ocean.

693 The Watermaster is not the only body exercising discretion over basin operations. The Replenishment District levies assessments ("pump tax") to purchase supplemental water to replenish the basin. The Central Basin Water Users Association represents

most of the producers and concentrates on the decisions of the Replenishment District.

694 The basin is roughly west of Pomona, south of the San Gabriel Mountains, east of Monterey Park, and north of Whittier Narrows.

695 There are no advisory bodies established by the court or the Watermaster, but the San Gabriel Water Users Association monitors the Watermaster and the Watermaster is careful to consider the views of the Association.

696 The basin is roughly west of the Harbor Freeway, south of the Santa Monica Mountains, east of the ocean and north.

697 The Watermaster is not the only body exercising discretion over basin operations. The Replenishment District of Southern California levies assessments ("pump tax") to purchase supplemental water to replenish this basin. The West Basin Water Users Association represents most of the producers and concentrates on the decisions of the Replenishment District.

698 16 U.S.C. Section 1271.

699 Public Resources Code Sections 5093.50 Ð 5093.69.

700 The Department of Fish and Game enforces the statute because it is unlawful to substantially divert or obstruct natural flow or substantially change the bank of any stream or lake or to use any material from streambeds without first notifying the Department. See *Rutherford v. California* (1987) 188 Cal.App.3d 1267, 233 Cal.Rptr. 781.

701 California Water Plan Update, Volume 1 (Bulletin 160-93) p.233.

702 See, e.g. *Butte County Water Users' Association v. Railroad Commission* (1921) 185 Cal. 218 (duty to protect existing customers).

703 Cal. Const. Article X, Section 2; *Erickson v. Queen Valley Ranch Co., Inc.* (1971) 22 Cal.App.3d 578, 99 Cal.Rptr. 446; *Imperial Irrigation District v. California Water Resources Control Board* (1990) 225 Cal. App.3d 548, 275 Cal.Rptr. 250.

704 Water Code Sections 375, 1009.

705 See e.g. Water Code Section 31035 (county water district); Water Code Sections 71610, 71611, 71610.5 (municipal water district).

706 Fortunately, the reasonableness tests fits well with representative government. A well functioning board of directors will accurately reflect and understand the goals and values of the community. Unless those goals and values violate constitutional standards for the protection of the weak, the expectations of the community will describe what is reasonable.

707 See also Water Code Sections 31026-31028 (county water district use restrictions), Water Code Sections 71640-71642 (municipal water district use restrictions).

708 If the Mono Lake dispute had been submitted to the State Board in the first instance, it is likely a more coherent theory than the public trust doctrine would have been developed to resolve the dispute.

709 42 U.S.C. Section 300f.

710 42 U.S.C. Section 300j.

711 Health and Safety Code Section 4010, *et seq.*

712 Health and Safety Code Section 4023, 4023.1.

713 Health and Safety Code §116470(a).

714 Health and Safety Code §116470(b).

715 Health and Safety Code §116540.

716 Health and Safety Code §116540(a). This section also applies to changes of ownership of a public water system that occur after January 1, 1998.

717 Health and Safety Code §116540(b).

718 *Hansen v. City of San Buenaventura* (1986) 42 Cal.3d 1172, 233 Cal. Rptr. 22.

719 See e.g., Water Code Section 71613 (municipal water districts).

720 But see, *San Marcos Water District v. San Marcos Unified School District* (1986) 42 Cal.3d. 154, 228 Cal.Rptr. 47 (cannot collect fees for capital facilities from tax-exempt public agencies); Government Code Section 54992 establishes conditions for capital facilities charges against public agencies.

721 *Boynton v. City of Lakeport Municipal Sewer District No. 1* (1972) 28 Cal.App.3d 91, 104 Cal.Rptr. 409.

722 *Louisiana-Pacific Corp. v. Humbolt Municipal Water District* (1982) 137 Cal.App.3d 152, 186 Cal.Rptr. 833 (40 years); *McBean v. City*

of Fresno (1896) 112 Cal. 159, 44 P. 358 (5 years); *Marin Water and Power v. City of Sausalito* (1914) 168 Cal. 587, 143 P. 767 (10 years); *Sawyer v. City of San Diego* (1956) 138 Cal.App.2d 652, 292 P.2d 233 (36 years); *Carruth v. City of Madera* (1965) 233 Cal.App.2d 688, 43 Cal.Rptr. 855 (19 years).

723 *Memphis Light, Gas & Water v. Craft* (1977) 436 U.S. 1, 98 S.Ct. 1554, 56 L.Ed.2d 30.

724 Public Utilities Code Section 10010.1.

725 Government Code Section 60372(c).

726 Public Utilities Code Section 10016 applies to investor-owned public utilities and *municipal* corporations. Usually, the term municipal corporation refers to cities. However, some public districts are quasi-municipal corporations e.g. municipal water district. Section 10016 may apply to these public districts; the Legislative Counsel takes this position. (Legis. Counsel Digest Ch. 888, Stats 1985). Government Code Sections 60371 and 60372 specifically apply to public *district* purveyors. When the Government Code conflicts with the Public Utilities Code, the Government Code prevails because the specific controls the general. When the Public Utilities Code deals with a subject which is not covered in the Government Code, the specifics of Public Utilities Code will prevail.

727 Government Code Section 60372(c).

728 Government Code Section 60372(b).

729 Government Code Section 60371(a); See also, *Tovar v. Southern California Edison Company* (1988) 201 Cal.App.3d 606; 247 Cal. Rptr. 281.

730 *Id.*

731 Government Code Section 60371(b).

732 Government Code Section 60370(a).

733 Government Code Section 60374.

734 Government Code Section 60375.5.

735 Government Code Section 60371(c). Payments for water service may be deducted from rent. Government Code Section 60371(d).

736 Government Code Section 65589.7.

737 Government Code Section 65589.7(c).

738 Government Code Section 56133.

739 Municipal water districts are not required to make findings on domestic water needs and potential customers before adopting a moratorium on new service connections. *Building Industry Ass'n of Northern California v. Marin Mun. Water Dist.* (1991) 235 Cal.App.3d 1641, 1 Cal.Rptr.2d 625.

740 The priority for human consumption contained in Section 350 is in direct conflict with the priority for irrigation use contained in the federal Reclamation Acts. *City of Fresno v. California* (1963) 372 U.S. 627, 10 L.Ed.2d 28, 83 S.Ct. 996. This is a strong indication a water purveyor cannot use Section 350 to divert the yield of a federal reclamation project from agricultural to municipal uses.

741 *Urban Planning and Land Development Control Law* (2d Ed), Hagman & Juergensmeyer, p. 260.

742 See e.g. *Butte County Water Users' Assn. v. RR Com.* (1921) 185 Cal. 218.

743 An agency cannot always escape liability for a moratorium even if it is based upon shortage of supply. In *Morrison Homes Corp. v. City of Pleasanton* (1976) 58 Cal.App.3d 724, 130 Cal.Rptr. 196, a city was required to pay damages to a developer when the second phase of the development was blocked due to a sewer moratorium imposed by the Regional Water Quality Control Board.

744 *Swanson v. Marin Municipal Water District* (1976) 56 Cal.App.3d 512, 128 Cal.Rptr. 485. See also *Associated Home Builders v. City of Livermore* (1976) 18 Cal.3d 582, 135 Cal.Rptr. 41, a California Supreme Court decision on the power of a city to restrict growth under its zoning powers due to infrastructure shortages. The Court upheld the power to restrict growth under such circumstances but assumed that the city would do everything in its power to alleviate the shortages. The implication is that even cities, which enjoy considerable land use powers, have an obligation to augment service to meet demands.

745 See e.g. Government Code Sections 65302.8, 65580-65584. See also Public Resources Code Section 21001(d) (CEQA).

746 See e.g. Government Code Sections 65589.6, 65754.5, 65755

65762, Evidence Code Section 669.5.

747 But see *Building Industry Assn. of Northern California v. Marin Municipal Water District* (1991) 235 Cal.App.3d 1641, 1 Cal.Rptr.2d 625. (mandamus will not lie to compel agency to augment supply.)

748 For example, the Cities of Camarillo and Thousand Oaks have successful growth management programs.

749 Of course, the more cynical no-growth advocates do not expect water agencies to have a coherent no-growth policy. They are satisfied if a debate over the water district's role in growth management causes confusion or inaction sufficient to prevent positive programs to acquire additional supply.

750 This argument is weakened when the boundaries of the land planning and water district agencies are not coterminous.

751 33 U.S.C. 403.

752 33 U.S.C. 1251. This law was subsequently "tuned up" with several amendments. It is now known as the Federal Clean Water Act.

753 The Act has received a good deal of attention not only for its broad reach, but because of the massive public works program that funded facilities necessary to comply with the Act. 33 U.S.C. 1281.

754 *United States v. Ashland Oil & Transportation Co.* (1974, Ky) 504 F.2d 1317 (waters tributary to navigable waters).

755 *United States v. Riverside Bayview Homes* (1986) 474 U.S. 121, 88 L.Ed.2d 419.

756 *Solid Waste Agency of Northern Cook County v. Army Corps of Engineers* (2001) 531 U.S. 159.

757 One increasingly important area regulated by the federal Clean Water Act is the dredging or filling of navigable waterways. 33 U.S.C. 1344. A permit must be obtained from the Corps of Engineers before dredge or fill operations can be undertaken. California likewise requires dredge or fill permits. Water Code Section 13385(a).

758 But see, *Tahoe-Sierra Preservation Council v. State Water Resources Control Board* (1989) 210 Cal.App.3d 1421, 259 Cal.Rptr. 132. State Board may enforce non-point source plan for waters subject to

federal act by means of permit system; plan does not violate Water Code by specifying matter of compliance.

759 *Kelley v. United States* (1985 WD Mich) 618 F. Supp 1103 (no federal jurisdiction over groundwater pollution).

760 *Marina County Water District v. State Water Resources Control Board* (1985) 163 Cal.App.3d 132, 209 Cal.Rptr. 212 (a "zone of prohibition" of wastewater discharge is not a water quality standard which must be reviewed by the state every three years); *Morshead v. California Regional Water Quality Control Board* (1975) 45 Cal.App.3d 442, 119 Cal.Rptr. 586 (board may consider hardship when establishing waste discharge standards; such orders are a valid exercise of police powers for which inverse condemnation actions will not lie).

761 *Lake Madrone Water District v. State Water Resources Control Board* (1989) 209 Cal.App.3d 163, 256 Cal.Rptr. 894.

762 *Los Angeles Bar Bulletin* (March 1970) "Practice Under California's New Porter-Cologne Water Quality Control Act."

763 Water Code Sections 13265, 13340, 13385, 13386, and 13387.

764 Water Code Section 13320.

765 Water Code Section 13330.

766 *Id.*

767 Water Code Section 13002.

768 *City of Milwaukee v. Illinois* (1981) 451 U.S. 304, 68 L.Ed.2d 114, 101 S.Ct. 1784; *Middlesex County Sewage Authority v. National Sea Clammers Assoc.* (1981) 453 U.S. 1, 69 L.Ed.2d 435.

769 But see *Stevens v. Oakdale Irrigation District* (1939) 13 Cal.2d 343, 90 P.2d 56 (no duty to continue artificial flow to downstream appropriators); Water Code Section 1210 (ownership of reclaimed water).

770 Water Code 13550.

771 Water Code Section 13551.

772 See also Water Code Section 461. When there is a shortage, Water Code Section 350 implies that use of more expensive reclaimed water can be mandated.

773 See also Health and Safety Code Section 5008 (sewer maintenance district's may sell effluent).

774 Water Code Section 13552.2.

775 Water Code Section 13552.6.

776 Water Code Section 13553.

777 Water Code Sections 13552.4, 13552.8, 13554.

778 Sometimes greed or pride motivates the objection; occasionally the protester wishes to stop the use of reclaimed water.

779 *McCulloch v. Maryland* (1819) 17 U.S. (4 Wheat.) 316.

780 United States Constitution Article VI, Section 2.

781 *Florida Lime & Avocado Growers v. Paul* (1963) 373 U.S. 132, 10 L.Ed.2d 248.

782 *McDermott v. Wisconsin* (1913) 228 U.S. 115, 33 S.Ct. 431, 57 L.Ed. 754.

783 Tenth Amendment to U.S. Constitution.

784 *National League of Cities v. Usery* (1976) 426 U.S. 833, 49 L.Ed.2d 245, 96 S.Ct. 2465.

785 *Garcia v. San Antonio Metropolitan Transit Authority* (1985) 469 U.S. 528, 83 L.Ed.2d 1016, 105 S.Ct. 1005.

786 *Bishop v. City of San Jose* (1969) 1 Cal.3d 56, 61-62, 81 Cal.Rptr. 465, 460 P.2d 137.

787 *Professional Firefighters, Inc. v. City of Los Angeles* (1963) 60 Cal.2d 276, 294, 32 Cal.Rptr. 830.

788 *Butterworth v. Boyd* (1938) 12 Cal.2d 140, 147; 82 P.2d 434.

789 *California Federal Savings and Loan v. City of Los Angeles* (1991) 54 Cal.3d 1, 283 Cal.Rptr. 569, 584.

790 Government Code Section 65401.

791 Government Code Section 65403.

792 Government Code Section 65402.

793 Government Code Section 53091.

794 *Baldwin Park County Water District v. County of Los Angeles* (1962) 208 Cal.App.2d 87, 25 Cal.Rptr. 167.

795 Government Code Section 53091.

796 Government Code Section 6103.

797 40 Ops. Cal. Atty. Gen. 15 (1962).

798 Government Code Sections 6500, *et seq.*

799 Government Code Sections 56300, *et seq.*

800 Public Utilities Code Sections 1500, *et seq.*